Democracy:
Can't We Do Better
Than That?

Other books by Bob Avakian

The Loss in China and the Revolutionary Legacy of Mao Tsetung

Mao Tsetung's Immortal Contributions

For a Harvest of Dragons: On the "Crisis of Marxism" and the Power of Marxism, Now More Than Ever

A Horrible End, or an End to the Horror?

Bullets from the Writings, Speeches, and Interviews of Bob Avakian, Chairman of the Revolutionary Communist Party, USA

Democracy: Can't We Do Better Than That?

by Bob Avakian

BANNER PRESS • CHICAGO

Banner Press, P.O. Box 21195, Midtown Station,
  New York, N.Y. 10129

Library of Congress Cataloging-in-Publication Data

Avakian, Bob.
    Democracy: can't we do better than that?

    Includes index.
    1. Communist state.   2. Democracy.   I. Title.
JC474.A93   1986   321.9'2   86-3650
ISBN 0-916650-30-8
ISBN 0-916650-29-4 (pbk.)

Contents

1

Democracy:
Can't We Do Better
Than That?

In the world today, the most horrendous crimes are committed in the name of democracy. In El Salvador, death squads and the "legitimate government" – which are the same animal – continue to massacre hundreds every week, but we are supposed to believe this is all right now because the government has been established in a U.S.-sanctioned "free election" and is committing these atrocities with an up-to-date arsenal provided by the God-father of Western democracy, the USA. In neighboring Guate-mala, numerous accounts in recent years have described scene after scene where government troops enter a village and, after executing everyone of fighting age, proceed to brutally murder old people, rape and kill women, and then take the small children and infants and bash their heads open. Much of this went on while Jerry Falwell, Pat Robertson, and other bornagain ghouls publicly prayed for (and actively, vocally championed) their bornagain counterpart heading the government in Guatemala – a government installed and kept in power by the U.S. – and the same thing is continuing today.

Throughout Central and South America, such grisly scenarios

are repeated – and justified – in the name of preserving freedom, democracy, and the American way. Within the past year, for example, the *New York Times* has several times reported on the widespread and vicious terror carried out by the government of Peru in its desperate attempts to stem the rising tide of revolutionary war there, led by the Maoist Communist Party of Peru (called "Sendero Luminoso" or "Shining Path" by the Western media). The Peruvian government has tried to literally kill off the growing support for that revolutionary war among the Peruvian people. But this does not prevent the *New York Times* and the rest of the prostitute press from describing and defending the Peruvian state as an important link in the Western democratic chain in Latin America. In fact, in an article entitled "A Latin Spring: Democracy in Flower," the *New York Times* informs us that Peru is one of a number of Latin American countries where democracy has seen a recent revival; according to the *Times*, in Latin America today (including the Caribbean) "only Chile, Paraguay, and Haiti are still firmly in the grip of rightist dictators." Such a claim, while outrageous in light of the actual and gruesome facts, does have the value of helping to make even clearer that there is no essential or practical difference between "rightist dictators" and "freely elected democratic leaders" in the service of Western imperialism.[1] It would be very difficult, for example, to convince the peasants, or others, in Guatemala – one of the countries where democracy has also recently seen at least the first flowers of spring, according to the *Times* – of the great difference between the regime of the bornagain butcher, Ríos Montt, and that of the succeeding butchers, under whom the same unspeakable brutalities have been perpetrated but who have allowed elections.

In the same period of the last few years the world has wit-

---

1. See the *New York Times*, 29 November 1984, p. A3. This is not to say that there is nothing of substance to what the *Times* describes as a democratic flowering in Latin America. It is just that there is nothing positive about it. In recent times, in a number of countries in that region – including Argentina and Uruguay, for example – there has been a definite move, clearly under U.S. direction, to involve broader strata among the upper and middle classes in the political process and to ease restrictions against them in particular, in an effort to secure greater stability and support against revolution amidst potentially volatile social conditions, and especially to secure their allegiance to the Western imperialist alliance in its confrontation with the rival Soviet bloc. And, again showing that it is the system and its exigencies that determine policy rather than the man (or party) in office, this is taking place under the baton of the Reagan administration – anti-Reagan democrats, take note.

nessed the events in Lebanon, beginning with the massive pounding and saturation bombing by Israel – slaughtering and uprooting tens of thousands of Palestinians and others in the holy crusade against "terrorism" (i.e., Palestinian national liberation). This was then followed by the massacres at the Sabra and Shatila refugee camps, instigated and backed up by Israel. The French and Italians have also done their part, along with the U.S., in attempting to enforce a new order in Lebanon (and more generally in the Middle East) on this foundation of bodies and rubble. Meanwhile, we have also witnessed the U.S. mugging and rape of Grenada and its continuing acts of provocation and aggression against Nicaragua, while from Turkey to South Africa to South Korea the most vicious regimes, carrying out the most sanguinary suppression, are maintained in power as part of the Western imperialist alliance. The list goes on and on; it could almost literally be extended endlessly and it involves all the Western imperialists, in all parts of the world. And does it need repeating that all of this is defended (with the appropriate expressions of pious doubts and petty amendments by the liberals) in the name of preserving democracy against something worse than all these evils – "totalitarianism"?

Then there are the British imperialists – their armed forces openly described as the envy of the rest of NATO because of their "battle-tested experience" in Northern Ireland and still more in the Malvinas (Falklands) war of 1982. It has recently been revealed that during that war the British threatened and were seriously prepared to carry out the nuclear devastation of the third largest city in Argentina.[2] (And what envy would have been provoked in the ruling circles of the NATO powers if the British had actually been the first to use nuclear weapons – well, not exactly the first, there was the U.S. use of the atom bomb, but that was so long ago, in the last world war, and nothing compared to the bang of present-day nukes!) Together with all this, and setting the framework for all of it in today's world situation, are the intense, accelerating preparations for world war, involving massive nuclear destruction, for the triumph of the "democratic way of life" against the totalitarian Soviet bloc.

The Soviet bloc, for its part, with its own particularities, is no

---

2. For an account of the British contingency plans for using nuclear weapons during the Malvinas (Falklands) war, see "The Plan for a British Hiroshima," *Revolutionary Worker,* No. 272 (14 September 1984).

less vigorous in insisting that it is the real representative and champion of democracy – of a real, full democracy, freed of capitalist restrictions and hypocrisy and only attainable with the establishment of Soviet-style "socialism." In fact, the Soviet bloc, despite its socialist pretensions, is no less imperialist than the USA and its alliance and has a hardly less impressive record of crimes carried out in the name of upholding democracy – and socialism – against reaction, obscurantism, imperialism. Afghanistan, Poland, Ethiopia . . . again the list goes on and on – right up to the Soviet bloc's equally intense and accelerating preparations for world war/nuclear devastation. Again, it must be said that the most horrendous crimes are committed – and even more monstrous crimes, dwarfing all previous atrocity and carnage, are being actively prepared – in the name of democracy.

But at the same time, democracy as a political goal is being struggled for by millions and millions of oppressed people in large parts of the world – in the Third World in particular, where even revolutionary movements have democratic objectives as their first order of business: the winning of genuine national liberation, the elimination of feudal or other precapitalist relations (or remnants) in the economic foundation and the political/ ideological superstructure of society, the overturning of privileges, and barriers, based on birth, rank, sex, and so on. And the view is widely held among oppressed masses everywhere that the fullest expression of what they are being denied, what they demand – and the essence of their aspirations – are democratic rights, equality, the same opportunity as other people (or nations) to rise to their full potential without entrenched privilege to impede them or tyranny to oppress them.

Within the "developed countries" – that is, the imperialist states, particularly in the Western bloc but with variations in the Soviet bloc as well – popular notions of democracy have some different features. There is, of course, the general notion that democracy means the rule of the people (whose highest expression is the election of public officials) and that the majority decides while the rights of the minority are protected. But among fairly broad and relatively well-off strata in these countries, what many think of when they think of democracy or freedom amounts not only to having the right to vote – as opposed to having leaders openly installed from above, ruling for life, etc. – but also (and closer to their hearts) the right to gripe about the policies of the government and things in society that affect them without fear of the consequences; the right to a private life not dictated in intimate detail by the state; and in the economic sphere, the right to choose what job or occupation they can qualify for and to do what they want with what money they can make, limited only by "economic opportunity" and not political (or, as it is often put, bureaucratic) regulation and regimentation. Particularly the more philistine among them – and there are more than a few of these – care little for lofty-sounding theories concerning the "rights of man." Nor, for that matter, do they have any materialist (not even any elementary actual) understanding of what in fact is the *basis* of such "economic opportunity" – of the relations of exploitation and oppression, not only in their own countries but internationally, which are the foundation for and set the terms of such "opportunity."

While such views of democracy and freedom serve to foster and reinforce the inclinations and prejudices of these privileged strata, they also exert considerable influence among the dispossessed in society – both because of the prevailing social "atmosphere" and values and because of massive promotion of these ideas through the media, the educational system, and other means – and they serve to channel and contain outrage and outbursts against oppression. Thus, an understanding of democracy – of its place and function in the present-day world and in the historical development of society – is crucial for the exploited and oppressed, who make up the vast majority of humanity, for all those who seek the final abolition of exploitation and oppression.

In reality and in essence, democracy, in whatever form, means democracy only in the ranks of the ruling class (or classes) in society. The other side of this democracy is a dictatorship exercised – as ruthlessly as necessary – over the oppressed classes and groups. The full force of the state will be brought down on those who pose any serious threat to the ruling class, while those who form a base of support for the ruling class, or at least don't do anything serious by way of protest or rebellion, will have a good chance of escaping direct repression. The loyal base of support will even be encouraged and at times mobilized in political action by the political leaders of the state – for example, the initiation of "hard hat" attacks on anti-Vietnam War demonstrators by the Nixon administration a decade ago, or pogroms against Iranians during that "hostage crisis," or violent assaults on abortion clinics and similar services in the U.S. today, stimulated and at least "winked at" by the administration in office (whether Carter in the case of the Iranians or Reagan in relation to the abortion clinics). The role and the force of the state is never neutral: it is always an instrument for protecting and preserving the existing system, for enforcing the dominant relations and class structure, for backing up those who serve and support them, and for suppressing those who are in any kind of fundamental opposition. This is certainly no less true in a democratic form of state than in any other.

Proof of this is everywhere to be found. Besides the international marauding and mass murder carried out by the imperialists, within the U.S. itself (to cite an outstanding example) there are the continual murders of poor people, especially Black people and other oppressed nationalities (at least hundreds every year), by police. There are the vicious police attacks and at times the use of the National Guard, Airborne, and other units of the armed forces (as happened in the U.S. in the 1960s) against protests and rebellions that seriously challenge the established order or major policies of the government. As the experience of the 1960s shows—as well as other experience throughout the history of the U.S. and every other "democratic" country—such repression, besides indiscriminate murder and brutality against rebellious masses, will assume a concentrated, systematic form against organizations and individuals that act as leading forces among the oppressed in revolt. Such organizations and individuals will be targeted for everything from extensive surveillance and infiltration by the political police (the FBI and so forth) all the way to coldly calculated assassination and massive use of force directed from the highest levels of government. The experience of the Black Panther Party in the U.S. in the late '60s to early '70s dramatically illustrates this: more than twenty of its members were murdered by the police, FBI, etc., operating openly as well as undercover, while thousands of its members and supporters were jailed, harassed, hounded. And what the imperialists have on their agenda in this period—above all world war with all that implies—can only be attended by the most vicious repression. This is presently being prepared through the harassment and persecution of immigrants, the sharpening of repressive laws and the legal machinery of repression, the carrying out of "preemptive strikes" against alleged "terrorists," sweeps against "criminal elements" as preparation for sweeps against political opposition elements, and other concerted actions by the governments in the Western imperialist democracies.

The experience of opponents of the system is fundamentally

the same in the social-imperialist bloc (socialist in words, imperialist in fact) headed by the Soviet Union. There are, of course, different peculiar features to the repression carried out in the two rival blocs. One of the more significant focuses of this is the use of psychiatry as a weapon against political dissidents and "misfits." The Soviet Union is notorious for this practice and is roundly condemned for it, including by influential intellectuals in the West. In this regard, the following observations on the use of psychiatry as a repressive tool are both insightful and telling:

> It is important to see that it was not so much that the Soviet protesters were being punished for their protest, although they themselves clearly believed that they were. Rather, the state seemed concerned to *invalidate* a social and political protest by declaring the protesters to be *invalids,* sick, in need of care and protection to cure them of their delusions that there were any blemishes on the features of the Soviet state. But we would argue that the forensic and other psychiatrists who are asked to diagnose the disease of the Soviet protesters are not behaving very differently from their counterparts in the West. Perhaps the chief difference lies in that while the most common candidates for psychiatric hospitalization in the West are drawn from among the working class, women, or ethnic minority people who find it hard to locate a megaphone to speak their troubles to the waiting media world, the Soviet intelligentsia who have been hospitalized are neither inarticulate nor dispossessed.[3]

And I would add that this difference is one of the chief reasons why most intellectuals in the West (and in the Soviet bloc, for that matter) who express outrage at the use of psychiatry by the Soviet authorities to silence political protest are themselves silent when it comes to the same essential technique in the West—by and large they either refuse to speak out against this, refuse to believe it exists, or refuse to concern themselves with it. But despite the prejudices and "blind spots" of such people, the repressive use of psychiatry is a very instructive example of both the particular differences and the common fundamental essence of state power and its function in the Western and Soviet imperialist camps.

Yet, even if all this is true, couldn't it be different? What if governments really were founded on and actually applied the

---

3. R. C. Lewontin, Steven Rose, and Leon J. Kamin, *Not In Our Genes: Biology, Ideology, and Human Nature* (New York: Pantheon Books, 1984), p. 166.

democratic principles and ideals that are proclaimed so loudly and hypocritically by those in power now? Don't democracy and equality still represent the best in human nature and human society? This view is widely propagated and is widely held by democrats, including many "democratic socialists" of various kinds (even theoreticians of Soviet-style "socialism"[4]). This view, however, is both distorted and confined: it is in accord neither with reality nor with the highest vision of what it is possible for humanity to achieve.

In discussing the communist view of this question—and in particular the contributions of Lenin to communist theory on this crucial point—in my book *For a Harvest of Dragons,* I wrote in a footnote that "Lenin also argued that with the achievement of classless society, democracy too would wither away—about this more later."[5] I was not able, however, to go into this in any depth in that book, and it was indeed left for later to return in a central and thoroughgoing way to this subject and the fundamental questions it concentrates. This, then, is the basic theme of this present book: with the achievement of that classless society, communism, on a global level, a radically new and different world and worldview will mark human society, where democracy will have "withered away" and been surpassed. As opposed to the practice of the "democracies" (of various kinds) in today's world *and* to the ideal of democracy, this book will show both the class nature of these "democracies" and the historically limited role of democracy itself—and will point to something indeed much better than that.

4. Listen, for example, to the comments of Mikhail Suslov, a major Soviet ideologue in the last several decades, insisting that communists should not

> renounce the realization of such slogans as freedom, equality, fraternity and democracy, simply on the grounds that these slogans were advanced by the bourgeois revolution and then distorted and debased by the bourgeoisie once it gained power. We believe, on the contrary, that these slogans should require [acquire?—B.A.] their true meaning and be put into practice, which can be done only on the paths of socialism and communism. (M.A. Suslov, *Marxism-Leninism—The International Teaching of the Working Class* [Moscow: Progress Publishers, 1975], p. 178)

Some would accuse Suslov et al. of hypocrisy, arguing that they don't really believe in these ideals and aren't sincere in their declarations of allegiance to them. I think, however, that it is the case, in basic terms, that they do uphold these ideals—which is *far more* of an indictment of these self-proclaimed pioneers "on the paths of socialism and communism."

5. Bob Avakian, *For a Harvest of Dragons* (Chicago: RCP Publications, 1983), p. 70.

2

The Roots and the Rise of Modern Democracy

Ancient Roots

"The Greece of antiquity was the cradle of our democracy." Hardly anyone growing up in the U.S. has not heard this, in school as well as elsewhere. It is something that the molders of thought and public opinion do not tire of repeating through various media. And there is basic truth to it: the city-state government, in particular of Athens, in the classical Greece of more than 2,000 years ago, and the legal system and law codes of ancient Rome, are indeed the "cradle of our democracy" and the "roots of Western civilization." The question is: what exactly can we learn from this?

To begin with a fundamental point, classical Greek city-states, Athens included, were sharply divided into classes: there were dominant class forces and class interests and other, dominated, classes and groups. This class-divided society arose out of the preceding social organization in the area of Athens (and most of Greece) that was not divided into antagonistic classes, and was based on the clan (or gens, with a number of these making up a tribe). In *The Origin of the Family, Private Property, and the State*, Engels gives a basic explanation of how

9

in the Grecian constitution of the Heroic Age, we still find the old gentile system full of vigor; but we also see the beginning of its decay: father right and the inheritance of property by the children, which favored the accumulation of wealth in the family and gave the latter power as against the gens; differentiation in wealth affecting in turn the social constitution by creating first rudiments of a hereditary nobility and monarchy; slavery, first limited to prisoners of war, but already paving the way to the enslavement of fellow members of the tribe and even of the gens; the degeneration of the old intertribal warfare to systematic raids, on land and sea, for the purpose of capturing cattle, slaves, and treasure as a regular means of gaining a livelihood. In short, wealth is praised and respected as the highest treasure, and the old gentile institutions are perverted in order to justify forcible robbery of wealth.[1]

Over a period of time, the Athenian city-state (as well as other Greek city-states) developed clear class structures (Athens came to be divided, across lines of gens and tribe, into three distinct classes) with entrenched ruling elites. As Engels goes on to explain, such a system necessarily involved

an institution that would not only safeguard the newly-acquired property of private individuals against the communistic traditions of the gentile order, would not only sanctify private property, formerly held in such light esteem, and pronounce this sanctification the highest purpose of human society, but would also stamp the gradually developing new forms of acquiring property, and consequently, of constantly accelerating increase in wealth, with

---

1. Frederick Engels, "The Origin of the Family, Private Property, and the State," in Karl Marx and Frederick Engels, *Selected Works* (hereafter referred to as *MESW*) (Moscow: Progress Publishers, 1976), Vol. 3, p. 275. The "Heroic Age" refers to the period in ancient Greece almost 1,000 years B.C.; it is the Greece reflected in the epics of Homer. For a fuller analysis of the transformation from Greek society of this period into the antagonistic class society of the Greek city-states of several centuries later, see also J.S., "Plato: Classical Ideologue of Reaction," in *The Communist* (Chicago: RCP Publications), No. 5 (May 1979), pp. 135-69, especially pp. 135-47; and Lenny Wolff, *The Science of Revolution: An Introduction* (Chicago: RCP Publications, 1983), pp. 176-81.

For a more detailed, and provocative, discussion of some of the major questions concerning the reasons and bases for the emergence of class divisions and social inequalities, in particular the oppression of women, in human social organization – and how this is not the inevitable product of "human nature" or innate characteristics in man, or woman – see (besides Engels's "Origin") Ardea Skybreak, *Of Primeval Steps and Future Leaps* (Chicago: Banner Press, 1984).

the seal of general public recognition; an institution that would perpetuate, not only the newly-rising class division of society, but also the right of the possessing class to exploit the non-possessing classes and the rule of the former over the latter.

And this institution arrived. The *state* was invented.[2]

But, as indicated in the passage previously cited from Engels, it was not simply a matter of the division of the citizenry in Athens (and the other city-states) into clear-cut classes; even more fundamental was the fact that these societies rested on a foundation of slavery—for every adult male citizen in Athens at the height of its prosperity, there were eighteen slaves.[3] As Engels noted, this slavery first involved prisoners of war but then came to involve others as well: with the emergence and development of private property in land and money-lending came mortgages and tenant-farming, and

> [m]ore than that: if the sum obtained from the sale of the lot did not cover the debt, or if such a debt was not secured by a pledge, the debtor had to sell his children into slavery abroad in order to satisfy the creditor's claim. The sale of his children by the father—such was the first fruit of father right and monogamy! And if the blood-sucker was still unsatisfied, he could sell the debtor himself into slavery. Such was the pleasant dawn of civilization among the Athenian people.[4]

Although, perhaps ironically, slavery eventually undermined and brought about the downfall of Athens, for a period slavery was the basis upon which Athens prospered economically and upon which it developed its democratic institutions, celebrated down to today. "The class antagonism on which the social and political institutions rested was no longer that between the nobles and the common people, but that between slaves and freemen, dependents and citizens."[5] Slaves had no rights; they were not counted as citizens but as property. The main function of the state—and in particular the armed forces of Athens, which consisted of a militia and a navy—was now to keep the slaves in

2. Engels, "Origin," *MESW,* 3, p. 275.

3. Engels, "Origin," *MESW,* 3, p. 284.

4. Engels, "Origin," *MESW,* 3, p. 278.

5. Engels, "Origin," *MESW,* 3, p. 284. "Dependents" refers to immigrants and freed slaves.

check (as well as dealing with external enemies). What an appropriate "cradle" indeed for modern "Western civilization" – and "American democracy" in particular – rooted as they are not merely in a system of wage-slavery in the "home countries," with oppressed nationalities and immigrants crucial elements among the exploited proletariat, but in a system of worldwide accumulation depending on superexploitation and plunder of the vast majority of the world's people, in the Third World, who are enslaved in various forms by these democratic imperialists!

The intellectual influence of ancient Athens (and classical Greece more generally) remains today a major component of "Western civilization's" predominant ideology. This finds a concentrated expression in the ideas of Plato and Aristotle – both their actual works and "distilled" or "popularized" versions of major themes in them. These two "luminaries of the Western world" are still counted among its greatest thinkers on both philosophical and political questions. There is perhaps a touch of irony in this, since neither Plato (nor his teacher, Socrates, at least as he is given voice in Plato's dialogues) nor Aristotle was even a champion of Athenian democracy, believing it gave too much power to nonaristocratic strata. Why, then, are they upheld today as leading thinkers of that age whose light has shined through the history of "Western civilization" to give guidance to modern society?[6] Essentially because, on the one hand, they attempted to formulate principles good for all time (transcendental, universal principles) on how society should be structured and led, seeking to base these on concepts of justice, reason, and wisdom that would also be universal. And, on the other hand, their outlook, values, and schema, while they contain specific features that by and large are not directly applicable in today's world – such as the role of slavery, which both Plato and Aristotle vigorously upheld and rationalized – nevertheless include many basic elements that are "universal" to any society based on an oppressive division of labor and division into classes: exploitation of the laboring classes, antagonism between mental and manual labor, patriar-

---

6. Both Plato and Aristotle have, during the course of the more than 2,000 years since they lived, been at different times more or less in favor among the ruling and intellectual elites in Western societies (for example, Aristotle was a target of many of the political theorists and philosophers associated with the rise of the bourgeoisie and capitalist society), but on the whole and in this era specifically they have continued to occupy an honored place and to exert great influence on the ruling political and philosophical thought, such as they are.

chy and the oppression of women, and, along with all this, chauvinism and xenophobia, which are certainly crucial, indispensable components of the modern-day models of freedom, justice, and enlightenment in the West (and the East as well).[7]

Ancient Rome in all its glory – which has exerted so much influence on "Western civilization" down to today, especially in the area of politics and law – was also a society divided into antagonistic classes. Moreover, it too was founded on slavery. It was the large land – and slave – owners who dominated the Roman state (and empire). The slaves, largely those captured in the continuing military adventures and conquests of the Romans, were again not citizens but were counted as property. As in Athens, not only slavery and class domination but patriarchy and the oppression of women were integral parts of the social structure and indispensable to the established order in ancient Rome: they were enshrined and enforced through the state and the political/ideological superstructure generally.

---

7. Of slavery, Plato matter-of-factly writes that "we'd all agree that a man should own the best and most docile slaves he can get" but sets it down that, if lenient treatment does not bring the desired results, "we should certainly punish slaves if they deserve it, and not spoil them by simply giving them a warning, as we would free men. Virtually everything you say to slaves should be an order." And he even gives explicit instructions for whipping slaves – for example, if a slave takes fruit from a landowner's trees without permission, "the number of lashes [is] to be the same as the number of grapes in the bunch or the figs picked off the fig tree" (Plato, *The Laws,* trans. Trevor J. Saunders [Middlesex: Penguin Books, 1970], Book 6, pp. 257, 259; Book 8, p. 346). For a fuller picture of Plato's views, not only on slavery but on the other questions raised in the text just above, see also *The Republic.*

Aristotle not only insists that "for those who are to till the land, the best thing (if we are to describe the ideal) is that they should be slaves. They should not be all of one stock nor men of spirit; this will ensure that they will be useful workers and no danger as potential rebels"; but in explaining that "a state's purpose is not merely to provide a living but to make a life that is good," he goes on to say, "Otherwise it might be made up of slaves or animals other than man, and that is impossible, because slaves and animals do not participate in happiness, nor in a life that involves choice" (Aristotle, *The Politics,* trans. T. A. Sinclair [Middlesex: Penguin Books, 1981], VII, x, p. 420; III, ix, p. 196). In fact it is important to emphasize that Aristotle and Plato's rationalizations for slavery are only "by and large" not applicable in today's world (since there still is literal slavery in some parts of the world) and to keep in mind that, until relatively recently (only a century ago) in the U.S., Aristotle's arguments on slavery were "still in use among the defenders of slavery" (T. A. Sinclair, "Introduction" to Aristotle, *The Politics,* p. 21 – and see *The Politics,* I, v for more of Aristotle's defense of slavery, in particular his attempt to ground this in alleged differences in the natures of different people). *The Politics* gives a comprehensive picture of Aristotle's views, not just on slavery but on the

Even among the free (nonslave) citizenry of Rome – and even after changes were made in the political institutions to allow more voice to the common people – differences in economic position and status, and property distinctions linked to political participation, worked to ensure that it was the minority of aristocrats who controlled the politics and economics of Rome, both during its Republican period and later in the Roman Empire. One historical account describes how "the social realities of republican Rome" were clearly reflected, and reinforced, in the distinctions "made by the Roman census between those able to equip themselves with the arms and armor needed to serve soldiers, those whose only contribution to the state was to breed children (the *proletarii*) and those who were simply counted as heads, because they neither owned property nor had families." And "below them all, of course, were the slaves."[8]

---

questions referred to in the text above.

As noted, neither Plato nor Aristotle was a champion of Athenian democracy (though their specific objections to it differed in some ways). Plato insisted that society should be ruled by a specifically selected and rigorously trained elite – in *The Republic* is found Plato's famous notion of the philosopher-king as the ideal ruler – and (like his mentor, Socrates) he was a bitter opponent of the involvement of the common people in decision-making. At one point in *The Republic*, Socrates issues this bitter denunciation: "democracy comes into being after the poor have conquered their opponents, slaughtering some and banishing some, while to the remainder they give an equal share of freedom and power..." (Plato, *The Republic*, trans. B. Jowett [New York: Vintage Books, 1955], VIII, p. 310). This is a distortion of what democracy really is, but it is revealing of Plato's (and Socrates's) biases all the same. As for Aristotle, T. A. Sinclair has written that "Aristotle has no clear-cut answer to give to the question 'which is the best form of constitution?' But he found plenty of warrant in *The Politics* for saying that the rule of one outstandingly good man, backed by just laws, is most desirable, if only it can be attained" ("Introduction" to *The Politics*, p. 16). Aristotle opposed tyranny as a form of government and in a general sense favored rule by an elite, allowing for some secondary role for the common people. The following criticism by Aristotle of tyranny is noteworthy: "The features of extreme democracy are also all characteristic of a tyrant's policy: the dominance of women in the home, and slack control of slaves." And "there is evidently something characteristic of democracy in all the typical measures of tyranny – lack of control over slaves (which may be expedient up to a point), and over women and children, and disregard of everyone living as they please" (*The Politics*, V, xi, p. 346; and VI, iv, p. 372). Again a distortion of democracy (unintentionally making it look better than it is), but revealing in its distortion.

8. J.M. Roberts, *The Pelican History of the World* (Middlesex: Penguin Books, 1984), p. 233. For more on how class distinctions influenced Roman politics and the domination of them by the upper classes, see Edward Gibbon, *The Decline and Fall of the Roman Empire* (New York: Modern Library, 1932), especially Vol. 2, chapter 44.

As Roman society developed and expanded through military conquest, slavery became more extensive and more decisive, and at the same time those among the conquered peoples who were not enslaved were included among the ranks of Roman citizens. It was to a significant degree in relation to this that a particular and very important contribution of the Roman rulers to "Western civilization" was made: the development of legal theory and the systematizing of rather extensive legal codes which served to reinforce the class distinctions and social relations generally under Roman rule, and which, beyond that, have provided much of the foundation for the laws and legal systems of the democratic republics of the modern era, including the USA and its "parent," England. The following account not untypically combines an idealized and "selective" account of the basis for Roman jurisprudence with some analysis of its actual historical-material roots and a generally accurate assessment of its influence down to today:

> The origins of the doctrine of the unalienable rights of man are too well known to need more than passing reference here. Oddly enough the theory arose in the decline of the Greek city states. Greek thinkers had earlier reached the conclusion that the world of nature was a cosmos, a world of laws discoverable by the human reason. As a result of the conquest of much of the East by Alexander the Great, there were far more contacts between their citizens and those of other states. The Stoics became deeply conscious that men lived in One World, that they were all citizens of one great city which they called cosmopolis. This world of man, too, has its laws, and they too must be recognized if man is to realize his human potential.
>
> This could be dismissed as empty theorizing. But oddly enough at about the same time the more practical Romans were confronted with a similar problem. Members of non-Roman peoples or tribes were beginning to flock to Rome to pursue commerce or enjoy her greater security. As non-citizens they as yet had no legal rights or status. Roman magistrates sought to discover a common denominator for the laws of all peoples and, so they believed, found it in what they called the law of nations, which they concluded must be the fundamental law. This was the basis of those laws of nature and of nature's God to which Jefferson appealed in our Declaration of Independence, and was to provide the basis of our modern conceptions of human rights and of equity. All this entered into the basic concepts of Roman jurisprudence which was to affect so deeply European civilization, and our own....

Roman jurisprudence [was] perhaps her greatest single contribution to civilization.[9]

As the encyclopedic eighteenth-century historian Edward
Gibbon relates, it was actually in the period of the decline of the
Roman Empire that Roman jurisprudence was systematized and
codified in enduring form, at the time of the Emperor Justinian in
the sixth century A.D.: "Under his reign, and by his care, the civil
jurisprudence was digested in the immortal works of the CODE,
the PANDECTS, and the INSTITUTES: the public reason of the
Romans has been silently or studiously transfused into the
domestic institutions of Europe, and the laws of Justinian still
command the respect or obedience of independent nations."[10]
Gibbon goes on to detail how this Roman jurisprudence regulated
the property relations of the society, including such things as
trade and debt but also, of course, the slaves, and gave absolute
domination (for several centuries this meant literally the power
of life and death) to the man as the head of the family in relation
to his wife and children, as well as to his slaves. In fact, as Engels
explains in exposing the roots of another fundamental institution
of modern society:

> The word *familia* did not originally signify the ideal of our modern
> Philistine, which is a compound of sentimentality and domestic
> discord. Among the Romans, in the beginning, it did not even
> refer to the married couple and their children, but to the slaves
> alone. *Famulus* means a household slave and *familia* signifies the
> totality of slaves belonging to one individual. Even in the time of
> Gaius the *familia, id est patrimonium* (that is, the inheritance) was
> bequeathed by will. The expression was invented by the Romans
> to describe a new social organism, the head of which had under
> him wife and children and a number of slaves, under Roman
> paternal power, with power of life and death over them all.[11]

In addition, Gibbon, referring to the famous Twelve Tables of

9. Christian Gauss, "Introduction" to Niccolò Machiavelli, *The Prince* (New
York: New American Library, 1980), p. 28.

10. Gibbon, *Decline of Roman Empire*, 2, chapter 44, pp. 668-69. As for that
other major ideological pillar of "Western civilization," the whole "Judeo-Christian
tradition" which was funneled and filtered through the Roman Empire to modern
Europe and America, that is beyond the scope of this book – I hope to deal with it
in a separate essay in the future.

11. Engels, "Origin," *MESW*, 3, p. 233.

Roman Law and specifically their "cruelty. . . against insolvent debtors," points out, "At the expiration of sixty days the debt was discharged by the loss of liberty or life; the insolvent debtor was either put to death or sold in foreign slavery beyond the Tiber: but, if several creditors were alike obstinate and unrelenting, they might legally dismember his body, and satiate their revenge by this horrid partition."[12] And Gibbon summarizes how Roman laws, besides setting down the rights and duties of the citizens in regard to legal and civil proceedings and in other spheres, also regulated how the spoils of foreign conquest by Rome were to be distributed.[13]

This legal tradition and its underlying concepts have been modified and "refined" since the time of the Roman Empire, of course—outright slavery has been abolished in Europe and America, where wage-slavery now prevails, and such things as the enslavement, or dismemberment, of debtors have been replaced by measures more appropriate to modern economic relations. But it is nevertheless very true that the basic principles governing Roman law and civil society were "to affect so deeply European civilization, and our own" and that this was perhaps Rome's "greatest single contribution to civilization." And this is a very telling exposure of the fundamental nature of that "civilization" today, which claims these Roman traditions as well as the political ancestry of ancient Athens as its democratic roots and "the basis of our modern conceptions of human rights and of equity."

Modern Democracy as a Phenomenon and Function of the Bourgeois Epoch

The dissolution of the Roman Empire was spurred on by the internal decay within the empire, particularly owing to the fact that slave labor was the only possible form of large-scale agriculture in that period, but:

> [s]lavery no longer paid, and so it died out; but dying slavery left behind its poisonous sting by branding as ignoble the productive

12. Gibbon, *Decline of Roman Empire*, 2, chapter 44, p. 719.
13. See Gibbon, *Decline of Roman Empire*, 2, chapter 44.

work of the free. . . . [S]lavery was economically impossible, while the labor of the free was under a moral ban. The one could no longer, the other could not yet, be the basic form of social production.[14]

At the same time, this decay was also driven forward by the very expansion of the empire itself and the wars of conquest by Rome, as well as the successive conquests of Roman dominions by "the barbarians." Out of all this emerged the feudal European societies. These were marked by a great deal of stagnancy and inertia, but they were not without internal contradiction and change, nor were they unaffected by developments elsewhere and by interactions and collisions with each other and with different peoples and states in other parts of the world. Eventually Europe gave birth to the first modern, bourgeois nation-states through a series of social eruptions, upheavals, and transformations, with worldwide dimensions.

English Liberal Tradition

The rise of the bourgeoisie, capitalism, and the modern nation-state are historically associated with and gave rise to the contemporary concepts of freedom (liberty), democracy, equality, "the rights of man," the principle of "tolerance" with regard to ideas and beliefs, and so on. It was particularly in England of the seventeenth century that these principles first began to be systematically formulated. England in this period was experiencing the relatively rapid expansion of commodity production and exchange relations and political conflicts and revolutions which, while involving religious conflicts and intertwined with foreign wars, represented the strengthening of the bourgeoisie and capitalism in opposition to the old feudal order and its ruling nobility. In England, over a several-century period, the triumph of capitalism, while extremely thorough in the economic base of society, was represented in the superstructure by the gradual incorporation of the monarchy into the structure of bourgeois political rule and the transformation of the aristocracy into an appendage of the bourgeois order (this is still reflected in present-day English political and social life). The seventeenth century

14. Engels, "Origin," *MESW*, 3, p. 310.

was a pivotal period in this overall process, and the theories of two leading English political philosophers of that century, Thomas Hobbes and John Locke, have not only played an important part in the development of constitutional government in England but to a significant degree established the foundations for what have continued to be the declared precepts of Western democracy in general. C.B. Macpherson, in pointing especially to Hobbes's and Locke's role in this, argues that the roots of the theoretical basis for the liberal-democratic state

> may properly be taken to be in the political theory and practice of the English seventeenth century. It was then, in the course of a protracted struggle in parliament, a civil war, a series of republican experiments, a restoration of the monarchy, and a final constitutional revolution, that the principles which were to become basic to liberal democracy were all developed, though not with equal success at the time. And it is clear that an essential ingredient, both of the practical struggle and of the theoretical justifications, was a new belief in the value and the rights of the individual. . . . The individual was seen neither as a moral whole, nor as part of a larger social whole, but as an owner of himself. . . . The human essence is freedom from dependence on the wills of others, and freedom is a function of possession. Society becomes a lot of free equal individuals related to each other as proprietors of their own capacities and of what they have acquired by their exercise. Society consists of relations of exchange between proprietors. Political society becomes a calculated device for the protection of this property and for the maintenance of an orderly relation of exchange.[15]

While Macpherson's characterization of the view of the individual is too absolute – particularly the notion that this individual was not seen "as part of a larger social whole" – there is a great deal of truth, and insight, in his analysis, as there is in his argument that:

> Individualism, as a basic theoretical position, starts at least as far back as Hobbes. Although his conclusion can scarcely be called liberal, his postulates were highly individualistic. Discarding

15. C. B. Macpherson, *The Political Theory of Possessive Individualism* (Oxford: Oxford University Press, 1979), pp. 1, 3. While not a Marxist-Leninist, Macpherson has a number of interesting insights on the subject of English liberal-democratic tradition.

traditional concepts of society, justice, and natural law, he deduced political rights and obligation from the interest and will of dissociated individuals.[16]

Hobbes, whose major work, *The Leviathan,* was published in the middle of the seventeenth century (1651) and less than a decade after a bloody civil war which resulted in the beheading of a king, was strongly influenced by the competitive struggle among commodity producers that was increasingly marking England, as well as by the acute social conflicts and political upheaval that punctuated the rise of the bourgeoisie and capitalist relations in England in that period. Hobbes saw this not in its real light – as a reflection of the intensifying contradictions in the economic base of the society in which he lived and the struggles and changes to which this was giving rise. Rather, he saw it as a result of the basic nature of man, or, as he put it, of man in the state of nature, which he basically characterized as the war of each against all. He did not argue that people everywhere had at one time or another lived in such a state, outside of civil society and its government – the inclinations and behavior of man in the state of nature represented, according to Hobbes, what would prevail if there was not a powerful enough social force capable of compelling people to act differently. Hobbes therefore insisted on the need for an absolute sovereign – though sovereign need not imply a monarchy, the sovereign could be a legislature – precisely in order to preserve and promote the interests of each and all:

> The only way to erect such a common power, as may be able to defend them from the invasion of foreigners, and the injuries of one another, and thereby to secure them in such sort, as that by their own industry, and by the fruits of the earth, they may nourish themselves and live contentedly; is, to confer all their power and strength upon one man, or upon one assembly of men, that may reduce all their wills, by plurality of voices, unto one will. . . .[17]

Macpherson links this doctrine of Hobbes to what he calls "the possessive market society, a society based on commodity produc-

---

16. Macpherson, *Possessive Individualism,* p. 1.

17. Thomas Hobbes, *The Leviathan* (New York: Collier Books, 1978), chapter 17, p. 132. Hobbes devotes an entire chapter (and more) of *The Leviathan* to the rights of sovereigns – see, in particular, chapter 18.

tion and exchange, where labor power itself is a commodity – in short, capitalist society:

> It is a society in which men who want more may, and do, continually seek to transfer to themselves some of the powers of others, in such a way as to compel everyone to compete for more power, and all this by peaceable and legal methods which do not destroy the society by open force. . . . Only in a society in which each man's capacity to labor is his own property, is alienable, and is a market commodity, could all individuals be in this continual competitive power relationship.[18]

And "[o]nly in a society in which every man's labor is an exchangeable commodity can the transfer of control of individuals' powers be as ubiquitous as is required by Hobbes's assumptions."[19] Macpherson further argues that a major reason why Hobbes's doctrine met with considerable – and often very intense – opposition was that Hobbes was formulating his theories at a point when capitalist commodity relations were still in their early stages of development and locked in acute conflict with what Macpherson terms *"customary or status society"*[20] (this classification seems to refer to both slave and feudal society, but in the concrete historical context of seventeenth-century England, feudal relations were the obstacle to capitalist development). Hence,

> Hobbes was addressing men who did not yet think and behave entirely as market men, whose calculation of the kind of political obligation they should acknowledge was still based on less than a full appreciation of what was most to their own interest, most consistent with their true nature as competitive men. He was asking those men to bring their thinking into line with their real needs and capacities as market men.[21]

Hobbes's political theory was not, however, simply grounded in capitalist commodity relations; it also was rooted in the scientific revolution of the time – which was spurred by and in turn spurred the extension of capitalist relations and the world

18. Macpherson, *Possessive Individualism*, p. 59.
19. Macpherson, *Possessive Individualism*, p. 51.
20. Macpherson, *Possessive Individualism*, p. 49.
21. Macpherson, *Possessive Individualism*, p. 105.

market – with its shattering of medieval shackles and its bold assertion of mechanical materialism. To quote Macpherson again, with Hobbes there is "a fundamental connection between his political theory and his scientific materialism."[22] Hobbes was strongly influenced by the scientific findings and method of Galileo and by the French philosopher/scientist René Descartes. Descartes placed mathematical principles and mathematical proof at the center of scientific inquiry. Beyond that, he sought to reduce or equate all material existence, including human beings, to machine processes. But at the same time, he posited a basic dualism – he rationalized the existence of god and of a human soul somehow different from and not governed by the mechanical mathematical principles that in his view governed material reality. Both Descartes's mechanical materialism and his dualism not only exerted influence on Hobbes and others in seventeenth-century Europe; with all the political and economic developments and advances in science since then, they have continued to exert considerable influence on political and scientific thought in the West down to the present time, because they continue to reflect and serve the worldview and interests of the bourgeoisie.[23]

In Hobbes's own introduction to *The Leviathan*, we read:

Nature, the art whereby God hath made and governs the world, is by the *art* of man, as in many other things, so in this also imitated, that it can make an artificial animal. For seeing life is but a motion of limbs, the beginning whereof is in some principal part within; why may we not say, that all *automata* (engines that move themselves by springs and wheels as doth a watch) have an artificial life? For what is the *heart*, but a *spring*; and the *nerves*, but so many *strings*; and the *joints*, but so many *wheels*, giving motion to the whole body, such as was intended by the artificer? *Art* goes yet further, imitating that rational and most excellent work of nature, *man*. For by art is created that great LEVIATHAN called a COMMON-WEALTH, or STATE, in Latin CIVITAS, which is but an artificial man; though of greater stature and strength than the natural, for whose protection and defense it was intended; and in which the *sovereignty* is an artificial *soul*, as giving life and motion to the

---

22. Macpherson, *Possessive Individualism*, p. 78.

23. For an interesting discussion of this influence, and in particular its negative aspects, see Lewontin, Rose, and Kamin, *Not In Our Genes*, especially pp. 40-51; see also Ernst Mayr, *The Growth of Biological Thought* (Cambridge, Mass.: Belknap Press, 1982), especially pp. 25, 40, 97-98.

whole body; the *magistrates,* and other *officers* of judicature and execution, artificial *joints; reward* and *punishment,* by which fastened to the seat of the sovereignty every joint and member is moved to perform his duty, are the *nerves,* that do the same in the body natural; the *wealth* and *riches* of all the particular members, are the *strength; salus populi,* the *people's safety,* its *business; counsellors,* by whom all things are needful for it to know are suggested unto it, are the *memory; equity,* and *laws,* an artificial *reason* and *will; concord, health; sedition, sickness;* and *civil war, death.* Lastly, the *pacts* and *covenants,* by which the parts of this body politic were at first made, set together, and united, resemble that *fiat,* or the *let us make man,* pronounced by God in the Creation.[24]

Just as, in this view, "the laws of nature are immutable and eternal,"[25] so too there are universal, immutable, and eternal laws that must govern society. And, argues Hobbes, as the essential tendency of any body is to continue in motion unless it meets with opposition, so freedom or liberty "signifieth, properly, the absence of opposition; by opposition, I mean external impediments of motion. . . . For whatsoever is so tied, or environed, as it cannot move but within a certain space, which space is determined by the opposition of some external body, we say it hath not liberty to go further."[26]

Yet, as Macpherson has argued, Hobbes's

materialism was not, of course, a sufficient condition of his theory of obligation. For besides the materialist assumption that men are self-moving systems of matter in motion, he needed the postulate that the motion of every individual is necessarily opposed to the motion of every other. This latter postulate was not contained in his mechanical materialism but was derived, as we have seen, from his market assumption. The postulate of opposed motion was what enabled him to treat all individuals as equally insecure, and hence as equally in need of a system of political obligation.

Thus both the materialist and the market assumptions were required to enable Hobbes to deduce political obligation. . . .

24. Hobbes, *The Leviathan,* p. 19.

25. Hobbes, *The Leviathan,* p. 123. The understanding of *internal* contradiction within things and the motion associated with *this,* the contradiction, struggle, and qualitative transformation of things through leaps and ruptures – and of the truth that motion, struggle, and change are absolute while rest, stability, and identity are relative – that is revealed by *dialectical* materialism is not found in the mechanical materialist view.

26. Hobbes, *The Leviathan,* p. 159.

It is only a society as fragmented as a market society that can credibly be treated as a mechanical system of self-moving individuals.[27]

Hobbes, however, like representatives of bourgeois relations generally, idealized these relations. Macpherson puts it this way:

> His model failed to correspond to the possessive market model in that he did not allow for the existence of politically significant unequal classes. He saw society as so necessarily fragmented by the struggle of each for power over others that all were equal in insecurity. He failed to see that the very same characteristic of a society which makes it an incessant competition of each for power over others, makes it also an unequal class-divided society. The characteristic is the all-pervasive market relationship. Only where all men's powers are marketable commodities can there be an incessant competition of each for power over others; and where all men's powers are commodities there is necessarily a division of society into unequal class.[28]

Macpherson adds that Hobbes was aware of class division in England, but he suggests that Hobbes was "apparently more impressed with the divisive effects of the loss of old values, and with the contests for power between different groups on the parliamentary side which broke out as soon as the monarchy had been thrown over, than by the cohesion that had enabled the opponents of the old structure to overthrow it."[29] In any case, there is no mistaking the fact that, at least by the time he wrote *The Leviathan,* Hobbes regarded what he described as "the calamities of confusion and civil war"[30] as evils that could only be prevented through the exercise of absolute sovereignty. Such a view is consistent with that of the English bourgeoisie in the concrete historical circumstances it faced at that time, fearing popular discontent and revolt and finding the necessity to compromise and "work through" – rather than abolish – the monarchy, as a counterweight to the old nobility and a buttress of the state against the poorer classes.[31]

---

27. Macpherson, *Possessive Individualism*, p. 79.

28. Macpherson, *Possessive Individualism*, p. 93.

29. Macpherson, *Possessive Individualism*, p. 94.

30. Hobbes, *The Leviathan*, p. 325.

31. The influence on Hobbes of Francis Bacon is significant. Bacon was an early seventeenth-century champion of the new age, in which mankind would ad-

It was in the second half of the seventeenth century that "with the creation of a contractual monarchy England at last broke with her *ancien régime* and began to function as a constitutional state."[32] This was consummated in 1688-89 with what has been called the "Glorious Revolution" (with no small amount of hyperbole – viewed even by the standards of that time it was neither so thorough a revolution nor perhaps so glorious). Be that as it may, this event did represent a significant change in the structure of English government, and in the complex of European power relations: it ousted James II from the English throne and enthroned in his place the Dutch William, with his wife Mary Stuart, at the same time as it firmly established constitutional monarchy in England. In this process, John Locke was a major force, practically and theoretically. This finds concentrated expression in one of Locke's major and historically most influential works, his *Treatises* on government. "It is clear," writes C.B. Macpherson,

> that when Locke wrote the *Two Treatises* he was no unworldly scholar but a man of property, greatly interested in safeguarding established property institutions, much concerned with policies to promote the increase of the nation's wealth, and deeply committed to the Whig position, both when it was a conspiracy against Charles II in 1679-83, and an open conspiracy against James II in 1688, and of course when it had triumphed with the installation of William and Mary in 1689. The *Treatises* are a product of that experience, of a mind shaped in Oxford and reshaped in conspiratorial and commercial London.[33]

As compared to Hobbes's *Leviathan*, Locke's *Treatises* is a more developed and more direct exposition of the principles of bourgeois property relations and their corresponding political principles and ideals. And it is largely for this reason that it has re-

---

vance to new heights through the power of knowledge and mastery over nature; Bacon was also an advocate of powerful government. And it is difficult not to hear in Hobbes's insistence on the decisive role of a powerful sovereign an echo of a major theme in Shakespeare, a contemporary of Bacon's. Many Shakespearean tragedies, with *Hamlet* an outstanding example, and even many comedies, like *Henry IV*, express this theme (with the caveat that the sovereign must be above corruption).

32. Roberts, *Pelican History of the World*, p. 564.

33. Macpherson, "Editor's Introduction" to John Locke, *Second Treatise of Government* (Indianapolis: Hackett Publishing, 1980), p. x.

mained one of the main pillars of bourgeois liberal thought. On the one hand, it is true, as Macpherson points out, that Locke's view of human motivation is very similar in important respects to that of Hobbes: "Appetites and aversions are the mainspring. Unless they are checked by a law armed with rewards and punishments they will override all moral behavior."[34] But Locke did not draw the conclusion that an all-powerful sovereign was required; rather, he insisted that the sovereign must be limited in relation to the members of society, especially in their most essential aspect: as property owners. As Macpherson explains, Locke's crucial chapter on property in his *Second Treatise*

> fixed property rights firmly in the center of all subsequent liberal theory; and it is essential to an understanding of Locke's chain of argument from the state of nature to the limited and conditional nature of governments' powers. . . .
>
> Locke has thus in effect removed all the initial natural law limits on individual appropriation, and has established a natural right to unlimited amounts of private property. It is important to notice that Locke has all this happening in the state of nature, *before* men entered civil society. . . . It is to protect this natural unlimited right that men agree to establish civil society and government.[35]

Right off the bat in his *Second Treatise,* Locke defines political power as "a *right* of making laws with penalties of death, and consequently all less penalties, for the regulating and preserving of property. . . ."[36] Then in the chapter on property, beginning with the thesis that, while nature has provided the earth and its stores to mankind in common, it is only through labor that this can be appropriated—and moreover, that in transforming nature through labor people add to what nature has provided—Locke works up his whole argument on the right not only of private property but of unequal wealth, and of commodity exchange through the medium of money. His conclusion on this is a classical statement of capitalist property principles and their political expression—idealizing not only the role of money but of capitalist commodity relations generally and the role of govern-

---

34. Macpherson, "Editor's Introduction" to *Second Treatise,* p. xi. Locke's views on this are grounded in the same basic mechanical materialist (and dualist) precepts as were Hobbes's.

35. Macpherson, "Editor's Introduction" to *Second Treatise,* pp. xvi, xvii.

36. Locke, *Second Treatise,* p. 8.

ment in relation to them:

> But since gold and silver, being little useful to the life of man in proportion to food, raiment and carriage, has its *value* only from the consent of men, whereof *labor* yet *makes*, in great part, *the measure*, it is plain, that men have agreed to a disproportionate and unequal *possession of the earth*, they having, by a tacit and voluntary consent, found out a way how a man may fairly possess more land than he himself can use the product of, by receiving in exchange for the overplus gold and silver, which may be hoarded up without injury to any one; these metals not spoiling or decaying in the hands of the possessor. This partage of things in an inequality of private possessions, men have made practicable out of the bounds of society, and without compact, only by putting a value on gold and silver, and tacitly agreeing in the use of money: for in governments, the laws regulate the right of property, and the possession of land is determined by positive constitutions.[37]

In Locke's thinking – as in the reality of capitalist relations, which it reflected – property rights and commodity production and exchange mean not just the right to one's own possessions and to the product of one's own labor but also the right to buy and sell the capacity to labor itself, labor power. Once again, Locke derives this from the right of possession of one's own labor power as well as the right to the product of one's own labor. Since it is one's own possession, one has the right to alienate one's labor power – to exchange it for a wage. Once thus alienated, this labor power belongs to whomever purchases it (though the laborer himself, as a person, does not belong to this purchaser and cannot be bought and sold, a fundamental difference from outright slavery). But therefore the logical conclusion – and the actual fact under capitalist relations – is that the product (or result) of the labor performed belongs not to the laborer who has alienated his labor power but to the person who has purchased it and uses it, applies it as concrete labor. Thus Locke could say, expressing himself in the terms of seventeenth-century wage-labor, while essaying to set forth universal principles,

> the grass my horse has bit; the turfs *my servant* has cut; and the ore I have digged in any place, where I have a right to them in common with others, become my *property*, without the assignation or

37. Locke, *Second Treatise*, pp. 29-30.

consent of any body. The *labor* that was *mine,* removing them out of that common state they were in, hath *fixed* my *property* in them.[38]

Macpherson has summed up this point and its significance as follows:

his insistence that a man's labor was his own – which was the essential novelty of Locke's doctrine of property – has almost the opposite significance from that more generally attributed to it in recent years; it provides a moral foundation for bourgeois appropriation.... The insistence that a man's labor is his own property is the root of this justification.... If it is labor, a man's absolute property, which justifies appropriation and creates value, the individual right of appropriation overrides any moral claims of the society. The traditional view that property and labor were social functions, and that ownership of property involved social obligations, is thereby undermined.

In short, Locke has done what he set out to do. Starting from the traditional assumption that the earth and its fruits had originally been given to mankind for their common use, he has turned the tables on all who derived from this assumption theories which were restrictive of capitalist appropriation. He has erased the moral disability with which unlimited capitalist appropriation had hitherto been handicapped.[39]

Marx and Engels, a century and a half after Locke, in drawing the following vivid picture of the triumph of capitalist relations as it had unfolded from the seventeenth century to the middle of the nineteenth, themselves laid bare the essence of this process:

The bourgeoisie, wherever it has got the upper hand, has put an end to all feudal, patriarchal, idyllic relations. It has pitilessly torn asunder the motley feudal ties that bound man to his "natural superiors," and has left remaining no other nexus between man and man than naked self-interest, than callous "cash payment." It has drowned the most heavenly ecstasies of religious fervor, of chivalrous enthusiasm, of philistine sentimentalism, in the icy water of egotistical calculation. It has resolved personal worth into exchange value, and in place of the numberless indefeasible

38. Locke, *Second Treatise,* pp. 19-20, emphasis added to "my servant" and "mine."

39. Macpherson, *Possessive Individualism,* pp. 220-21.

chartered freedoms, has set up that single, unconscionable freedom – Free Trade. In one word, for exploitation, veiled by religious and political illusions, it has substituted naked, shameless, direct, brutal exploitation.[40]

In sum, the society of which Locke was a theoretical exponent, as well as a practical political partisan, was a society based on wage-slavery and capitalist exploitation. And it is not surprising that, while he was opposed to slavery in England itself, he not only defended the institution of slavery, under certain circumstances, in the *Second Treatise*,[41] but turned a not insignificant profit himself in the slade trade[42] and helped to draw up the charter for a government headed by a slave-owning aristocracy in one of the American colonies.[43] For as Marx sarcastically summarized:

> The discovery of gold and silver in America, the extirpation, enslavement and entombment in mines of the aboriginal population, the beginning of the conquest and looting of the East Indies, the turning of Africa into a warren for the commercial hunting of black-skins, signalized the rosy dawn of the era of capitalist production.[44]

"With the development of capitalist production during the manufacturing period," Marx observed, "the public opinion of Europe had lost the last remnant of shame and conscience. The nations bragged cynically of every infamy that served them as a means to capitalistic accumulation." He then cites the profitability of the slave trade for such places as Liverpool, England, as late as the eighteenth century, and concludes:

40. Marx and Engels, *Manifesto of the Communist Party* (Peking: Foreign Languages Press, 1975), pp. 35-36 (hereafter referred to as *Communist Manifesto*). It should be noted that Marx and Engels are here stressing the contrast between capitalist and previous exploitative relations; so when they say, for example, that the bourgeoisie has put an end to all patriarchal relations, they have in mind, as they indicate, feudal patriarchal relations and not patriarchy in the more general sense, as Engels uses it in *The Origin of the Family, Private Property, and the State*, for example.

41. See Locke, *Second Treatise*, pp. 17-18; see also pp. 42-51.

42. Macpherson, "Editor's Introduction" to *Second Treatise*, p. x.

43. See Howard Zinn, *A People's History of the United States* (New York: Harper Colophon Books, 1980), pp. 73-74.

44. Marx, *Capital* (New York: International Publishers, 1970), Vol. 1, p. 751.

> Whilst the cotton industry introduced child-slavery in England, it gave in the United States a stimulus to the transformation of the earlier, more or less patriarchal slavery, into a system of commercial exploitation. In fact, the veiled slavery of the wage-workers in Europe needed, for its pedestal, slavery pure and simple in the new world.[45]

Also consistent with his bourgeois outlook, Locke not only saw the necessity and desirability of what is objectively an exploitative division of labor in society but saw a "natural" basis for this. To a significant degree, his thinking was influenced by the mechanical materialism (and dualism) of Descartes and the application and development of these by Newton in the second half of the seventeenth century, by what Ernst Mayr has described as "[t]he 'mechanization of the world picture'—the belief in a highly orderly world such as one would expect if the world was designed by the creator to obey a limited set of eternal laws...," which really took off starting with Galileo and "achieved its greatest triumph in Newton's unification of terrestrial and celestial mechanics."[46] Newton allowed for—indeed insisted on—the existence of god as a prime mover, setting the universe and its laws in motion, but he also insisted that this god did not interfere with the ongoing functioning of this physical world, which Newton defined as a complex but highly ordered machine, a whole "system of the world" whose workings in whole and in part were governed by a small number of basic overarching universal laws.[47] Clearly, according to Newton's methodology, this "system of the world" had equal validity when applied to the world of men as when applied to the rest of the natural world. Shouldn't the

---

45. Marx, *Capital*, 1, pp. 759-60.

46. Mayr, *Growth of Biological Thought*, p. 39. Evidence of Locke's mechanical materialism and dualism is found throughout his very influential philosophical work, *An Essay Concerning Human Understanding*, including the following rather astounding assertion: the existence of god is "the most obvious truth that reason discovers," and evidence of it is "equal to mathematical certainty"! (See Locke, *An Essay Concerning Human Understanding*, ed. Maurice Cranston [New York: Collier Books, 1965], p. 349.) Cranston points out in his introductory essay (p. 17) that philosophically, as well as politically, Locke's thought exerted considerable influence on central figures in the American and French revolutions of the late eighteenth century and on "the central American tradition of pragmatism" as well as the "central British tradition of empiricism."

47. See Isaac Newton, *Mathematical Principles of Natural Philosophy and His System of the World (Philosophiae Naturalist Principia Mathematica)* (Berkeley: University of California Press, 1962).

world of men, too, be organized as an efficient machine with each part doing what it was supposed to and with the whole machine performing its function?

It is important to note, however, that the division of labor that would be consistent with this is not one based on natural order in the sense that particular individuals have a predetermined place in this overall machinery – this corresponds to the feudal view, and Newton's principles and their political parallels were a weapon of the rising bourgeoisie against the feudal system and its outlook. The division of labor of capitalist society is one not formally or legally determined by hereditary title, rank, and so on, but by the functioning of the process of capitalist commodity production and exchange, by the process of capitalist accumulation, and by the political (including military) processes and conflicts to which this gives rise. Through the filter of bourgeois ideology, this appears as the selection of people for different roles on the basis of their merit or performance, their success or failure in the marketplace and in the society generally. Thus Locke sees no contradiction between his insistence on the fundamental equality of men and the fact that they come to occupy different stations in life. For the equality he insists on – the equality that represents the bourgeois ideal – is "that *equal right*, that every man hath, to *his natural freedom*, without being subjected to the will or authority of any other man."[48] That, in fact, no such "natural freedom" exists in the society around him, that in bourgeois society itself the majority of people, the laboring population and the wage-workers in particular, are subjected to the authority of other men, the bourgeois ruling class, was not something about which Locke was completely ignorant, but, again, he regarded this as the natural result of the exercise by all men of their wills and abilities. Macpherson explains:

> The assumption that men are by nature equally capable of shifting for themselves was not an idle one. It enabled Locke in good conscience to reconcile the great inequalities of observed society with the postulated equality of natural right.[49]

Locke naturally drew political conclusions from all this. Macpherson recalls how in Locke's account of the relations of men in

---

48. Locke, *Second Treatise*, p. 31.
49. Macpherson, *Possessive Individualism*, pp. 244-45.

the state of nature, after a certain point, "with the introduction of money in any territory, all the land therein is soon appropriated, leaving some men without any," and "those who are left with no land cannot be industrious and rational in the original sense: they cannot appropriate and improve the land to their own benefit, which was originally the essence of rational behavior."[50] And

> at this point it became morally and expediently rational to appro-
> priate land in amounts greater than could be used to produce a
> plentiful supply of consumption goods for oneself and one's fam-
> ily; that is, it became rational to appropriate land to use as capital,
> which involves appropriating the surplus product of other men's
> labor, i.e. of the labor of those who have no land of their own. In
> other words, at the point where laboring and appropriating
> became separable, full rationality went with appropriating rather
> than with laboring.[51]

Thus, "whether by their own fault or not, members of the labor-ing class did not have, could not be expected to have, and were not entitled to have, full membership in political society; they did not and could not live a fully rational life."[52]

It is all this, it is the ensemble of Locke's political theory and not some isolated, abstract notions of the equality of man – or even, for that matter, of the rights of property – that has been a major constituent of Western democratic tradition. One of Locke's main theses, which exercised a major influence on both the French and American revolutions and the societies that emerged from them, is the doctrine of the right of revolution. Locke grounds this right in his opposition to governmental power that is absolute or arbitrarily exercised, and more specifically in the notion that "the reason why men enter into society, is the preservation of their property," and if the governors of society *"endeavor to take away and destroy the property of the people,* or to

50. Macpherson, *Possessive Individualism*, pp. 233-34.

51. Macpherson, *Possessive Individualism*, p. 234.

52. Macpherson, *Possessive Individualism*, p. 226. Macpherson cites Locke's *Some Considerations of the Consequences of the Lowering of Interest and Raising the Value of Money* and *The Reasonableness of Christianity* for such views on the labor-ing class, and he says that Locke did not even bother to argue these views because he could feel certain that his readers shared them. Macpherson also argues that even the Levellers, one of the more radical elements in seventeenth-century England but representing self-employed, small-scale property owners, were not for extending the vote to propertyless laborers (see pp. 107-59).

reduce them to slavery under arbitrary power, they put themselves into a state of war with the people, who are thereupon ab-
solved from any farther obedience, and are left to the common
refuge, which God hath provided for all men, against force and
violence."[53] But again, true to his bourgeois outlook, Locke did
not mean "all men"[54] in the most literal sense:

> Although he insists, in the *Treatise,* on the majority's right to
> revolution, it does not seem to cross his mind here that the labor-
> ing class might have the right to make a revolution. And indeed
> there is no reason why it should have crossed his mind, for to him
> the laboring class was an object of state policy, an object of ad-
> ministration, rather than fully a part of the citizen body. It was in-
> capable of rational political action, while the right to revolution
> depended essentially on rational decision.[55]

Hence, on this decisive point, no less than on other major questions concerning the nature of society and government, one can
recognize the reasons why Locke's essential theses have continued to occupy a central place in the ideological foundations of
Western democracy.

The Most Radical of All Bourgeois Revolutions

As opposed to the upheavals in the 1600s in England, the French
Revolution at the end of the 1700s was a truly radical revolution
in society – it dramatically put an end to the monarchy and rather
thoroughly uprooted the old feudal order. It was far more profound and sweeping a revolution than its American counterpart
of the same time period – in fact, this French Revolution was the
most radical of all bourgeois revolutions. As Engels put it, "when

53. Locke, *Second Treatise,* p. 111. The influence of Locke on the American
Revolution in particular will be dealt with in more detail in a later chapter, but the
similarities between the quotes from Locke's *Second Treatise* above and passages
in the *Declaration of Independence* seem rather obvious.

54. That Locke meant *men,* literally, is obvious and is made clear throughout
the *Second Treatise,* for example in the statement that in the family the man should
rule – "it naturally falls to the man's share, as the abler and the stronger" – though
Locke argues this power should be limited: as the good bourgeois he insists the
conjugal relations must conform not to an absolute and arbitrary power of the
man but to the terms of the marriage contract (see Locke, *Second Treatise,* p. 44).

55. Macpherson, *Possessive Individualism,* p. 224.

the bourgeoisie of the eighteenth century was strengthened enough likewise to possess an ideology of its own, suited to its own class standpoint, it made its great and conclusive revolution, the French. . . ."[56] What was the essential ideology guiding this Revolution, and how was it suited to the class standpoint of the bourgeoisie?

In a recently published book, *Rousseau: Dreamer of Democracy,* James Miller argues with some justification that it was not the American but the French Revolution that was "the event in which modern concepts of democracy first gained currency."[57] And there is also justification for what seems to be the central theme of Miller's book: that it was the political philosophy of Rousseau that inspired these modern concepts of democracy. Or rather, that it was the way in which the French Revolution gave expression to Rousseau's ideas, for "the French Revolution has played a major role in determining how we can read Rousseau. The event illuminates the text—for it was the Revolution, after all, which forced the idea of democracy onto the agenda of modern history."[58] In order to understand this more fully and to address the questions posed at the end of the previous paragraph, it is relevant, indeed necessary, to focus to a significant degree on Maximilien Robespierre, as well as on the ideas of Rousseau, particularly as expressed in his most central political thesis, *The*

56. Engels, "Ludwig Feuerbach and the End of Classical German Philosophy," *MESW*, 3, p. 355. Obviously, a thorough analysis of the French Revolution, and particularly of the reasons why it was so radical and thoroughgoing as compared with other bourgeois revolutions, is beyond the scope of this work. There were attempts by wealthier and politically conservative bourgeois forces, as well as sections of the nobility, themselves thrown into revolt against the crown (in significant part because of its efforts to tax them to make good debts incurred from numerous foreign wars), to work out some kind of resolution to the French Revolution similar to those which characterized the revolutions in seventeenth-century England. But other more radical bourgeois elements and rebellious small property owners and emerging proletarians were set loose and gained initiative in the course of the French Revolution in a way far beyond anything in bourgeois revolutions before (or after) that, and the revolution was pushed much farther than many of its initiators wanted or imagined in the beginning. (It should be noted here that in the continuation of the statement above, not quoted here, Engels exaggerates somewhat the degree to which religious elements were absent in the French Revolution and its guiding ideas. But he is fundamentally correct in insisting that its essential appeal was not to religion, as had been much more the case with previous bourgeois revolutions, but to "juristic and political ideas."

57. James Miller, *Rousseau: Dreamer of Democracy* (New Haven: Yale University Press, 1984), p. 133.

58. Miller, *Rousseau*, p. 203.

Social Contract.

Robespierre was not only a central figure in the French Revolution, but, perhaps more than any other leading figure in it, he concentrated the contradictions within this Revolution. More specifically, Robespierre, who was from a family of smaller-scale provincial bourgeois, was the most forceful and influential of the Jacobins, radical bourgeois and petty-bourgeois forces who came to the fore in the more "extreme" period of the Revolution. Robespierre is personally identified with the Terror, instituted first against conservative and reactionary elements within the broad camp of the Revolution and then also against certain more radical elements. Robespierre himself was finally guillotined as more conservative bourgeois forces launched a coup aimed at consolidating their power. But Robespierre's personal political trajectory – his rise to power followed by a no less dramatic removal – is only an expression of the more profound and essential way he concentrated the contradictions within the French Revolution.

At the heart of the matter was that Robespierre – and the Jacobins generally – tried to institute a society that would realize the bourgeois ideals of equality, freedom, and the universal rights of man, avoiding the extremes of wealth and poverty, monopolized power and mass powerlessness. The historic irony lies not in the fact – as is often alleged by bourgeois democrats and bourgeois historians generally – that in the attempt to do this they resorted to dictatorial and violent means and then themselves became the victims of this; rather, it lies in the fact that this bourgeois ideal actually corresponds most to the position of the petty bourgeoisie – independent small-scale proprietors, artisans, and so on – and yet this class (or more accurately, these petty-bourgeois strata) are incapable of ruling society and reshaping it in their image. This is because the very property relations – and even more, the laws of commodity production and exchange – of which these strata are an expression, and the whole process of accumulation in which they are enmeshed once bourgeois production relations take hold, inexorably lead to the polarization of society into a small number of big bourgeois and a large mass of propertyless proletarians – with these petty-bourgeois strata caught in between. One or the other of these two main forces must rule modern society. At the time of the French Revolution this was already becoming true – and the bourgeoisie was then in a position to seize power and retain hold of it (even if, for a time, in the peculiar costume of the Napoleonic empire) while the conditions had not developed for the proletariat to clearly distinguish its interests from all other classes and strata and emerge on the political stage as an independent class-conscious force. It was not in any position to seize, let alone retain, command of society. As for the petty bourgeois, and their radical democratic representatives like Robespierre and the Jacobins, they could play a major role in impelling—even, in a certain sense, compelling—the bourgeoisie to carry out its own revolution, but their vision of society itself was one impossible of realization, and their attempts to implement it, however heroic and tragic in certain respects, were doomed to failure. This will become clearer by looking more closely at some of the essential ingredients of Robespierre's outlook and programmatic and practical steps associated with it in the French Revolution.

Robespierre was not unaware of the tremendous advances that had been made in the productive capacity of society over the past several centuries, nor did he fail to recognize altogether the connection between this and necessary political changes. In fact, from his own viewpoint, he based himself on this. Miller cites Robespierre on how mankind's degeneration can be reversed:

> The world has changed, it must change again. What is there in common between what is and what was? Civilized nations have succeeded the wandering savages of the deserts; fertile harvests have taken the place of the ancient forests that once covered the globe. A world has appeared beyond the limits of the world; the inhabitants of the earth have added the seas to their immense domain.... Everything has changed in the physical order; everything must change in the moral and political order. Half the revolution of the world is already accomplished; the other half must be achieved.[59]

As Miller sums it up, "A revolution in technology has occurred. A revolution in social relations must follow: the time has come for all men to reclaim their natural dignity. That is the unique opportunity created by the French Revolution."[60] But Robespierre believed that what was in fact an idealized version of the social relations called forth by this technological revolution could be frozen into timeless principles that could maintain a just and vir-

<hr/>

59. Maximilien Robespierre, "Report on Religious and Moral Ideas and on the National Festivals" (7 May 1794), as cited in Miller, *Rousseau*, p. 132.

60. Miller, *Rousseau*, p. 133.

tuous society – one which corresponds ultimately, however, to the median position of the small independent producer.

The right of property must be upheld as a basic right, but limits must be established to this. Thus, in order to prevent the right of property from becoming license for the rich, the monopolizers and profiteers, the speculators, and the tyrants (*"les riches," "les accapareurs," "les agioteurs," "les tyrans"*), Robespierre proposed the following changes in the "Declaration of the Rights of Man and of Citizens":

> Article 1 – Property is the right that each citizen has to enjoy and dispose of that portion of possessions that are guaranteed him by the law.
> Article 2 – The right of property is limited, like all rights, by the obligation to respect the rights of others.
> Article 3 – This right of property must compromise neither the security, the liberty, the existence, nor the property of one's fellow men.
> Article 4 – Any ownership, any commerce, which violates this principle shall be illegal and immoral.[61]

Further, according to Robespierre, the right to exist is foremost among the rights of man, and all other rights, including the right of property, must be subordinated to this – since "property has been instituted or guaranteed only in order to reinforce" the right to existence. Thus Robespierre insists that everything that is indispensable for the preservation of life must be

> the common property of society as a whole. Only that property which is in excess of this should be private property and given over to the industry of merchants. Any mercantile speculation which I undertake to the detriment of my fellow man is not commerce, but thievery and fratricide.
>
> In accordance with this principle, what must we seek to accomplish in the matter of legislation over the means of subsistence? We must guarantee that all members of society enjoy that portion of the fruits of the earth that is necessary for their existence, that owners and farmers obtain fair payment for their labors and see to it that the excess is given over to free trade.[62]

---

61. Robespierre, "Discours sur la proprieté" (1793), in *Textes Choisis* (Paris: Editions Sociales, 1973), Tome 2, p. 135; my translation.

62. Robespierre, "Sur les subsistances" (1792), in *Textes Choisis*, 2, p. 85; my translation.

As indicated before, these ideas represented a position that was untenable – not because, in some abstract sense, Robespierre and the Jacobins were unrealistic visionaries seeking to impose a utopia on an unwilling world of real men, but because, at bottom, theirs was an attempt to contain and narrowly circumscribe the very changes in social relations and forces of production that were being unleashed in this bourgeois revolution. In short, though they were radical in their opposition to the tyranny of wealth, their notions of equality and of how society should be organized and regulated economically were, in the final analysis, conservative. Faced with the moves of the big bourgeoisie and sections of the nobility to suppress the uprisings of the poorer classes and rein in the revolution, Robespierre sided with the latter. But then, in the circumstances of foreign war and attempts at counterrevolution, and faced at the same time with the demands for a further "levelling" of economic status, Robespierre turned on those he regarded as carrying things too far (especially those promoting atheism). Finally, Robespierre was left without firm ground to stand on and a firm base to rely on – and with the guillotining of Robespierre came the end of Jacobin rule and of the high tide of mass upheaval in the French Revolution. For not only the Jacobins (and the radical petty-bourgeois and bourgeois forces they represented), but also the laboring masses – who were mainly artisans and small producers, with only a small number of propertyless wage-workers at that time – were incapable of carrying the revolution beyond bourgeois bounds, and thus they were incapable ultimately of staying at the head of what was, and could only be, a bourgeois revolution.[63]

---

63. There are some who romanticize the role of the *sans-culottes* (the militant masses of Parisian laboring people) and some of the more radical sections of their leadership, such as the *Enragés*. For example, Daniel Guérin, a bourgeois democrat of the Trotskyite variety in modern-day France, purports to see in the Commune form of government that arose in Paris in 1792 in the course of the French Revolution a model for democracy in socialist society. Guérin even argues that bourgeois parliamentary democracy is "artificial and unnatural," citing (as do many undisguised bourgeois democrats) the ancient roots of direct democracy and calling, essentially, for a return to this, as adapted to modern conditions (see Daniel Guérin, *La Révolution française et nous* [Paris: Petite Collection Maspero, 1976], pp. 100-101). In this regard, the following argument by James Miller concerning Marx's view of the Paris Commune of 1871 is worth citing:

> the insurgents of 1871 were remarkably like the Parisian insurgents of 1792, 1830, and 1848: artisans, journeymen, apprentices, independent producers, professionals, and only a few laborers in the new factory in-

How, then, was the guiding light of this Revolution Jean-Jacques Rousseau? Rousseau had died shortly before the outbreak of the Revolution, and Rousseau himself was never a practical revolutionist – he tended strongly to fear great social upheaval. On the other hand, Rousseau did exert a revolutionary influence on French society in the latter half of the eighteenth century. Rousseau's works were closely read by many of the leading figures in the French Revolution and, especially once the Revolution was under way, they were widely disseminated, in condensed and popularized form, among much broader strata. Certainly Rousseau was the dominant influence in the thinking of Robespierre. This can be seen not only in the latter's notions of equality – and of the economic basis for a just and virtuous society – but also in his most sweeping pronouncements concerning the nature of man and his destiny in society. For example: "Nature tells us that man was born for freedom, and the experience of centuries shows him a slave. His rights are written in his heart, his humiliation in history."[64] This is an obvious echo of the famous opening sentence of the first chapter of Rousseau's *Social Contract*: "Man was born free, and he is everywhere in chains."[65] But if, as we have seen, Robespierre's position could not be maintained and the rule of the Jacobins was replaced by that of more powerful and less radical bourgeois forces, then how

---

dustries. Though the Commune of 1871 may be regarded as the last efflorescence of the French popular culture of politics Rousseau helped to define three generations before, it is far more difficult, particularly in the light of modern historiography, to find in it a harbinger of an international proletarian revolution. (Miller, *Rousseau*, pp. 260-61)

While Miller's observations are one-sided and his last sentence in particular is wrong – it is Miller's bourgeois bias that makes it hard for him to find in the 1871 Paris Commune "a harbinger of an international proletarian revolution" – nevertheless, his comments are not without any validity. They do reflect the fact that even this Paris Commune embodied both elements of the old, bourgeois revolution as well as of the new, proletarian revolution and that it could not, as such, serve as a fully developed model of a proletarian state (especially one in the early stages of the international proletarian revolution and surrounded by powerful bourgeois states). And, while Guérin's book is not without insights, it must be remarked that on this point the openly bourgeois bourgeois democrat, Miller, is more insightful than the "Marxist" bourgeois democrat, Guérin.

64. Robespierre, "Report on Religious and Moral Ideas," as cited in Miller, *Rousseau*, p. 132.

65. Jean-Jacques Rousseau, *The Social Contract*, trans. Maurice Cranston (New York: Penguin Books, 1968), Book 1, chapter 1, p. 49.

is it that Rousseau's ideas can be considered the general guiding principles of the French Revolution? What was there in Rousseau's thinking that was essentially bourgeois and at the same time essentially revolutionary, in the circumstances of that time?

In tracing the progress of materialism in Europe – which, he demonstrated, was spurred on by the development of science and industry and changes in the organization of production related to this development – Engels noted how in the eighteenth century the Enlightenment took form in France and influenced political events:

> In the meantime materialism passed from England to France, where it met and coalesced with another materialistic school of philosophers, a branch of Cartesianism. In France, too, it remained at first an exclusively aristocratic doctrine. But soon its revolutionary character asserted itself. The French materialists did not limit their criticism to matters of religious belief; they extended it to whatever scientific tradition or political institution they met with; and to prove the claim of their doctrine to universal application, they took the shortest cut, and boldly applied it to all subjects of knowledge in the giant work after which they were named – the *Encyclopédie*. Thus, in one or the other of its two forms – avowed materialism or deism – it became the creed of the whole cultured youth of France; so much so that, when the Great Revolution broke out, the doctrine hatched by English Royalists gave a theoretical flag to French Republicans and Terrorists, and furnished the text for the Declaration of the Rights of Man.[66]

Rousseau was not, properly speaking, one of the *philosophes* (Diderot, D'Alembert, and others) who were responsible for the propagation of this materialist doctrine through the *Encyclopédie* – though allied with them in certain respects, he also had strong disagreements and clashes with them, over religion as well as politics (Rousseau was a Calvinist protestant, then converted to Catholicism, and later reconverted to Calvinism). But, as the following summary puts it:

> The 1760's, the decade of . . . [Voltaire's] *Philosophical Dictionary*, was a time of great beginnings. It marked the quickening of

---

66. Engels, "Socialism: Utopian and Scientific" (introduction to English ed.) *MESW*, 3, p. 107.

mechanical inventions, improvements in agricultural productivity, and the establishment of an industrial discipline that we are
once again calling (after some shifts in fashion) the Industrial
Revolution. It saw the beginnings of what R.R. Palmer has recently called the "Age of the Democratic Revolution," a widespread
rebellion against time-honored constituted authority, a rising demand for self-government, and rudimentary essays in popular
political activity. It was the decade in which Rousseau published
his most revolutionary books, the *Contrat social* and *Emile,*
Diderot completed his *Encyclopédie,* and Holbach deluged Europe
with his atheist tracts. Voltaire had angry contempt for the first,
cool respect for the second, and...vehement disagreements with
the third of these men; but Rousseau, Diderot, Holbach, and Voltaire, an improbable team of reluctant allies, were yoked together
in a single enterprise: the movement for modernity.[67]

Within all this it was Rousseau's contribution to the "age of
democratic revolution," and in particular to the idea of popular
sovereignty, that had the most direct and powerful impact on the
French Revolution at the end of that century.

On the surface, it might seem that Rousseau was not only an
"improbable" and "reluctant" ally of the *philosophes* – they followed Francis Bacon's vision of progress through rational
knowledge while Rousseau regarded such progress with suspicion, seeing in it the cause of man's corruption and oppression in
society – but also an unlikely champion of democracy. In fact, in
his central political work, *The Social Contract,* Rousseau writes:
"If there were a nation of Gods, it would govern itself
democratically. A government so perfect is not suited to men";
and, "We may add that there is no government so liable to civil
war and internecine strife as is democracy or popular government."[68] But James Miller has argued that Rousseau distinguished
between a democratic society – that is, a society based on popular
sovereignty – and democratic government: Rousseau regarded
government in a restricted sense, viewing it as a kind of executive
appointed by and accountable to the sovereign. And, in the matter of sovereignty, Rousseau considered direct democracy – as opposed even to representative democracy – as the only form
corresponding to and expressive of freedom and the only

---

67. Peter Gay, "Editor's Introduction" to François Voltaire, *Philosophical Dic-
tionary,* trans. Peter Gay (New York: Basic Books, Inc., 1962), p. 39.

68. Rousseau, *Social Contract,* Book 3, chapter 4, pp. 114, 113.

legitimate basis for government.

Thus, if Rousseau allowed that aristocracy – an elected, not hereditary, aristocracy – was the best form of government, as he defined it, this aristocratic government could only find a legitimate basis in democracy, in popular sovereignty. While Miller's rather convoluted effort to show that Rousseau also regarded democracy as the ideal form of *government*, corresponding to the original society of free men, need not concern us here, the following summation is important:

> By making democracy the only real embodiment of sovereignty, Rousseau not only ruled out any form of absolute monarchy, he also realigned the world of republican discourse. The primacy of an indivisible and inalienable sovereign meant, in practice, that every legitimate republic must, at base, be simple: a pure democracy. The question, How much democracy? was no longer paramount. The burden of proof was shifted. After reading Rousseau, the question was reversed. All republican government, if it would be legitimate, had to rest on the free will of a people. In this setting, the real question was not How much democracy?, but How much aristocracy?, How much monarchy? – and these questions only a sovereign people could rightfully decide.[69]

It is not difficult to see how such a doctrine would have subversive and revolutionary implications in French society of that time, ruled as it was by an aristocracy and a monarchy that insisted that sovereignty resided by divine and natural right in them. Nor is it difficult to see how the French revolutionaries, including radical elements among them, would take up and apply this doctrine in their fight against the aristocracy, the monarchy, and generally the tyranny of wealth.

But what of Rousseau's assertion that not only is a democratic government unworkable in many situations but "freedom is not a fruit of every climate, and it is not therefore within the capacity of every people"?[70] Rousseau attempts to justify this by linking it to the question of social surplus. The details – and the particular flaws – in Rousseau's political economy also need not concern us here, but his political conclusions bear significantly on Rous-

---

69. Miller, *Rousseau*, pp. 120-21. Miller's fuller discussion of this question of sovereignty and government is contained largely in chapter 5, from which the above quote is taken.

70. Rousseau, *Social Contract*, Book 3, chapter 8, p. 124.

seau's basic assumptions:

> Places which yield only the bare necessities of men's lives must be inhabited by barbarous peoples, since no political society is possible. Places where the surplus of product over labor is moderate are suited to free peoples. Places where an abundant and fertile soil gives a lavish return for little labor will want monarchical government, so that the luxury of the prince may consume the surplus of the product of the subjects–for it is better that this surplus should be absorbed by the government than dissipated by private persons. There are exceptions, I know, but these exceptions themselves confirm the rule, in that sooner or later they produce revolutions which put things back into the order of nature.[71]

Contained within this is the core of Rousseau's viewpoint – for a situation where the surplus over labor is moderate not only provides, in Rousseau's view, the basis for a free people in general, it specifically corresponds to Rousseau's ideal republic: an idealized vision of the small Swiss republic of Geneva where he was born but from which he was exiled for much of his life. While noting that Geneva was in reality ruled by a wealthy minority at the time Rousseau wrote *The Social Contract*, Miller describes crucial elements of the ideal – and idyllic – Geneva conceived by Rousseau:

> To think about this city, we must imagine not merely a country *(pays)*, but a fatherland *(patrie)*: not merely a territory with inhabitants, but an association of families, its solidarity secured through "bonds of blood." And at the core of this community, as its basic cell, we must imagine not isolated individuals, but patriarchal households; not men without ties, but families governed by fathers, each sustained by his labor on a plot of land he can call his own.[72]

It would be tempting to simply dismiss such a vision with the observation that no such society ever has existed or ever could

71. Rousseau, *Social Contract*, Book 3, chapter 8, pp. 125-26.

72. Miller, *Rousseau*, p. 28. The influence on Rousseau of Calvinism is obvious here. In another work I discussed how Calvinist principles, in particular frugality, as they were applied in sixteenth-century Geneva, contributed to the development of capitalist accumulation and capitalist society (see Avakian, *Harvest of Dragons*, pp. 50-51). It is also not difficult to understand why, among the ancient Greek city-states, Rousseau was attracted not by the more luxurious Athens but by Sparta, renowned for its severity and frugality.

exist, and insofar as anything even partially approximating such a
society has ever been seen – where everything ran, almost literally, like the proverbial Swiss watch – it has long since given way
to other forms of society . . . and good riddance. Nor is it possible
to avoid the observation that the invocation of such traditional
values as patriotism, patriarchy, family, and home and hearth is
at the heart of the reactionary ideological offensive being carried
out in the U.S. today by the imperialist bourgeoisie and its
political spokesmen, bible-brandishers, and others. But to leave it
at that would be to miss the point that for Rousseau, two centuries ago, such a view was bound up with ideas of freedom and
equality that played a major part in inspiring a thoroughgoing
revolution against feudal relations, aristocratic privilege, and
monarchal rule.

"If we enquire wherein lies precisely the greatest good of all,
which ought to be the goal of every system of law," Rousseau
wrote in *The Social Contract,* "we shall find that it comes down to
two main objects, *freedom* and *equality:* freedom because any individual dependence means that much strength withdrawn from
the body of the state, and equality because freedom cannot sur-
vive without it."[73] He immediately explains, however, that

> as for equality, this word must not be taken to imply that degrees
> of power and wealth should be absolutely the same for all, but
> rather that power shall stop short of violence and never be exer-
> cised except by virtue of authority and law, and, where wealth is
> concerned, that no citizen shall be rich enough to buy another and
> none so poor as to be forced to sell himself; this in turn implies
> that the more exalted persons need moderation in goods and in-
> fluence and the humbler persons moderation in avarice and
> covetousness.[74]

Rousseau was opposed to outright (chattel) slavery, where one
person literally belonged to another, but he was not opposed to all
social inequality and class division. Nor was he opposed to wage-
labor, which in fact constitutes *wage-slavery.* Rousseau did not see
this – he regarded the wealthy and the poor, employer and
employed, the "exalted" and the "humbler" persons as essentially
equal if they were legally equal: "Whichever way we look at it,

---

73. Rousseau, *Social Contract*, Book 2, chapter 11, p. 96.
74. Rousseau, *Social Contract*, Book 2, chapter 11, p. 96.

we always return to the same conclusion: namely that the social pact establishes equality among the citizens in that they all pledge themselves under the same conditions and must all enjoy the same rights."[75]

In Rousseau's notion of the social contract, we find the familiar theme that people entered into society – formed a state – in order to secure their rights, particularly the right to property. Later in this chapter I will discuss why this concept of the social contract is fundamentally erroneous and disguises a fundamentally exploitative relationship, but here it is important to note what for Rousseau is the nature of the exchange that goes on when man enters into society:

> Suppose we draw up a balance sheet, so that the losses and gains may be readily compared. What man loses by the social contract is his natural liberty and the absolute right to anything that tempts him and that he can take; what he gains by the social contract is civil liberty and the legal right of property in what he possesses. If we are to avoid mistakes in weighing the one side against the other, we must clearly distinguish between *natural* liberty, which has no limit but the physical power of the individual concerned, and *civil* liberty, which is limited by the general will; and we must distinguish also between *possession*, which is based only on force or "the right of the first occupant," and *property*, which must rest on a legal title.[76]

What comes through in all this is the bourgeois outlook that generally characterized Rousseau's thinking; and, at the same time, one can also clearly recognize the inspiration for the ideas of the radical Robespierre and other leaders of the French Revolution.[77] To make a "balance sheet" of this from the stand-

---

75. Rousseau, *Social Contract*, Book 2, chapter 4, p. 76.

76. Rousseau, *Social Contract*, Book 1, chapter 8, p. 65.

77. As for Rousseau's influence on the leaders of the American Revolution, it is clear that this influence was considerable in the case of Thomas Paine, in particular after he went to France and became involved in the events of the revolution there. While Thomas Jefferson was mainly influenced by English theorists such as John Locke, as well as leading figures of the Enlightenment in Scotland, at the very least he had certain basic beliefs in common with Rousseau, including on the exalted virtues of agrarian self-sufficiency. "Those who labor in the earth," wrote Jefferson, "are the chosen people of God, if ever he had chosen people, whose breasts he has made his peculiar deposit for substantial and genuine virtue. It is the focus in which he keeps alive that sacred fire, which otherwise might

point of the revolutionary class of today – that is, to apply the dialectical materialist viewpoint and method of the proletariat – we can turn to this sweeping summation by Engels:

> The great men, who in France prepared men's minds for the coming revolution, were themselves extreme revolutionists. They recognized no external authority of any kind whatever. Religion, natural science, society, political institutions – everything was subjected to the most unsparing criticism: everything must justify its existence before the judgment-seat of reason or give up existence.... Every form of society and government then existing, every old traditional notion was flung into the lumber-room as irrational; the world had hitherto allowed itself to be led solely by prejudices; everything in the past deserved only pity and contempt. Now, for the first time, appeared the light of day, the kingdom of reason; henceforth superstition, injustice, privilege, oppression, were to be superseded by eternal truth, eternal Right, equality based on Nature and the inalienable rights of man.
>
> We know today that this kingdom of reason was nothing more than the idealized kingdom of the bourgeoisie; that this eternal Right found its realization in bourgeois justice; that this equality reduced itself to bourgeois equality before the law; that bourgeois property was proclaimed as one of the essential rights of man; and that the government of reason, the Contrat Social of Rousseau, came into being, and only could come into being, as a democratic bourgeois republic. The great thinkers of the eighteenth century could, no more than their predecessors, go beyond the limits imposed upon them by their epoch.[78]

It is when the attempt is made in the present epoch to impose an order based on this vision – not only the patriarchy and the patriotism but also the notions of freedom and equality that conform to the outlook and interests of the bourgeoisie – and more-

---

escape from the face of the earth. Corruption of morals in the mass of cultivators is a phenomenon of which no age nor nation has furnished an example" (Thomas Jefferson, "Notes on the State of Virginia," Query 29: "Manufactures," in *The Portable Thomas Jefferson,* ed. Merrill D. Peterson [New York: Penguin Books, 1975], p. 217; see also Jefferson's "First Inaugural Address" [4 March 1801], pp. 290-95). It should be noted, however, that Jefferson, always keeping uppermost the interests of the United States and jealous of its special opportunities to expand and prosper, recognized that it was necessary to develop manufacturing together with agriculture (see for example, "Domestic manufactures – a change of opinion," letter to Benjamin Austin [9 January 1816], pp. 547-50).

78. Engels, "Socialism: Utopian and Scientific," *MESW,* 3, pp. 115-16.

over to oppose these to the revolution of this era, the proletarian revolution, that this becomes thoroughly reactionary.

The "Rights of Man"

Thomas Paine was a direct link between the French and American revolutions; he was not only a theoretical advocate for but an active participant in both. On the one hand, it is important to note that Paine's political-ideological stand "involved him in taking up positions on the far left of the American revolutionary movement, while in France he was to the right of the Jacobins who took power less than a year after his arrival"[79] – this is emblematic of the differences between the two revolutions. On the other hand, however, Paine did represent and voice views that in a basic sense were common to these two revolutions – basic ideals and principles of bourgeois revolution and of bourgeois society seen in a radical light. Paine's *Rights of Man* – written as a defense of the French Revolution but drawing from the experience of the American Revolution and seeking to draw out of the two revolutions universal truths about human society and its government – provides a useful focus for examining these ideals and principles.

One summation of this general point puts it this way:

> What Paine defended in the French Revolution was the concept of popular sovereignty in its most extreme, republican form. Like the Jacobins, too, Paine thought that a people's government in the political sphere must express itself economically through the abolition of poverty and the widest possible distribution of property so that every citizen would have an equal chance of becoming a property-owner. Finally, in the view of Paine as of the Jacobin leader, Robespierre, a people's government would inaugurate the reign of reason and the worship of God would be freed, for the first time, from all its superstitious and priestly accretions.[80]

Paine himself linked together reason and the kind of religious belief discussed just above as the foundation for what he acclaimed to be a universal truth:

---

79. Henry Collins, "Introduction" to Thomas Paine, *Rights of Man* (Middlesex: Penguin Books, 1969), p. 38.

80. Collins, "Introduction" to *Rights of Man*, p. 40.

The illuminating and divine principle of the equal rights of man, (for it has its origin from the Maker of man) relates, not only to the living individuals, but to generations of men succeeding each other. Every generation is equal in rights to the generations which preceded it, by the same rule that every individual is born equal in rights with his contemporary.

Every history of the creation, and every traditionary account, whether from the lettered or unlettered world, however they may vary in their opinion or belief of certain particulars, all agree in establishing one point, *the unity of man;* by which I mean, that men are all of *one degree,* and consequently that all men are born equal, and with equal natural right, in the same manner as if posterity had been continued by *creation* instead of *generation,* the latter being only the mode by which the former is carried forward; and consequently, every child born into the world must be considered as deriving its existence from God. The world is as new to him as it was to the first man that existed, and his natural right in it is of the same kind.[81]

And, in discussing the connection between the natural rights and civil rights of man, Paine sets forth that:

Natural rights are those which appertain to man in right of his existence. Of this kind are all the intellectual rights, or rights of the mind, and also all those rights of acting as an individual for his own comfort and happiness, which are not injurious to the natural rights of others. – Civil rights are those which appertain to man in right of his being a member of society. Every civil right has for its foundation, some natural right preexisting in the individual, but to the enjoyment of which his individual power is not, in all cases, sufficiently competent. Of this kind are all those which relate to security and protection.[82]

These, then, are, in their general expression, the basic tenets

81. Paine, *Rights of Man,* p. 88. It would be a distortion to say that Paine, like many others enunciating the doctrine of the "rights of man," meant literally men only – and not women – since Paine did speak out against at least aspects of women's oppression (as well as for the abolition of slavery); it nevertheless remains true that in *Rights of Man* (and generally) Paine sought to base his notion of the equality of man in part at least on the "Mosaic account of the creation, whether taken as divine authority, or merely historical"; and Mosaic tradition, as should be obvious to even the casual reader of its accounts, not only draws "the distinction of sexes" in its version of creation (as Paine himself notes) but systematically codifies the inferior status and oppression of women (see *Rights of Man,* pp. 88-89).

82. Paine, *Rights of Man,* p. 90.

for all human society and government as Paine sees them – and it is not difficult to recognize here central underlying themes (with certain particular variations) of bourgeois-democratic tradition. A closer look at some of the specific arguments Paine makes in defending and elaborating on these tenets will shed further light not only on Paine's view but on the essential content of that bourgeois-democratic tradition.

As with the classical theorists of bourgeois civil society before him, beginning with Hobbes, Paine adheres to the notion of the social contract (or compact) as the origin and basis for government. Paine insists that this is not a compact between the people and the government – which would make the latter at least the equal of the former – but, in its foundation, between different independent individuals:

> The fact therefore must be, that the *individuals themselves,* each in his own personal and sovereign right, *entered into a compact with each other* to produce a government: and this is the only mode in which governments have a right to arise, and the only principle on which they have a right to exist.[83]

Here it must be pointed out that this notion of a social contract, entered into by sovereign individuals, completely ignores the fact that individuals, at whatever point in human history, do not exist in such a state of personal sovereignty – their personal freedom is limited by nature and their ability to control and transform it as well as by relations with others (assuming that they live in society with others, or as soon as they enter into such society). And, therefore, no such compact, either explicit or tacit, has ever been entered into or could ever be entered into by individuals each possessing the kind of personal sovereignty spoken of by Paine. Further, governments have actually arisen in human society at a point at which differences between people – both individuals and social groups, such as men/women – are beginning to assume social significance; and the exercise of governmental functions by certain people has in turn furthered the division of labor which this exercise reflects, contributing to the emergence of class

---

83. Paine, *Rights of Man,* p. 92. Paine even attempts to give this too a divine basis, insisting that "before any human institution of government was known in the world, there existed, if I may so express it, a compact between God and Man, from the beginning of time" and "all laws must conform themselves to this prior existing compact . . ." (p. 135).

antagonism and a *state apparatus* to enforce class division and the ruling position of the economically dominant class. And finally, if we take Paine's argument that each new generation begins with the same natural rights as all preceding generations, and that this is the basis for their civil rights – an argument which in fact is essential to make the case for the "rights of man" in bourgeois society, since no bourgeois spokesmen will deny that pre-bourgeois society was marked by inequality that was *not* founded on the sovereign rights of all individuals – then how can it be realistically argued that an impoverished, propertyless proletarian (or even a relatively prosperous member of the middle class, for that matter) can enter into a compact, on the basis of equality, with a billionaire (or even millionaire) financier, for example?

Yet this is exactly what the idealizers and ideologues of bourgeois democracy must argue, and will argue, in the last analysis – even the more radical ones who represent the bourgeoisie in its rising, progressive, even revolutionary, phase, such as Thomas Paine. They must argue this, because otherwise they would have to say that bourgeois society, like previous forms of society divided into classes, represents the rule of the rich and powerful over the poor and powerless – and this they will not or cannot recognize. In their eyes, despite material inequalities between individuals (or, some would allow, between classes), there is no oppression, exploitation, or violation of the rights and fundamental equality of people involved, because that fundamental equality is equal *opportunity* and its reflection in the political-ideological superstructure as *equality before the law.* The fundamental inequality involved in this, the basic class oppression and exploitation, is masked by not only formal political equality but by the underlying relationship of wage-labor and capital – a relationship in which it appears that an equal exchange (wages for labor) is taking place. In fact, based on the monopoly of the means of production by capital and the condition of the workers – that they have no means to live except to sell their labor power to capital – the workers are forced to give their labor power over to the capitalists to create profit for them, while the workers are maintained merely at a level that enables them to continue in this relationship. Politically, despite formal political equality, this basic inequality – as well as other social inequality and oppression – is reflected and reinforced through the organs of government that serve and protect the interests of capital.

If we look again even at the more radical exponents of these bourgeois principles – who believe, however, that they are espousing universal principles for all human society and government – like Thomas Paine, both their bourgeois "blind spots" and the basis for their bias can be made still clearer. Resuming with Paine's elaboration of the relationship between natural and civil rights, we find the explanation that "the natural rights which are not retained" by the individuals entering into the compact to form a government "are all those in which, though the right is perfect in the individual, the power to execute them is defective."[84] And:

> He therefore deposits this right in the common stock of society, and takes the arm of society, of which he is a part, in preference and in addition to his own. Society *grants* him nothing. Every man is a proprietor in society, and draws on the capital as a matter of right.[85]

Could anyone ask for a more obvious indication that the notion of the "rights of man," as presented even by a radical democrat like Paine, is founded upon and is conceived in terms of bourgeois property relations – an idealized vision of them to be sure, where everyone is equal as property owner, but typically bourgeois in its idealization nonetheless?

In fact, all of Paine's notions of the "rights of man" are reflections of this bourgeois outlook and find their ultimate point of origin in bourgeois property relations. In some cases, this finds more direct, obvious expression, as in the example just above. In other cases, the connection between the idea and its material

---

84. Paine, *Rights of Man*, p. 90.

85. Paine, *Rights of Man*, pp. 90-91. In the classical French movie *La Nuit de Varennes* the character Thomas Paine says at one point that in the American *Declaration of Independence* the word "property" was replaced by "pursuit of happiness" among the inalienable rights. It should be clear from the above that Paine regarded property, bourgeois property, as the practical as well as theoretical basis for people's rights in society. And Paine also quotes, approvingly, the "Declaration of the Rights of Man and of Citizens," issued in 1789 by the French National Assembly in the first stages of the French Revolution. This "Declaration" includes the proviso, "The right to property being inviolable and sacred, no one ought to be deprived of it, except in cases of evident public necessity, legally ascertained, and on condition of a previous just indemnity" (p. 134). While this Assembly represented, in the main, more wealthy and more conservative elements in the French Revolution, it is true, as noted earlier, that the Jacobins too wished to make bourgeois property relations compatible with their notions of justice but not by any means to abolish them.

basis in bourgeois property relations is less obvious and more indirect, as, for example, Paine's upholding of the right of conscience (regarding religious belief as well as beliefs in general), which still finds its ultimate foundation in the notion of the equality of commodity owners in the marketplace, where the commodity in question in this case is ideas.[86] So too the very concept of political liberty that Paine puts forward reflects the idealized bourgeois world of atomistic commodity producers — equal, independent, and sovereign, each and all, by virtue of their proprietorship, free to pursue their fortunes as they see fit, limited only by the requirement of recognizing the rights of all others to do the same:

> Political Liberty consists in the power of doing whatever does not injure another. The exercise of the natural rights of every man, has no other limits than those which are necessary to secure to every *other* man the free exercise of the same rights; and these limits are determinable only by the law.[87]

All this becomes clearer in the following eulogy of the representative political form:

> In the representative system, the reason for everything must publicly appear. Every man is a proprietor in government, and considers it a necessary part of his business to understand. It concerns his interest, because it affects his property. He examines the cost, and compares it with the advantages; and above all, he does not adopt the slavish custom of following what in other governments are called LEADERS.[88]

Engels exploded this idealized picture of bourgeois society, including in its more idealized sphere — the pursuit of happiness — which has been

---

86. For Paine's view on freedom of conscience, see *Rights of Man*, pp. 107, 133. At times the questions concerning the property relations involved with the commodity "Ideas" could become very concrete, as well as complex (as indeed they often do today) — as reflected, for example, in Thomas Jefferson's notions of the limitations that should be placed on patent rights for inventions. In this regard, see "No Patents on Ideas," letter to Isaac McPherson (13 August 1813), in *The Portable Jefferson*.

87. Paine, *Rights of Man*, p. 133. Paine is here quoting (again, approvingly) the French National Assembly's "Declaration of the Rights of Man and of Citizens."

88. Paine, *Rights of Man*, p. 206.

recognized in words ever since and inasmuch as the bourgeoisie, in its fight against feudalism and in the development of capitalist production, was compelled to abolish all privileges of estate, that is, personal privileges, and to introduce the equality of all individuals before the law, first in the sphere of private law, then gradually also in the sphere of public law. But the urge towards happiness thrives only to a trivial extent on ideal rights. To the greatest extent of all it thrives on material means; and capitalist production takes care to ensure that the great majority of those with equal rights shall get only what is essential for bare existence. Capitalist production has, therefore, little more respect, if indeed any more, for the equal right to the urge towards happiness of the majority than had slavery or serfdom.[89]

In a typical, idealist inversion of the real motive forces underlying the transformation of society with the rise of the bourgeoisie and capitalist relations of production, Paine pictured the French Revolution as a process where material reality followed in the wake of ideas, rather than the reverse: "It [the French Revolution] has apparently burst forth like a creation from a chaos, but it is no more than the consequence of a mental revolution priorily existing in France. The mind of the nation had changed beforehand, and the new order of things has naturally followed the new order of thoughts."[90] As a matter of fact, as we have seen, the tremendous turmoil and struggle in the ideological realm, as represented by the Enlightenment, in the period leading up to the French Revolution, was both a harbinger of and contributed considerably to the eventual eruption of that Revolution. But this Enlightenment and the very guiding ideas of the French Revolution were themselves the product of profound changes taking place in the material base of society.

Making a sweeping survey of this basic dynamic since the sixteenth century and its inverted reflection by bourgeois thinkers, Engels pointed out that these latter ("from Descartes to Hegel and from Hobbes to Feuerbach") believed that they were "impelled. . .solely by the force of pure reason"; but "[o]n the contrary, what really pushed them forward most was the powerful and ever more rapidly onrushing progress of natural science and industry"[91] – and the continual transformations in production

---

89. Engels, "Ludwig Feuerbach," *MESW*, 3, pp. 358-59.
90. Paine, *Rights of Man*, p. 115.
91. Engels, "Ludwig Feuerbach," *MESW*, 3, pp. 347-48.

relations all this called forth. It is of course not the case that people like Paine were ignorant of this "onrushing progress" – quite the contrary. In fact, Paine was also strongly influenced by the mechanical materialism that reached a pinnacle in Newtonian principles, "in which the universe, having been set in motion by God, behaved eternally in accordance with the laws laid down by the Creator"; and Paine eventually reached the conclusion that "the political universe might be susceptible to the same analytical techniques."[92] In *Rights of Man*, Paine insists that "nature is orderly in all her works" and then argues that monarchy "is a mode of government that counteracts nature."[93] In other words, Paine believes there are universal and unchanging principles of society and government, corresponding to universal and unchanging laws in nature; and it turns out that "the representative system is always parallel with the order and immutable laws of nature, and meets the reason of man in every part."[94]

Paine asserts that in the form of government established in the United States of America, as a result of the revolution there, the ideal model has been instituted – the democratic republic. This is "representation ingrafted upon democracy," and it is the perfect synthesis, he argues, because it allows for democracy – not in its simple form but in the representative form – to be extended over a large country and to be "capable of embracing and confederating all the various interests and every extent of territory and population. . . .[95] Thus Paine is moved to say, "What Athens was in miniature, America will be in magnitude."[96] While merely noting the ironically prophetic nature of Paine's pronouncement – indeed America today is on a grand and international scale the enslaving empire that Athens represented in miniature – what is important to stress here is how Paine's bourgeois idealism blinds him to stark realities: Paine could not have been ignorant of the slave foundation of ancient Athens, and he was a

---

92. Collins, "Introduction" to Paine, *Rights of Man*, p. 12. The influence of Newtonian principles on Paine's political thought is obvious, for example, in his analysis that individuals are driven to form society by their wants, which "impel the whole of them into society, as naturally as gravitation acts to a center" (see Paine, *Rights of Man*, p. 185).

93. Paine, *Rights of Man*, p. 204.

94. Paine, *Rights of Man*, p. 205.

95. Paine, *Rights of Man*, p. 202.

96. Paine, *Rights of Man*, p. 202.

vocal opponent of slavery in America, yet he can still hold up Athens as the model for modern democracy, as embodied in the United States of America. He further argues that had this synthesis of democracy and representation only been discovered in ancient times, "there is no reason to believe that those forms of government, now called monarchical or aristocratical, would ever have taken place."[97] And, with the same logic, he even describes the revolutions in America and France as a kind of restoration—"a renovation of the natural order of things, a system of principles as universal as truth and the existence of man, and combining moral with political happiness and national prosperity."[98]

What all this serves to demonstrate is not that Paine was after all not a revolutionary, even in his time; rather it is a powerful demonstration of the limitations of even revolutionary representatives of the bourgeoisie and capitalist society (to say nothing of those reactionary apologists of this system now that it has long since outlived any positive and certainly any revolutionary role). It is this that Marx was speaking to in contrasting the proletarian revolution (which he referred to as "the social revolution of the nineteenth century") with all previous revolutions:

> The social revolution of the nineteenth century cannot draw its poetry from the past, but only from the future. It cannot begin with itself before it has stripped off all superstition in regard to the past. Earlier revolutions required recollections of past world history in order to drug themselves concerning their own content. In order to arrive at its own content, the revolution of the nineteenth century must let the dead bury their dead. There the phrase went beyond the content; here the content goes beyond the phrase.[99]

---

97. Paine, *Rights of Man*, p. 199.

98. Paine, *Rights of Man*, p. 166.

99. Marx, "The Eighteenth Brumaire of Louis Bonaparte," *MESW*, 1, p. 400.

That Paine fared no better than others before him (or since) in attempting to set forth universal, immutable principles that should govern society irrespective of its stage of development, and that instead all political and ideological principles can be shown to reflect a particular set of social—and fundamentally production—relations, is again not owing to personal limitations but to the basic truth that the material base of society is the foundation and ultimate point of determination for the political and ideological superstructure. Another significant demonstration of this can be found in an analysis of the attempt by one of the most influential and far-ranging thinkers of the Enlightenment, Immanuel Kant, to formulate transcendental moral principles—moral categorical imperatives, as he

Marx and Engels wrote in the *Communist Manifesto,* "When people speak of ideas that revolutionize society, they do but express the fact, that within the old society, the elements of a new one have been created, and that the dissolution of the old ideas keeps even pace with the dissolution of the old conditions of exis-

---

called them.

In his *Foundations of the Metaphysics of Morals,* Kant stated that there is "only one categorical imperative. It is: Act only according to that maxim by which you can at the same time will that it should become a universal law" (Immanuel Kant, *Foundations of the Metaphysics of Morals,* trans. Lewis White Beck [New York: Liberal Arts Press, 1959], p. 39). And Kant set forth the specific, practical content of this categorical imperative in what has become an oft-cited dictum: "Act so that you treat humanity, whether in your own person or in that of another, always as an end and never as a means only" (p. 47). While this principle is not at all practical – nor is it realizable, in any society – and furthermore is not desirable, what should be pointed out here is that, while Kant believed he was basing this categorical imperative in pure reason – he insisted that "reason must regard itself as the author of its principles, independently of foreign influences," just as for rational beings freedom must be exercised "independently of foreign causes determining it" (pp. 67, 64) – in reality these notions were founded in the material conditions and changes in the society around him, as Engels indicated in the statement quoted above, speaking of the philosophers "from Descartes to Hegel and from Hobbes to Feuerbach."

Kant's particular political views – he favored the monarchy, specifically that of "Frederick the Great" of Prussia (who might be termed a tyrannical patron of the Enlightenment) over a republican form of government (see pp. 91-92) – were, to a significant extent at least, a reflection of the fact that in the Germany of that time (the end of the eighteenth century) the process of the bourgeois revolution and the unification of the nation-state had been retarded, as had the development of capitalism economically. In the field of science, Kant made many important contributions, but he held to the view that "all conceptions, like those of senses, which come to us without our choice enable us to know the objects only as they affect us, while what they are in themselves remains unknown to us" (p. 69). Engels commented on this:

> To this Hegel, long since, has replied: If you know all the qualities of a thing, you know the thing itself; nothing remains but the fact that the said thing exists without us; and when your senses have taught you that fact, you have grasped the last remnant of the thing-in-itself, Kant's celebrated unknowable *Ding an sich.* To which it may be added that in Kant's time our knowledge of natural objects was indeed so fragmentary that he might well suspect, behind the little we knew about each of them, a mysterious "thing-in-itself." But one after another these ungraspable things have been grasped, analyzed, and, what is more, *reproduced* by the giant progress of science; and what we can produce we certainly cannot consider as unknowable. (Engels, "Socialism: Utopian and Scientific" [introduction to English ed.], *MESW,* 3, p. 102)

Thus, whether in the realm of morals and politics, of science, or of the theory of knowledge and other philosophical questions, Kant's views, too, were not the product or expression of pure reason, or of some universal, transcendental prin-

tence."[100] At the time of the Enlightenment, in the eighteenth century, it was the old feudal conditions that were experiencing such a "dissolution": capitalist society had not yet brought forth the development of the material conditions – a level of productive forces and the corresponding production relations and class antagonisms – that would lead to its own "dissolution." This can be seen in a discussion of the question of justice by David Hume, philosopher and political theorist and a luminary of the Enlightenment in eighteenth-century Scotland (along with such people as the classical bourgeois political economist Adam Smith, the historian Edward Gibbon, and others). Indirectly and inadvertently, as it were, Hume's remarks, while seeking again to set forth universal, transcendental principles, actually lay a basis for grasping the historically limited, transitory nature of bourgeois economic relations and their reflection in politics and ideology. Hume begins this discussion by defining justice as what is "useful to society" – "public utility is the *sole* origin of Justice."[101] Then, in elaborating on this, he makes the following argument:

> Few enjoyments are given us from the open and liberal hand of nature; but by art, labor, and industry we can extract them in great abundance. Hence, the ideas of property become necessary in all civil society; hence, justice derives its usefulness to the public; and hence alone arises its merit and moral obligation.[102]

And in the same discussion Hume says that had nature made material abundance so profuse and so readily accessible that virtually no human labor would be required for everyone to appropriate and enjoy it, then

> in such a happy state every other social virtue would flourish and

---

ciples, but were conditioned and limited by historical developments and social relations – not in the sense that they literally mirrored only the conditions and relations he was most directly involved with, which itself would be a mechanical materialist interpretation, but in the sense that developments economically, in science and so on, and in social relations and the contradictions and struggles arising in relation to all this, established the basic foundation and set the general framework for his investigation and interpretation of society and nature, as they do for everyone.

100. Marx and Engels, *Communist Manifesto*, p. 58.

101. David Hume, "An Inquiry Concerning the Principles of Morals," Section 3: "Of Justice," Part 1, in *The Essential David Hume* (New York: New American Library, 1969), p. 166.

102. Hume, "Principles of Morals," Section 3: "Of Justice," Part 1, p. 170.

receive tenfold increase; but the cautious, jealous virtue of justice would never once have been dreamed of. For what purpose make a partition of goods where everyone has already more than enough? Why give rise to property where there cannot possibly be any injury?[103]

Here we see that Hume reckons on the basis of the material abundance that was produced and distributed in the society of his time in accordance with the level of development of the productive forces and the corresponding production relations – an abundance of great magnitude compared to previous societies but not as yet such that private ownership of the means of production, unequal property relations, and the division of society into classes could be eliminated. Hume can only picture such a state of society as an idyllic myth. He speaks only in terms of nature providing such a profuse abundance, not in terms of society's productive forces reaching the level where such an abundance could be produced through human labor and the means of production created by it.

In fact, as Marx and Engels explained, it was the historic role of capitalism – which was still in its early, rising period in Hume's day – to develop the productive forces to exactly that stage where not only bourgeois property relations but all exploitative and oppressive property relations, all division of society into classes, would be abolished through the overthrow of the bourgeoisie and the carrying through of the proletarian revolution to the achievement of communism. In his polemic against Dühring, Engels gave this powerful summation of this most fundamental point:

> The cleavage of society into an exploiting and an exploited class, a ruling and an oppressed class, was the necessary outcome of the previous low development of production. Society is necessarily divided into classes as long as the total social labor only yields a product but slightly exceeding what is necessary for the bare existence of all, as long as labor therefore claims all or almost all of the time of the great majority of the members of society. Side by side with this great majority exclusively enthralled in toil, a class freed from direct productive labor is formed which manages the general business of society: the direction of labor, affairs of state, justice, science, art, and so forth. . . .
>
> But if, upon this showing, division into classes has a certain

103. Hume, "Principles of Morals," Section 3: "Of Justice," Part 1, p. 166.

historical justification, it does so only for a given period of time, for given social conditions. It was based on the insufficiency of production; it will be swept away by the full development of the modern productive forces. In fact the abolition of social classes presupposes a level of historical development at which the existence not merely of this or that particular ruling class but of any ruling class at all, and therefore of class distinction itself, has become an anachronism, is obsolete. It therefore presupposes that the development of production has reached a level at which the appropriation of the means of production and of the products, and consequently of political supremacy and of the monopoly of educational and intellectual leadership by a special social class, has become not only superfluous but also a hindrance to development economically, politically, and intellectually.

This point has now been reached.[104]

With the abolition of capitalism and all relations of exploitation and social inequality – necessitating the two radical ruptures, with traditional property relations and traditional ideas, that Marx and Engels pointed to in the *Communist Manifesto*[105] – will come the abolition of the political institutions, practices, and principles that correspond to capitalist economic relations, including democracy.

There remains one more fundamental phenomenon of capitalism and the bourgeois epoch that must be spoken to here: the modern nation-state and its attendant principle of patriotism. We have seen how the methodology of mechanical materialism, and particularly the principles of Newton, both reflected and furthered the development of the machine age and capitalist society, a society marked by atomistic commodity owners, on the one hand, and the increasing regulation and organization of production by the different capitalists according to the latest scientific and technological advances, on the other. This, in turn, relates to what is the fundamental contradiction of capitalism – between socialized production and private (capitalist) appropriation – and more particularly, to what Engels analyzed as the two major manifestations of this contradiction: the class antagonism between the proletariat and the bourgeoisie, and the contradiction between anarchy of production in society as a whole and the

104. Engels, *Anti-Dühring* (Peking: Foreign Languages Press, 1976), Part 3: "Socialism," Section 2: "Theoretical," pp. 364-65.

105. See Marx and Engels, *Communist Manifesto*, p. 59.

organized character of production within individual enterprises. In regard to this latter manifestation specifically, Engels also analyzed how this assumed an international dimension with the extensive colonization and the commercial wars carried out by rival European powers in the seventeenth and eighteenth centuries. Today, in this, the imperialist stage of capitalism, while anarchy of production remains a fundamental, driving force in the overall process of capitalist production and accumulation, the capitalist state has been compelled to increasingly intervene in this process in an effort to regulate it and mitigate its eruption into crisis; and one of the main expressions of the anarchy/organization contradiction today is the condition that capital in the imperialist stage remains anchored in a national market but accumulates and can only accumulate internationally. Thus there remains a powerful material basis for national rivalry between imperialist states while at the same time this rivalry is even more global in nature (and in its destructive potential) than in the period of rising capitalism.[106] And in their insistence not only on the universality of the principle of patriotism but on the fact that patriotism means placing one's nation above all others, the imperialist leaders of today are in fact carrying forward the ideas and traditions established by their "founding fathers."

As Stalin explained, the formation of modern nations is a phenomenon of rising capitalism. The formation of nation-states has everything to do with securing a "home market" for capital:

> The chief problem for the young bourgeoisie is the problem of the market. Its aim is to sell its goods and to emerge victorious from competition with the bourgeoisie of a different nationality. Hence its desire to secure its "own," its "home" market. The market is the first school in which the bourgeoisie learns its nationalism.[107]

106. For Engels's presentation of this, see *Anti-Dühring*, Part 3: "Socialism," Section 2: "Theoretical," pp. 343-70, especially pp. 347-52. For a fuller discussion of the present-day expression of these contradictions, see "Fundamental and Principal Contradictions on a World Scale" (excerpt from the 1980 Report from the Central Committee of the RCP, USA), *Revolutionary Worker*, No. 132 (27 November 1981), p. 8; and for a thorough analysis of the underlying political-economic dynamics, see Raymond Lotta with Frank Shannon, *America in Decline* (Chicago: Banner Press, 1984), Vol. 1, especially chapter 1.

107. J. V. Stalin, "Marxism and the National Question," in *Works* (Moscow: Foreign Languages Publishing House, 1953; reprinted London: Red Star Press, 1973), Vol. 2, p. 316.

But we have seen that this process of consolidating the national market was intertwined with colonization of other territories and peoples and with commercial wars (along with the wars of colonial conquest). Thus, while in general representatives of the bourgeoisie in its rising, revolutionary period have given voice to the principle of the self-determination of nations, they could not help but insist at the same time that loyalty must be given to one's own nation first and foremost. Thus the eloquent words of Hume:

> When the interests of one country interfere with those of another, we estimate the merits of a statesman by the good or ill which results to his own country from his measures and counsels, without regard to the prejudice which he brings on its enemies and rivals. His fellow citizens are the objects which lie nearest the eye while we determine his character. And as nature has implanted in everyone a superior affection to his own country, we never expect any regard to distant nations where a competition arises. Not to mention that while every man consults the good of his own community, we are sensible that the general interest of mankind is better promoted than by any loose indeterminate views to the good of a species, whence no beneficial action could ever result for want of a duly limited object on which they could exert themselves.[108]

The leading political theorists and political leaders of bourgeois revolution and bourgeois society, beginning at least with Hobbes and Locke,[109] continuing through Rousseau[110] and

108. Hume, "Principles of Morals," Section 5: "Why Utility Pleases," pp. 195-96. Note the influence of Newtonian principles here, especially in the attempt to ground such patriotism in natural law and more specifically in the echoes of the principles of gravity: one's attachment to one's own country as opposed to the attraction of distant ones.

109. Both Hobbes and Locke not only saw the nation-state (or commonwealth) as the essential and highest expression of human society and government but set it down that each nation was, in relation to all others, in a "state of nature." (See for example, Hobbes, *The Leviathan*, pp. 111, 132, 144, 162; and Locke, *Second Treatise*, p. 76 and also p. 45.) It is also interesting to note that Niccolò Machiavelli, a century and more before Hobbes and Locke, was marked not only by his more notorious "Machiavellian" maxims (his advice on how to carry out ruthless machinations in order to rule society), but also by his fervent nationalism (though in envisioning and striving for a glorious Italy he looked backward to an idealized vision of ancient Rome). In this regard, see Machiavelli, *The Prince*, especially pp. 124-27.

110. See Rousseau, *Social Contract*, Book 1, chapter 7, pp. 63, 66; also pp. 124-25.

Paine,[111] as well as Jefferson and other leaders of the American Revolution, and down to the present era, have all reflected in their thoughts and actions not only the fact that under capitalism – and so long as society remains divided into classes – nations will continue to exist in rivalry with each other but that there will be no way for mankind to transcend this rivalry or prevent it from continuing to lead to violent collision. Given this, then, despite declarations – and in some cases sincere intentions – concerning the universal rights of mankind, the equality of nations, and so on, it is a duty for all those who follow bourgeois principles to place the welfare of their own nation above that of all others. Thomas Jefferson exemplifies this very well. On the one hand he could write that "no one nation has a right to sit in judgment over another";[112] but since this is the real world, and nations do indeed seek to impose their will on each other, better my nation than yours. Jefferson applied this logic in practice, as a leader of the American Revolution and of the United States that emerged out of it, not only in relation to oppressed peoples, such as the Indians and Black slaves, but also in relation to rival powers, such as Spain and France, as well as England of course. And he gave this a theoretical – if at the same time a rather crass – expression, in statements such as the following:

> The first object of my heart is my own country. In that is embarked my family, my fortune, & my own existence. I have not one farthing of interest, nor one fibre of attachment out of it, nor a single motive of preference of any one nation to another, but in proportion as they are more or less friendly to us.[113]

From all this it can be seen that the democratic principle of the equality of nations and the right of nations to self-determination, while it must be upheld and fought for today in opposition to the domination of oppressed nations under imperialism, neverthe-

---

111. See Paine, *Rights of Man*, pp. 132, 165-66. Though Paine spoke, positively, of the possibility of a confederation of European nations to oppose "the intrigue of Courts, by which the system of war is kept up" (p. 168), he still regarded the nation as the highest form of political organization and "the general will of a nation" as the highest expression of political principle (p. 287) – as is clear not only in the pages cited here but throughout *Rights of Man*.

112. Jefferson, "Opinion on the French Treaties," in *The Portable Jefferson*, p. 270.

113. Jefferson, "These...are my principles," letter to Elbridge Gerry (26 January 1799), in *The Portable Jefferson*, p. 479.

less is historically delimited and in the final analysis is not sufficient even to illuminate the way to the abolition of national inequality and oppression. It falls far short of pointing to a world in which humanity is no longer marked by division into nations as well as classes. Ultimately, it too is a phenomenon of the bourgeois epoch and will be superseded, together with all other such phenomena, with the advent of communism worldwide.

3

The Illusions
of Democracy

Democracy and Dictatorship

It is conventional wisdom in countries like the U.S. that democracy and dictatorship are the complete opposite of each other: where there is democracy there is not a dictatorship and where there is a dictatorship there is of course no democracy. But in fact democracy is a form of dictatorship. In any state where democracy is the form of political rule, democracy is really only practiced among the ranks of the ruling class, while dictatorship is exercised over the oppressed class (or classes). In the present-day self-proclaimed "democratic countries" this is the dictatorship of the bourgeoisie over the proletariat (and other oppressed strata and groups).

Lenin gave this comprehensive and concise definition of what is meant by classes:

> Classes are large groups of people differing from each other by the place they occupy in a historically determined system of social production, by their relation (in most cases fixed and formulated in law) to the means of production, by their role in the social organization of labor, and, consequently, by the dimensions of the

share of social wealth of which they dispose and the mode of acquiring it.[1]

The division of society into classes is not a universal and inevitable feature of human society, and an examination of the earliest forms of society reveals that they are not characterized by a division into classes, as defined by Lenin – that there is not a situation where there are "groups of people one of which can appropriate the labor of another owing to the different places they occupy in a definite system of social economy."[2] But as the social economy develops, the social division of labor further develops to the point where, once surpluses can be accumulated (beyond what is required for mere survival) by distinct individuals or groups within the society, then antagonistic class divisions emerge.

In stressing that class antagonism and class distinctions generally "will fall as inevitably as they arose at an earlier stage" because "we are now rapidly approaching a stage in the development of production at which the existence of these classes not only will have ceased to be a necessity, but will become a positive hindrance to production," Engels also stresses that where and so long as society is divided into classes, there will of necessity be a state apparatus:

> The state, then, has not existed from all eternity. There have been societies that did without it, that had no idea of the state and state power. At a certain stage of economic development, which was necessarily bound up with the split of society into classes, the state became a necessity owing to this split.[3]

The state here means something very precise – it is not the same thing as government in the most general sense. A state, wherever it exists and whatever the form of government, is "essentially a machine for keeping down the oppressed, exploited class."[4] The

---

1. V. I. Lenin, "A Great Beginning," in *Collected Works* (hereafter referred to as *LCW*) (Moscow: Progress Publishers, 1965), Vol. 29, p. 421.

2. Lenin, "A Great Beginning," *LCW*, 29, p. 421.

3. Engels, "Origin," *MESW*, 3, p. 330.

4. Engels, "Origin," *MESW*, 3, p. 332. The dictatorship of the proletariat, as a special kind of state, representing the political rule of a formerly exploited class over the overthrown bourgeoisie and other would-be exploiters, will be discussed more fully in chapter 7.

essential parts of this machinery are not legislatures and other similar vehicles of public discussion and nominal decision-making – these can be dispensed with when necessary, as they often have been – but are the executive power and the bureaucracy, the courts, and in particular the armed forces. These armed forces are the concentration of the power of one class over another: they represent a monopoly of force by the ruling class, and their purpose is to forcefully guarantee its interests (both within the country and, especially in this era of imperialism, anywhere else in the world those interests are contested).

All these things – the armed forces, the courts and laws, the executive and the bureaucracy (and the legislatures and so on, where they exist), the political institutions in general – belong to the superstructure, which in any society rests upon and reinforces the economic base. "In the social production of their existence," Marx wrote,

> men enter into definite, necessary relations, which are independent of their will, namely, relations of production corresponding to a determinate stage of development of their material forces of production. The totality of these relations of production constitutes the economic structure of society, the real foundation on which there arises a legal and political superstructure and to which there correspond definite forms of social consciousness.[5]

In a society whose basis is capitalist relations of production, with its fundamental class antagonism between the bourgeoisie – the capitalist exploiters – and the exploited class of propertyless wage-workers (the proletariat), the legal and political superstructure (and the dominant forms of social consciousness) serve to maintain the rule of the bourgeoisie over the proletariat and to preserve and protect those relations of exploitation. This truth, and its underlying basis, as made clear by Marx, is of such fundamental importance and bears so significantly on the class struggle between exploiters and exploited – on the whole question of how society and the possibility of radically transforming it is viewed – that it is not surprising that it is denied and distorted by defenders and apologists of the existing order.[6] It would be extremely sur-

---

5. Marx, *Preface and Introduction to "A Contribution to the Critique of Political Economy"* (Peking: Foreign Languages Press, 1976), p. 3.

6. The distortions of such defenders and apologists in "socialist," even "Marxist," guise will be focused on in chapter 6.

prising if they did not do so.

Many will say: how can the political system in a democratic country like the U.S. "serve to maintain the rule of the bourgeoisie over the proletariat" when everyone has the right to choose the political leaders by participating in elections? The answer to this is that elections in such a society, and the "democratic process" as a whole, are a sham – and more than a sham – a cover for and indeed a vehicle through which domination over the exploited and oppressed is carried out by the exploiting, oppressing, ruling class. To state it in a single sentence, elections: are controlled by the bourgeoisie; are not the means through which basic decisions are made in any case; and are really for the primary purpose of legitimizing the system and the policies and actions of the ruling class, giving them the mantle of a "popular mandate," and of channeling, confining, and controlling the political activity of the masses of people.

In relation to all this the recent presidential election in the U.S. is highly instructive. The consensus was obviously reached within the ruling class, well before the election, that Reagan was the man for the times; this was transmitted and drummed into people through the media. Again, there was the attempt to disguise it as the popular will (people are told what *to* think by telling them it is what they already *do* think). There was the incessant refrain that Reagan was "unbeatable." All of this to set up an overwhelming "mandate" for what Reagan personifies. And, in any case, should Mondale have somehow won the election, it wouldn't have made the slightest bit of difference on any substantial question – above all on the cardinal question of preparing for war against the rival Soviet bloc.[7]

---

7. This is not to say that Reagan has no base of support among people in the U.S. With the intensification of world events – and in particular the all-around crisis of the imperialist system, involving both the Soviet- and U.S.-led blocs, and the heightening rivalry between them, pushing things rapidly toward world war – there is increasing polarization within the U.S. But the basic terms of this polarization are not Republicans versus Democrats (this does involve some real differences, but precisely differences among and on the terms of the ruling class). Rather, the basic polarization is between the ruling class on one side, including both its major parties and all the major political figures paraded before the people, and on the other side the exploited and dispossessed – with a large number of people in between these two basic poles and tending to split and to oscillate between the one and the other. As for elections specifically, to a large degree the proletarians and other oppressed who make up that pole do not vote, or even if they do vote do not put much stock in the notion that this will have any real effect on

On the most obvious level, to be a serious candidate for any major office in a country like the U.S. requires millions of dollars – a personal fortune or, more often, the backing of people with that kind of money. Beyond that, to become known and be taken seriously depends on favorable exposure in the mass media (favorable at least in the sense that you are presented as within the framework of responsible – that is, acceptable – politics). These mass media are called that because they reach and influence masses of people daily and constantly. But they are certainly not controlled by the masses, nor do they reflect or serve their fundamental interests. They are themselves key pillars of the power structure: they are owned by major financial interests (where they are not owned by the state) and are in any case closely regulated by the state. By the time "the people express their will through voting," both the candidates they have to choose among and the "issues" that deserve "serious consideration" have been selected out by someone else: the ruling class. Small wonder they are more than willing to abide by the results!

Further, and even more fundamentally, to "get anywhere" once elected – both to advance one's own career and to "get anything done" – it is necessary to fit into the established mold and work within the established structures. This is partially because those already entrenched in positions of power and influence are thereby in a position to make others conform and work through the accepted avenues, but more basically it is because, once again, the political system must serve the underlying economic system. This is not a mere theoretical abstraction, it has concrete meaning: policies and actions which work against or undermine that economic system *will in fact* cause disruption, disorder, chaos, breakdowns in the more or less orderly functioning of things – and unless you are prepared to see the entire order overthrown, with all that implies, you can only view such disruption, disorder, and chaos as something to be avoided or kept to the minimum where it cannot be avoided. But if you are prepared to see – and work for – the overthrow of the existing order, and if you say so openly, you will never be allowed to hold any real posi-

---

the decision makers and the direction of things. The molding of public opinion around the elections has its main effect on that "large number of people in between," but it also affects the exploited and dispossessed, particularly by making them feel they are up against a powerful government that has a "popular mandate."

tion of power; or, if, on the other hand, you have this perspective but hide it and attempt to "get in the power structure and work from within," you will be swallowed up – or chewed up and spit out – by that structure. There is an abundance of historical experience to demonstrate this – and none which disproves it.

If, however, the electoral process in bourgeois society does not represent the exercise of sovereignty by the people, it generally does play an important role in maintaining the sovereignty – the dictatorship – of the bourgeoisie and the continuation of capitalist society. This very electoral process itself tends to cover over the basic class relations – and class antagonisms – in society, and serves to give formal, institutionalized expression to the political participation of atomized individuals in the perpetuation of the status quo. This process not only reduces people to isolated individuals but at the same time reduces them to a passive position politically and defines the essence of politics as such atomized passivity – as each person, individually, in isolation from everyone else, giving his/her approval to this or to that option, *all of which options have been formulated and presented by an active power standing above these atomized masses of "citizens."* It is not infrequently said, as a major selling point of this electoral process (in the USA specifically), that, regardless of everything else – and in particular, regardless of admittedly immense differences in wealth and economic power and social status – the ballot box is the great equalizer . . . that once you step into that polling booth, the vote of a common wage-worker and the vote of a Rockefeller count for the same thing. And, fundamentally, this is true – neither of these votes counts for a damn thing; Rockefeller (or the class of Rockefellers) doesn't need to vote to exercise political power, and the common wage-workers will never exercise political power under this system no matter how many votes they cast or for what. There never has been and never will be "a revolution through the ballot box," not only because the powers-that-be would forcibly suppress any such attempt, but also – and this touches on a very important function of elections in bourgeois society – because the very acceptance of the electoral process as the quintessential political act reinforces acceptance of the established order and works against any radical rupture with, to say nothing of the actual overturning of, that order. In sum, then, the electoral process and the notion that this process represents the expression of the popular will serves not to set or to fundamentally influence the politics that govern society but to reinforce the shackles binding the masses of people to the political – and underlying economic – interests and dictates of the governing, dominant class.

Similarly, the much-vaunted freedom of expression in the "democratic countries" is not in opposition to but is encompassed by and confined within the actual exercise of dictatorship by the bourgeoisie. This is for two basic reasons – because the ruling class has a monopoly on the means of molding public opinion and because its monopoly of armed force puts it in a position to suppress, as violently as necessary, any expression of ideas, as well as any action, that poses a serious challenge to the established order. What Marx and Engels wrote in the *Communist Manifesto* is more true than ever in today's conditions: "The ruling ideas of each age have ever been the ideas of its ruling class."[8]

The control of the mass media by finance capital has already been mentioned: this is so obvious that anyone honestly looking into it will be immediately struck by this fact. What is more important – and more concealed – however, is that the media constitute an instrument of the ruling class in general in putting over its point of view and discrediting or outright suppressing views opposed to it – in molding people's minds and exercising dictatorship in the realm of ideas as part of its overall dictatorship.[9] But it

8. Marx and Engels, *Communist Manifesto*, p. 57.

9. For some indication of the measure of control exerted by powerful financial groups over the media and some examples of how this affects the content of what is presented by these media, see Ben H. Bagdikian, *The Media Monopoly* (Boston: Beacon Press, 1983). Bagdikian, however, treats this as a question of particular corporate power centers pursuing their private interests against the public interest; he fails to point out (he probably does not believe) that this "public interest" represents the interests of the ruling class – for the "public" is divided into classes and it is the interests of the economically dominant class (the bourgeoisie in capitalist society) that will dominate politically and ideologically and will define the "public interest." Thus, as I pointed out in another work, *The Media Monopoly* "does contain some interesting exposure of the control and manipulation of the media by large corporations and it has stirred some controversy, but it . . . places the problem squarely within the confines of bourgeois democracy – and bourgeois rule" (Avakian, *A Horrible End, or An End to the Horror?* [Chicago: RCP Publications, 1984], p. 47).

It is also striking to what lengths bourgeois ideological dictatorship reaches: a computer inventory of 2,425 Hallmark Christmas card designs in 1984 "shows exactly three featuring the word peace. 'The peace theme doesn't have the same impact this year as it did in the '60s and '70s,' one spokesman for Hallmark explained" ("A Counterforce Christmas," *Revolutionary Worker*, No. 286 [21 December 1984], p. 4). We also see here the classical device of presenting ruling class indoctrination and molding of public opinion as merely the reflection of the "popular will."

remains a fact that on any really significant issue (and, for that matter, most not very significant ones) the men (and the few women) of the media put forward the same viewpoint – and to a great degree seem to be reading from the same prepared text. Where they do disagree – with each other, or with a particular government policy at any given time – this too is from the point of view of the general interests of the ruling class and the established order as a whole. In part, this occurs more or less "spontaneously"; that is, these people – especially those who have climbed up the ladder to any position of real influence – can overwhelmingly be counted on to know what the basic interests of the ruling class are and how to present them as effectively as possible. But on any occasion where the system and its rulers are put to a severe test or find their interests threatened, then there is a marked "pulling together" around an orchestrated official line – which is often all the more insidious because it is done without the acknowledgment that it is an official line – and generally with the denial that such an official line even exists.

A few examples will help to bring this even more clearly to light. When the Soviet Union shot down the South Korean airplane, KAL 007 – and if anyone still does not believe that this was indeed a plane sent on a spy mission by the U.S., that in itself is a tribute to the propagandizing powers of the media! – the media in the U.S. (and generally throughout the Western bloc) howled in chorus about the horrors of the Soviet state, repeating over and over the same message of mock outrage. Where, especially in the critical days right around the time of this event, were the hardened cynics among the political correspondents and nightly news anchormen who were pointing to the gaping holes in the U.S.-South Korean-Japanese account of the events, posing the "tough questions" that would at least raise the real specter of a deliberate provocation by the U.S.? Apparently they were in the same place as all the members of Congress, including the "critics" of the Reagan administration, who did the same – nowhere. There were none. They all dutifully (and, in most cases, passionately) trumpeted the official line. And when, some time later, it became impossible to continue covering over the evidence pointing to such a deliberate provocation – which, it should be stressed, involved the risk of igniting world war, with all that means – there was not a single network, major newspaper, etc., in the U.S. which, even if it noted certain "inconsistencies," did anything but continue to portray the Soviet Union as the sole culprit and to point to this incident as further proof of the barbarous nature of the Soviet state.

Or look at that recent dispute in which some in the media did seem to become truly outraged: the issue, which surfaced with some fireworks around the U.S. invasion of Grenada, of whether or not members of the media would be allowed to accompany U.S. military forces in the early, perhaps critical, stages of an operation. What were the terms of this debate, all the way around? They were whether or not such media presence is helpful to such operations (even if, in certain secondary aspects, this involves raising certain questions or criticisms concerning them) and to what degree the government should directly determine (and enforce) the rules of conduct for the media in these situations, and on the other hand to what degree the media can be relied on to "police itself" in this regard. Those who argued vehemently against serious restriction, or even elimination, of such media participation pointed with pride – and with accuracy – to the long history of media involvement in such situations. Indeed, the media have played a crucial role in helping to win public support for these operations. Where in all this – even in the "outrage," or the questions and criticisms raised – is any viewpoint different from (to say nothing of any viewpoint fundamentally opposed to) that of the imperialist ruling class?

Or recall the "Iran hostage crisis" of five years ago (under a Democratic administration, let it be noted now). Not only was there a very clear line coming down from the top levels of government (even comedians such as Johnny Carson got the word not to make jokes about the situation in Iran), but the media as a whole showed its mettle in maintaining a consistent practice of turning reality upside down, portraying the Iranian people – who had suffered for decades under the brutal oppression of the Shah, installed and kept in power by the U.S. – as the perpetrators of a horrendous crime against innocent America. Over and over, media spokesmen could be heard openly declaring that they were going to put forward "the American point of view and not the Iranian" – in other words, that they are there to represent U.S. imperialism, not those who oppose it. In every instance of "hostage-taking" or similar "acts of terrorism" against U.S. imperialist interests, the U.S. media consistently present the situation as though "America itself" is "held hostage," as though the interests of everyone in the USA are the same as those of the ruling class; these media never present the problem from any angle other than this: how are "we" going to deal with "international terrorism," are "we" doing enough to eliminate this scourge, or at least to retaliate forcefully against it? Never is the label "terrorism" used without qualification to describe anyone serving the interests of U.S. imperialism – this is reserved for those opposing it. And never is the question even treated as legitimate by the U.S. media: Does the U.S. government have no right to speak in condemnation of "terrorism," given its whole record of mass murder and wanton destruction throughout the world? To even suggest that such a question might be seriously presented in the U.S. media is to invite laughter and ridicule. The free press, you see, is free only to promote the interests of the imperialist ruling class that controls it.

Or another example: where, during the "Watergate scandal" of a decade ago, was the prominent commentator, newsman, or columnist who, instead of parroting the line that this whole affair showed the strength of democracy and the ability of the system to "heal itself," pointed to the mass murder and destruction in Vietnam – as well as similar atrocities in other parts of the world and murderous repression within the U.S. itself – as the real, and towering, crimes of Richard Nixon. . .and still more of the U.S. imperialists for whom Nixon acted as chief executive and commander in chief? This is obviously a question that answers itself. And, as Noam Chomsky has pointed out, not only during the early stages of the Vietnam War – when the media were in perfect synchrony in their role as cheerleaders for U.S. aggression there – but later as well, once it was clear the U.S. was headed for defeat and even after that defeat was brought to a culmination, there have been no significant media personnel who have come out and portrayed the war as something other than a tragic mistake, if not a noble enterprise, by the U.S., who have condemned U.S. actions there as criminal and have said that what the U.S. was fighting for in Vietnam, the interests it sought to uphold, were not worth fighting for – that in fact they should have been fought against and defeated.[10] And of course none of the media have raised the question: does this war say something fundamental about the whole nature of the system in the U.S.? The control and use of the media by the ruling class that is reflected in these (and countless other) examples is one important

10. See Noam Chomsky, *Towards a New Cold War* (New York: Pantheon Books, 1982).

aspect of the all-around dictatorship exercised by the bourgeoisie in all spheres of the superstructure of capitalist society. The cultural arena, the educational system (and the church structures), and all other spheres of ideology are dominated by this ruling class and its viewpoint. Through them people are conditioned to view the world with the outlook of the ruling class and at the same time are prepared and conditioned to find their place and accept their fate within the confines of the system and according to the interests and demands of the ruling class. In the realm of ideas, just as in the political sphere and in the underlying social relations, there is no freedom and equality for everyone – there is class domination.

As we have seen, equality under the law is one of the foundation stones of the bourgeois concept of democracy. The law is presented as a neutral force, affecting everyone equally, regardless of their place in society, and moreover as originating ultimately in the will of the people because it is legislated by their chosen representatives. In addition to what has already been shown about elections – which clearly refutes the notion that laws are legislated by the representatives of all the people and indicates that instead they are legislated by representatives of the ruling class – the reality is that in any case laws must reflect and serve the underlying economic relations and the interests of the class that is dominant in those relations. Otherwise, if the laws were in conflict with the fundamental property relations, the economic basis of society would be completely disrupted and society could not function.

Imagine, for example, if the basic necessities of life continued to be produced as they are now in capitalist society – overwhelmingly through a process where workers exchange their labor power for wages and are employed in facilities owned by capitalists who then appropriate the things produced and sell them at a money-price – but at the same time the laws stated that no one had to pay for such necessities, that anyone could just take as much of them as they needed. That such a situation immediately strikes one as absurd, as absolutely unworkable, is an expression of the basic truth that the underlying production relations of society (the economic base) must and will determine the nature of the ideological and political superstructure, including the laws. To have a situation where people would actually be able to have the things they needed without having to pay a money-price for them requires a fundamentally different economic system, a radically different society corresponding to such a fundamental change in the economic system – a whole new world – which can only be brought about through the international proletarian revolution. But so long as the relations of capital continue to dominate society, the laws of that society will reflect and reinforce those relations.

That is why "in the real world" of capitalist society, it is quite legal for a company to refuse to hire people for the reason that it cannot profitably employ them, even though it may mean that these unemployed people (and perhaps their families) will go hungry and homeless; whereas at the same time it is completely illegal for these people to occupy part of that company's property for shelter, or to take food or clothing from other businesses without paying for them – even though they and their families may starve or freeze without them. That is why it is legal for a finance company to repossess someone's car if they have fallen behind in their payments, even if they need the car to get to work to earn their livelihood; why it is perfectly legal for a utility company to shut off people's heat in the dead of winter if they have not paid their bills, and on and on. And all this is leaving aside the ways in which what is written down as law is actually interpreted and applied by the police, the courts, and those in authority generally. In reality, for example, even where the law might theoretically allow a poor Black person to carry a gun and even to use it for self-defense, he is extremely likely to pay with his life if he encounters the police, and the odds are overwhelming that the police killing of a Black person will be declared "justifiable homicide," regardless of the actual circumstances. In fact, police in the U.S. murder hundreds of Black people every year, and the overwhelming majority of the victims are unarmed (even though it is a common ploy of the police to plant a weapon near the victim after he has been killed, or to claim they thought he *might* have had a weapon, etc.). Nor is such legal murder of the oppressed the exclusive province of the police: recent times have seen the state sanction and encourage "vigilantes" and other reactionaries out to rid the streets of those they see as threats to the established order, whether they are engaging in conscious political activity or just being generally unruly. Similarly, the bombing of abortion clinics in the U.S. can be declared by the government not to be terrorist – and in effect the perpetrators of these bombings are not repressed but encouraged from the highest levels of government – while people who "invade" weapons production facilities and pour blood on weapons of mass destruction are arrested and branded as "terrorists."

Finally, there is the broader sphere in which the law codifies the power of the state to force people to become part of its armed forces, and when ordered to do so, to kill other people, in some other part of the world or in the "home country" itself. In the final analysis, this legalized violence too is for the purpose of protecting and reinforcing the basic property relations of capital and furthering capitalist accumulation – which, in this era of imperialism especially, is an international process and is battled out in a worldwide arena.

In sum, then, the apparatus of the state – the armed forces in particular but also the courts and the legal system, the bureaucracy, and so forth – are in the hands of a class, the class that is dominant in the economic relations of society. This state is not and cannot be neutral. Nor is it the instrument of particular private interests or specific powerful individuals (though of course there are *individual leaders* of any class at any given time). Rather, this state apparatus is an instrument of class rule, a machine for the oppression of the economically exploited and dominated classes: it enforces the dictatorship of the ruling class over the exploited and oppressed classes, and will be used by the ruling class to suppress any real resistance to its dictates, any serious challenge to its interests and to the established order which reflects and serves them, regardless of which particular individuals are in office.[11] As Raymond Lotta has incisively sum-

11. It is not merely the case, as numerous studies have shown, that many of the same people remain in positions of power in the armed forces, the bureaucracy, etc., whichever administration (or party) is in office, nor simply that major finance capitalists may have "investments," so to speak, in more than one of the major parties. More fundamental, again, is that the state must reflect and serve certain very definite economic relations and the class interests that dominate within these relations.

To be sure, different sections, or blocs, of capital battle each other, in pursuance of their particular interests, and seek to use various organs of the state in carrying out this battle. But such battles are subordinate to the primary and essential function of the bourgeois state – as an instrument of the dictatorship of the bourgeoisie as a whole, *as a class,* over the proletariat and other oppressed masses – and as a general rule these battles take place within the overall context of firmly upholding the general class interests of the bourgeoisie against its class antagonists (and of the bourgeois nation-state against rival nation-states). Indeed, if and when conflicts among different sections of the ruling class reach the point where they are beginning to assume antagonistic proportions themselves, that is a sign of extremely deep and acute cracks and fissures in the entire established order; and such a situation must be seized by the oppressed not to side with one

marized it:

> The state is an objective structure of society whose character is
> determined not by the class origins of its leading personnel but by
> the specific social division of labor of which it is an extension and
> the production relations which it must ultimately serve and
> reproduce.[12]

In a society based on bourgeois production relations – with the
fundamental class antagonism between bourgeoisie and proletariat – it is impossible for the superstructure (including the
laws and the courts, the police and the army, the bureaucracy,
and the whole apparatus of government and also ideas, values,
morals, etc.) *not* to uphold and enforce such production relations
and the division of labor that characterizes and is indispensable to
this society, even though this means exploitation and oppression
for the masses of people and the massive violence that is required
to defend and perpetuate such a system and the interests of its
ruling class. To eliminate such madness and destruction, to
change the conditions that give rise to them, it is necessary to
thoroughly transform the production relations and the division of
labor – the economic base of society. This, however, can only be
done through a revolution in the superstructure – the struggle to
seize political power from the ruling class through military
means – the revolutionary warfare of the proletariat, in alliance
with other oppressed masses, to defeat the armed forces of the
bourgeoisie and smash and dismantle its state apparatus, replac-
ing it with a new and radically different state, the dictatorship of
the proletariat, as a transition to the abolition of class divisions
and of the state.[13]

---

section of the bourgeoisie against another – thus helping the ruling class to "repair"
the rupturing old order and reinforce its dictatorship, in one form or another – but
instead to rise in revolutionary struggle to overthrow the rule of the bourgeoisie
altogether.

12. Lotta, "Realities of Social-Imperialism Versus Dogmas of Cynical Realism:
The Dynamics of the Soviet Capital Formation," in *The Soviet Union: Socialist or
Social-Imperialist? Part 2: The Question is Joined* (Chicago: RCP Publications, 1983),
p. 41.

13. In chapter 2, it was pointed out that bourgeois political philosophers have
sought to formulate "universal, transcendental principles," and it was suggested
that there are no such principles that can govern society irrespective of the era and
the circumstances in which that society exists. But couldn't it be said that the
analysis, presented in this chapter, that the superstructure arises on the basis of

There can be no such thing as a "peaceful revolution." Revolution means the transformation of the economic base and the superstructure of society; it requires the replacement of one ruling class by another. And no ruling class has ever voluntarily "stepped down" to make way for the class that was rising up to replace it. Not only was this true of society and its transformation in previous epochs, when revolution could only mean the replacement of one exploiting class by another. It is all the more true of the revolution of this epoch, the proletarian revolution, which aims at the abolition of all relations of exploitation, of all oppressive division of labor, and of all political institutions and ideological forms which reflect the division of society into classes. To think of carrying out such a revolution peacefully – particularly when it is up against the massive machinery of violence and destruction that is controlled by the bourgeois states in this era and up against ruling classes that have repeatedly demonstrated their absolutely ruthless determination to remain in power regardless of the cost in carnage and human misery – is the height of folly, at best. To promote such a notion as a political program and to oppose it to the necessity for violent proletarian revolution is deception of the greatest magnitude.[14]

---

and serves a particular economic base is precisely the attempt to formulate such a universal principle? Yes, on the one hand, this is a universal principle (though it should not be applied mechanically, as if the superstructure only serves the economic base in the most narrow and direct sense, rather than overall and in the final analysis). But, on the other hand, this is a principle that does not attempt to identify (and freeze) specific social relations, ideas, values, etc., as eternal and possible (or even desirable) in every society in every age. Rather, it indicates that different production relations and their corresponding political and ideological superstructure will characterize societies in different ages and at different levels of development of their productive forces. And it must include the understanding that, while there is a certain coherence in human history, because one generation inherits the productive forces from the previous ones, the historical development of human society is a dynamic process, marked and driven forward by contradiction, undergoing continual change and punctuated repeatedly by radical ruptures and sudden leaps. Thus, there is no eternal form of society, none which does not involve contradiction and undergo qualitative change, not even communism. There is a radical and fundamental difference between this and the bourgeois view.

14. Here it seems necessary to very briefly discuss, and debunk, what is probably the most frequently mentioned (and certainly a widely propagated) example of an alleged "peaceful revolution": the movement led by M. K. Gandhi in India, which was crowned with the granting of formal independence to India by England after World War 2. This, to put it simply, was no revolution: the domination of India by imperialism was never eliminated, although the form of domina-

The Ideal as Ideal, The Ideal as Reality

At this point it might be objected that, yes, there are many imperfections in the democratic system of government and it is true that many horrendous things are done in the name of democracy, but, with all its faults, democracy is still the best form of government possible and democracy as an idea represents the loftiest vision of how society should function – something to be striven for, even if it can never be fully realized. In refuting this basic argument elsewhere, specifically in terms of the principles embodied in the *Declaration of Independence,* I pointed out that "the answer to the question, what if the basic principles of the *Declaration of Independence* were really applied?, is that they have been, in the U.S. itself and generally in all bourgeois societies; and the time is long since past when *that* is the best and highest that humanity is capable of achieving." And I went on to stress that even if we "take the bourgeois ideal expressed in that *Declaration* and examine what its fullest realization would mean,"

---

tion changed from outright colonialism to neocolonialism (and although British imperialism was soon replaced by the U.S. as the dominant imperialist power in India, while more recently the Soviet Union has dug its claws in as well, so that today India is ravaged by both imperialist blocs and is a focus of sharp contention between them).

Nor, of course, has there been any revolution in the basic production and social relations in India. Not long ago, in Bhopal, a dramatic illustration was provided – at the cost of tremendous suffering on the part of the Indian masses, once again – of the consequences of the continuing domination of that country by imperialism. . .and, it must be said, of the legacy of Gandhi, representing collaboration with imperialism and utilizing peaceful forms of mass opposition only as a lever in seeking certain changes in the forms of imperialist domination, ones more advantageous to bourgeois class forces in India perhaps but offering no basic change in the social system, in the dependent relation of India with imperialism, or in the situation of the masses of people. (For a thorough exposure and analysis of the horrors of Bhopal and the causes and interests responsible, see Larry Everest, *Behind the Poison Cloud: Union Carbide's Bhopal Massacre* [Chicago: Banner Press, 1985].)

The road represented by Gandhi is in direct opposition to that charted in the same general time period by Mao Tsetung in China: the road of anti-imperialist, antifeudal revolution leading to real liberation from imperialism and then to socialism. While today China has been turned back to a situation very similar to India, where relations of exploitation and dependence on imperialism are the foundation of society, this is precisely as a result of the reversal of the revolution led by Mao in China, whereas in India it represents the continuation of the "revolution" led by Gandhi. And Mao's legacy continues to represent the revolutionary road forward, while Gandhi's legacy continues to represent capitulation to imperialism and reaction.

the result would still inevitably be the same system of exploitation and oppression that people all over the world are all too familiar with now; that with the fullest, most consistent application of the principle of equality embodied in that document – the ideal of equal opportunity for all –

> the result would be that some, a minority, would one way or the other utilize this opportunity to establish themselves as the exploiters of the majority, an exploitation they would have to enforce through the use of direct force (with hired enforcers) and deception (divide and conquer schemes included). *There could be no other result*, precisely if this principle, equal opportunity for all, were fully and consistently applied. In other words, we could get nothing but the bourgeois society we already have, including its social inequalities along with its basic exploitation of the proletariat. To get some other result, one which would abolish social inequality, along with the elimination of exploitation, it is necessary to overthrow and transcend the ideals and principles of bourgeois society and the material conditions of which they are an expression. It is necessary to overthrow bourgeois rule and advance entirely beyond what Marx termed "the narrow horizon of bourgeois right" (equal opportunity for all) and all the economic and other social relations of which it is a reflection and extension.[15]

I will return to and expand on this point shortly, but first it is important to address a concept that is a main component of the argument that democracy is the best possible form of government – the assertion that democracy, if not perfect, is perfectible, or at least that it allows for faults within the society and government to be corrected – that it is reformable. A major expression of this is the notion of the continual "extension" of democracy to include those previously excluded or discriminated against – slaves, women, nonpropertyholders, and others. This is a line of reasoning that can be extended back to encompass historical development since ancient times, to make a unified and linear progression from ancient Greek city-state government up to the present-day democratic states, viewing this as the history of the ever-widening scope of involvement of people in the process of government, reaching its pinnacle in modern democracy and the

---

15. Avakian, "Declaration of Independence, Equal Opportunity and Bourgeois Right," *Revolutionary Worker*, No. 230 (11 November 1983).

achievement of true government "of, by, and for the people." Or else it may be argued that the initial "experiment in democracy" that occurred in places like the Athens of antiquity was abandoned (or defeated) and replaced for a long period by the rule of an aristocracy, but finally a democratic revolution – or restoration – took place, giving birth to democratic society on a grander scale (recall Paine's statement that what Athens was in miniature, America would be in magnitude), a democracy that is now capable of being continuously extended and improved.

An argument of this sort is made by Alexis de Tocqueville, a nineteenth-century French democrat, who wrote extensively and influentially on democracy in the U.S. Contrasting the old feudal society in Europe with the new society, de Tocqueville pointed out that in the former, with its fixed, hereditary hierarchy, "the noble never suspected that anyone would attempt to deprive him of the privileges which he believed to be legitimate" and "the serf looked upon his own inferiority as a consequence of the immutable order of nature," but

> the scene is now changed. Gradually the distinctions of rank are done away with; the barriers that once severed mankind are falling; property is divided, power is shared by many, the light of intelligence spreads, and the capacities of all classes tend towards equality. Society becomes democratic, and the empire of democracy is slowly and peaceably introduced into institutions and customs.[16]

On one level it would be possible to expose the contradictions in this picture of society – a picture that was by no means entirely accurate at the time de Tocqueville painted it and is even more dramatically in conflict with reality today – merely by asking those who live in such democratic societies to compare this depiction with the reality they are experiencing. But it is necessary to examine and refute on a deeper level the notion of the continual extension and improvement of democracy.

In the previously mentioned article on the *Declaration of Independence,* I cited the following apologia:

> Though it did not immediately result in the emancipation of slaves or in universal suffrage, advocates of both abolition of slavery and

---

16. Alexis de Tocqueville, "Author's Introduction" to *Democracy in America* (New York: Vintage Books), ed. Phillips Bradley, Vol. 1, p. 9.

suffrage extension in later generations effectively used the equalitarian principles of the Declaration to advance their causes. In our own day it is a prod to the consciences of the American people to improve the conditions of minority groups.[17]

To this I gave the following answer:

> As a matter of fact, slavery was not abolished in the U.S. until the interests of the capitalists in the north – which had come into antagonism with those of the southern slavocracy – demanded it. It was only then that the government of the United States (the Union government) haltingly and hesitatingly declared the emancipation of the slaves (at first only in the Confederate states and not even in other states where there was slavery but which did not join the Confederacy) and then amended the U.S. Constitution to reflect that. And those freed slaves who attempted to carry forward the fight against their oppression in new forms were brutally suppressed, with the backing of the federal government and often the direct use of federal troops. More generally, every change of the type referred to in the above apologia has come about in response to mass struggle and has been adopted (and co-opted) by the ruling class in order to preserve its ruling position overall and maintain its exploitation and oppression of the masses of people – in short to protect and serve its own class interests, within the U.S. and internationally.[18]

Capitalist society does require a workforce that is "free" – in the twofold sense that it is mobile, not legally bound to a piece of land, a particular occupation, and so forth, and that it is "freed" of all ownership of means of production so that it can live only by selling its labor power to capital – and that is educated and trained sufficiently to perform its labor with modern productive forces. And, especially in this era of imperialism, the ruling class is required to draw the masses of people into political and world affairs. As Lenin pointed out in the midst of World War 1 – a decisive turning point in world history that drew masses, in all countries, into world affairs on a far greater level than ever before – "the mechanics of political democracy" in bourgeois

---

17. "The Origins of the Constitution," in Edward Conrad Smith, ed., *The Constitution of the United States*, 11th ed. (Barnes & Noble), p. 3; cited in Avakian, "Declaration of Independence, Equal Opportunity and Bourgeois Right."

18. Avakian, "Declaration of Independence, Equal Opportunity and Bourgeois Right."

society are geared to harnessing the workers and other oppressed to the existing structure and the interests of the ruling class:

> Nothing in our times can be done without elections; nothing can be done without the masses. And in this era of printing and parliamentarism it is *impossible* to gain the following of the masses without a widely ramified, systematically managed, well-equipped system of flattery, lies, fraud, juggling with fashionable and popular catchwords, and promising all manner of reforms and blessings to the workers right and left – as long as they renounce the revolutionary struggle for the overthrow of the bourgeoisie.[19]

All this represents, then, not an extension of democracy without class distinction, but an extension of the fundamental relations of capitalist exploitation; not an expression of the ever more broadly expanded sovereignty of the people, regardless of their social status, but an expression, a necessary component, of the supremacy of the ruling class – of its dictatorship over the working class and other oppressed people for the ultimate purpose of ensuring and enforcing its domination of the basic economic system.

Really, it is time to let the dead bury their dead, including, indeed especially, in the idealization of democracy. Listen, for example, to the rather typical conclusion of James Miller:

> If we try to think through the possible significance of democracy today, Rousseau nevertheless matters a great deal, not least because he stands at the beginning. First in Geneva and then in Paris in 1789 and after, democracy for the first time in two thousand years left the study for the streets, no longer a technical term but once more a living word for the right and power of a people to rule itself. What was won and what was ultimately lost in that migration may be grasped by consulting the thinker who was instrumental in allowing actors in this drama to understand themselves as democrats, struggling to obtain a legitimate freedom. Above all, reading Rousseau can remind us that the advocates of inalienable popular sovereignty lost, by force of arms. In the era of democratic revolutions, the proponents of simple democracy did not win, they were defeated – a defeat made all the more bitter when the victors expropriated the language of the vanquished.[20]

19. Lenin, "Imperialism and the Split in Socialism," *LCW*, 23, p. 117.
20. Miller, *Rousseau*, p. 209.

And what is it that is most enduring in Rousseau and the ideal of democracy? Miller answers:

> Of course, many details in Rousseau's vision – the rustic patriarch working the fields, say – do not seem particularly "democratic" to a contemporary reader. His idea of democracy stands at some distance from ideas common today. Rousseau could also be as blind to prejudice as any man. He did not, for example, question whether relations within the family might be based on something more than sentiment, whether the will of women might merit a wider field of sovereignty, too. He did not imagine any ways beyond the family to establish frontiers of privacy within a community. What matters today, though, are not so much the specifics of Rousseau's vision, though many of these doubtless account for his popularity two hundred years ago. What still matter are the abstract ideas conveyed *through* his images, the inchoate longing aroused by them. The figure of the patriarchal farmer suggests not only hierarchal command, but also self-reliance, evoking the notion of mastery in a sphere of one's own – no trivial idea and certainly no obsolete aspiration, either for men or for women.[21]

Here, in attempting to be most lofty, Miller betrays very acutely the historical limitations of the democratic ideal and the frankly pitiful worship of dogma that has long since come into basic conflict with the further advance of society and the further liberation of humanity. Miller does not want to negate altogether the model of the self-reliant farmer, but he wants at the same time to allow women "a wider field of sovereignty, too." He doesn't recognize that this model is inseparable from patriarchy and oppressive social relations generally. This can be taken as an encapsulation of the entire worldview of the democrat: he wants the existing social system but without its worst excesses, with room for reform and for accommodating the demands of the oppressed so long as they do not threaten to spring the established order into the air and overturn all existing social relations.[22] And what is at

21. Miller, *Rousseau*, p. 203.

22. Here I cannot help thinking of those reformers who are attempting to have the Christian bible rewritten so that the all-male references to the deity would be rendered instead in neutral (neuter) terms. Do these people really believe that such a change of literary form can in any way alter the reality that this bible enshrines and reinforces the oppression of women, as expressed, for example, in the following passage, where the deity is already mentioned in such neutral terms: "And when Rachel saw that she bare Jacob no children, Rachel envied her sister;

the heart of this? It is the ideal of individual sovereignty – of "mastery in a sphere of one's own" – reflecting the atomization of people whose identity is as commodity owners in capitalist society and who are at the same time subordinate to the dictates of capital and the dynamics of capitalist accumulation. Truly, what is expressed here is the "inchoate longing" for a time – for a past gilded in the imagination – when the underlying contradictions of this system did not assume such wildly explosive proportions, when the reality was not so glaringly and irrepressibly in conflict with the ideal. . .and yet at the same time the living embodiment of that ideal.

The contradiction between the ideal of democracy (and the professions of the bourgeois oppressors who rule in the name of democracy) on the one hand, and on the other hand the actual practice of "the democracies" and the reality of life under their rule, is one important source of exposure of this system and a lever for bringing people forward in struggle against it. But at the same time it is in itself a recurrent – and seemingly "infinite" – source of illusions about the "perfectability" of the democratic system, or the "actual realization" of democratic ideals – in short, for democratic prejudice and delusion. This has much to do with the fact that among opponents of the system radical variants of bourgeois democracy arise, one after another, even socialist tendencies that include as a central component the idealization of democracy in one form or another.

There is, of course, a powerful material basis for this in the objective world conditions in this era, particularly the basic division between a handful of imperialist states and the vast number of oppressed nations dominated by imperialism. Thus, as I summarized it in *Conquer the World,*

> on the one hand are these advanced countries where most of the
> productive forces are concentrated but the revolutionary sen-

---

and said unto Jacob, Give me children, or else I die. And Jacob's anger was kindled against Rachel: and he said, Am I in God's stead, who hath withheld from thee the fruit of the womb? And she said, Behold, my maid Bilhah, go in unto her; and she shall bear upon my knees, that I may also have children by her. And she gave him Bilhah her handmaid to wife; and Jacob went in unto her" (Gen. 30:1-4). Or would it help to change "Lord" to "Lord or Lady" (or "It") in the following admonition? – "Wives, submit yourselves to your husbands, as unto the Lord. For the husband is the head of the wife, even as Christ is the head of the Church. . ." (Eph. 5:22-23).

timents and level of struggle of the masses and consciousness of the masses is generally, and most of the time – at least so far – not on a very high level. . . .

And on the other hand, in most of the world the productive forces are backward; such development of the productive forces as there is is under the domination of finance capital and imperialism internationally, which distorts and disarticulates these economies. The people are in much more desperate conditions, much more desirous of radical change; yet. . . frankly, while desirous of change and capable of being rallied more readily to support for revolution, generally the stage of revolution there is one of bourgeois democracy, even if of a new type [that can advance to socialism if it is led by a proletarian vanguard].[23]

In every country in the world, then, there are broad strata whose mode of existence – that is, their position in the overall productive process and relations of production – and whose style of life can generally be described as petty-bourgeois; and to this correspond ideological inclinations toward democratic illusions and prejudices typical of the petty bourgeois: notions of freedom, equality, and right that correspond to the position of a small-scale commodity producer. At the same time, however, this same fundamental class outlook assumes radically different expressions in the Third World on the one hand, and in the imperialist countries on the other, where the middle strata – broadly speaking, to include many better-paid workers – enjoy a rather privileged position, and only rarely are vast numbers of them in a desperate situation. Speaking to this phenomenon not only in general terms but specifically in terms of its expression among forces opposed to imperialism, I observed:

> This era of imperialism and the proletarian revolution and the problem of the transition to communism worldwide have been further complicated by what I described in *Conquer the World* as the "lopsidedness in the world." What this refers to is the fact that in the world today the advanced productive forces are concentrated in a handful of the advanced – that is, imperialist – countries while the economies of most of the countries in the world are not simply backward but distorted, disarticulated in their development because of imperialist domination and

---

23. Avakian, *Conquer the World? The International Proletariat Must and Will,* published as *Revolution*, No. 50 (December 1981) (Chicago: RCP Publications), pp. 36-37.

plunder. Accompanying this is the fact that in these imperialist countries large sections of the people, including of the working class, are not, in "normal times" (which may last literally for decades), living in desperate conditions and impelled to seek a radical change, while in the colonial and dependent countries the masses are in such conditions and driven toward seeking revolutionary change (or at least are favorable to it) but the proletariat there is generally a small part of the population and the revolution that is on the agenda there and which corresponds to the class position and interests of most of the masses (who are small producers) is a bourgeois-democratic revolution, even if of a new type. Corresponding to this in the sphere of politics and ideology, and within the Marxist movement in particular (broadly defined), has been the marked tendency (of avowed Marxists) toward social-democracy in the imperialist countries and toward nationalism in the oppressed nations (though the latter has the virtue of often assuming a revolutionary expression, even if not a thoroughly Marxist-Leninist one).[24]

It is on the foundation of and in the context of all this that the contradiction between the ideal of democracy and the reality of the "democratic states" and their role in the world arises. But given that, this contradiction does assume a "life of its own" and does itself exert considerable influence along the lines described. Thus, for example, it is not surprising that the two main radical trends with a significant mass following in the U.S. in the "mad years" of the 1960s, SDS and the Black Panther Party, were both marked by their adherence to democratic prejudices and the ultimate failure to rupture with the whole framework of democracy. This, not surprisingly, found different expression in the one case and the other: SDS was based among radicalized sections of the white petty bourgeoisie, in particular students, while the Black Panther Party involved a number of different strata — intellectuals and other petty-bourgeois forces, proletarians, and even lumpen proletarians — but of an oppressed nation. But despite these differences — which were significant, the Black Panther Party representing in a far more fundamental way than SDS a leading force of a genuine mass revolutionary movement — in the outlook and program of both was ultimately expressed the failure to make that radical rupture.

On one level, this is obvious in the case of SDS, beginning with

24. Avakian, *Harvest of Dragons*, pp. 144-45.

its very name: Students for a Democratic Society. It is clearly revealed in the founding document of that organization, *The Port Huron Statement,* written in 1962, whose essential thesis is that "the American political system is not the democratic model of which its glorifiers speak," and which sets forth the goal of making America live up to this ideal and expresses the hopeful view that "we can develop a fresh and creative approach to world problems which will help to create democracy at home and establish conditions for its growth elsewhere in the world."[25] While, at its height in the late '60s, SDS advanced far beyond this naive, if radical, social-democratic position, and while there were many different trends within SDS, some of them genuinely revolutionary, it nonetheless remains true that in its prevailing outlook SDS never ultimately crossed beyond "the narrow horizon of bourgeois right," to borrow Marx's phrase again. That the same is true in the final analysis of the Black Panther Party (BPP) can be seen in a general analysis of the line, program, policies, and actions of the BPP, even during its most revolutionary and inspiring period, and more specifically is expressed in the Ten-Point Program of the BPP, which, while embodying demands of oppressed masses against the imperialist system, not only was marked by a generally radical bourgeois-democratic content but concluded by repeating the words of the *Declaration of Independence.*[26]

As we have seen, down through the ages—from the time of Plato and Aristotle (and even before) to the present era—political theorists and philosophers have formulated concepts of freedom, justice, wisdom, reason, right (or life, liberty, and the pursuit of happiness) in different ways, depending on the age in which they lived and the social system and the class they represented. In and of themselves these concepts have no specific social content and class character—though the notion that transcendental, eternal principles of freedom, justice, equality, wisdom, reason, and right can be formulated is itself a reflection of an outlook that serves the exploiting classes. Different and opposing classes will

25. Students for a Democratic Society, *The Port Huron Statement* (Chicago: SDS, 1966), pp. 12, 33.

26. See Bobby Seale, *Seize the Time* (New York: Random House, 1970), pp. 56-69. An analysis of the Black Panther Party in particular and of the movement of the 1960s in the U.S. more generally—specifically in relation to the question of a radical rupture with democracy and bourgeois ideology as a whole—is found in my book *A Horrible End, or an End to the Horror?,* especially chapter 2.

have different and opposing viewpoints on what such concepts mean – life, liberty, and the pursuit of happiness could not help but have the opposite meaning for slaves and slaveowners in America at the time the *Declaration of Independence* was written, for example.[27] But owing to the weight of tradition and the fact that society has for thousands of years been ruled by exploiting classes – and owing to the continuation of this today in the modern (democratic) bourgeois state – the meaning that will be given to these concepts spontaneously, even among the exploited and oppressed masses, will in the final analysis conform to the outlook and interests of one or another exploiting class (hence slaves in the U.S. could in their rebellion against outright slavery be under the sway of bourgeois-democratic ideology, and people in colonial or neocolonial countries today can fight against one imperialism and yet be led into the killing embrace of another, rival imperialism). In order to serve the struggle against exploitation and oppression in a consistent and thoroughgoing way, these concepts must be given a content that is clearly distinguished from and in direct opposition to the dominant view and use of such concepts and that conforms to the outlook and interests of the one class that can emancipate itself only by abolishing all exploitation and the very division of society into classes – the proletariat.

But even this is not all. Not only are these concepts historically conditioned and socially determined in general; some of them are more specifically an expression of society's division into classes. This will become clear by focusing on "equality." Equality – with the actual and essential content of equal opportunity and equality before the law – is a foundation stone of democracy, bourgeois democracy specifically. As argued before, such a concept, while proclaiming equality for everyone, regardless of social position, actually covers over a fundamental relationship of exploitation and oppression. And more than that, it is impossible for there to be equality for everyone, without class distinction. How can there be equality between oppressors and those they oppress, between exploiters and the exploited – between those who have a monopoly on the means to produce the requirements of life and the possibility for human advancement and those who do not have control or ownership of these and are therefore forced into a

27. This point is elaborated on in the article "Declaration of Independence, Equal Opportunity and Bourgeois Right."

situation where they are enslaved, in one form or another, by those who do? Or in socialist society, after the bourgeoisie has been overthrown but when class distinctions have not been finally and completely eliminated everywhere, how can there be equality between the formerly exploited proletariat, aiming to abolish all forms of exploitation, all oppressive division of labor, and the overthrown exploiters (or newly generated ones) aiming to restore a system founded on such exploitation and oppressive division of labor?

And after class divisions and oppressive social relations have been abolished and their bases uprooted, then there will be no equality either. Why? Because then equality will have no social basis. Equality will have "withered away." As I wrote in a response to a letter from a "Black Nationalist with Communistic Inclinations," while the struggle against social inequality – against national oppression, the oppression of women, and other aspects of such inequality – plays a very important part in the overall struggle for socialism and ultimately a communist world,

> once the division of society into classes has been finally abolished, then the very concept of "equality" will lose its meaning. Everything exists only in relation to its opposite; and once social inequalities are eliminated with the advent of communism (I say "social inequalities" because individual differences between particular people will never be eliminated – though in communist society this will not have the same consequences as in class society) then social *equality* will also be eliminated as a category. To look at this another way, all equality implies inequality – it is impossible to have the one without the other (for example, no two workers who get the same wage do exactly the same amount or quality of work, nor do they have exactly the same needs, so "equality" in wages is both equality on the one hand and inequality on the other hand). In communist society, the principle will be "from each according to his ability, to each according to his need" – people will not work for individual survival (society will have developed to the point, materially and ideologically, where that will not be a question as it is now) – but consciously to contribute to the development of society, and in turn they will receive what they (actually) need to live (this too will mean that a high degree of social consciousness has been reached, so that people voluntarily subordinate individual needs to the overall advance of society) while increasingly being enabled to develop and contribute to society in a fuller, more all-around way, both physically and intellectually. "Equality" does not enter in here – in fact "equality"

will have been *surpassed* and *superseded,* along with the bourgeois epoch to which it belongs.[28]

The communist view of freedom, then, is radically different from and opposed to the ideal bourgeois conception of freedom. It does not focus on the individual and to what degree other individuals stand as obstacles and impediments to the exercise of his will; it is not based on the individual struggle of each against all for survival and personal advancement. This is not to say that individuals will be less free in communist society than in the present bourgeois society: they will be free in a far greater – but more than that, a qualitatively different – way. As I put it in another discussion of this question, communist society will not "recognize the uninhibited right of individuals to do whatever they want: in fact individuals will, in the overall sense, still be subordinate to society as a whole," but – and this represents a world of difference – they will not be subordinate to other individuals.[29] Speaking to this same basic question, Marx cut through layers of bourgeois mystification and to the heart of the matter in pointing out, "Right can never be higher than the economic structure of society and its cultural development conditioned thereby."[30] In today's world, with its oppressing and lopsided social and international relations, starving children in Africa – and for that matter, the great majority of humanity, which still lives only a few short

---

28. Avakian, *Bob Avakian Replies to a Letter from: "Black Nationalist with Communistic Inclinations"* (Chicago: RCP Publications, n.d.), reprinted from *Revolutionary Worker,* No. 75 [10 October 1980], p. 7. What is presented here is in disagreement with the view of most socialists and many communists on this question. For example, in *Not In Our Genes,* the authors also focus on what they characterize as "[t]he contradiction...between the ideology of freedom and equality and the actual social dynamic that generates powerlessness and inequality." But they draw the conclusion that today, in bourgeois society, "the idea of equality is still as subversive as ever, if taken seriously" (Lewontin, Rose, and Kamin, *Not In Our Genes,* pp. 80, 68). Although I agree that there is a positive aspect to this contradiction – in terms of providing a basis for exposure of the present system and a lever for mobilizing people in struggle against it – there is also a negative side to this: its role as a continual source of democratic illusions and prejudices and an impediment to making the radical rupture with the whole framework of democracy. For a review of *Not In Our Genes,* including further criticisms as well as an assessment of the overwhelmingly positive and extremely important role of this book, see Skybreak, *"Not In Our Genes* and the Waging of the Ideological Counteroffensive," *Revolution,* No. 53 (Winter/Spring 1985).

29. Avakian, *Horrible End or End to Horror?,* p. 180.

30. Marx, *Critique of the Gotha Programme* (Peking: Foreign Languages Press, 1972), p. 17.

steps from starvation, at most – do not have the right to make plans for the distribution of the world's productive forces and resources in a way that could eliminate such starvation and misery and make possible a whole new life. Nor, for that matter, do the people in the "advanced" imperialist countries have this right (or even the right to take *practical, meaningful* steps to forestall mass starvation in the very short run) even if they wish to do so. Such rights, and whole new vistas of freedom, can become a reality only through the world-overturning revolution that in its ultimate achievement will sweep away the bourgeois notions of what constitutes freedom and justice.

4

The USA as Democratic Example... Leader of the Pack

My fellow Americans, on this Thanksgiving, when we have so much to be grateful for, let us give special thanks for our peace, our freedom, and our good people. I've always believed that this land was set aside in an uncommon way, that a divine plan placed this great continent between the oceans to be found by a people from every corner of the earth who have a special love of faith, freedom, and peace. Let us reaffirm America's destiny of goodness and good will. Let us work for peace, and, as we do, let us remember the lines of the famous hymn, "O God of love, O King of peace, make wars throughout the world to cease."

Ronald Reagan, concluding a speech
announcing his choice of the "dense pack" approach
to the deployment of MX missiles in the USA

While the basic analysis in this book applies equally to the USA as to all other capitalist democracies, historical development in the U.S. has differed in some significant ways from that of the European states, and of course the U.S. today plays a particular role as head of the "Western democratic alliance." Indeed, that the remarks quoted above could not only be uttered as part of a major address by the head of state but could be printed in a major newspaper such as the *New York Times* (with its allegedly more informed and sophisticated audience) without any apparent need to offer an apology or at least an "explanation" by way of introduction – all this is an indication of the peculiar historical development and particular present-day role of the U.S. It illustrates graphically what both pride-filled patriot and incredulous detractor mean when they use that phrase "only in America." A detailed dissection and exposure of the falsehoods and fabrications in the above-quoted statement is a worthwhile effort (and I have made such an effort elsewhere[1]), but here attention will be focused on major aspects of and major events in the development of the U.S. to its present position and role in the world.

The Foundation of the USA and the "Founding Fathers"

The 1776 *Declaration of Independence* of the United States of America marked both a significant turning point in the history of modern nation-states and their relations, and also a significant affirmation of the basic ideals and principles upon which the bourgeois nation-states of this era are founded. In the article on the *Declaration of Independence,* I emphasized:

> This document is precisely a declaration of independence of one country from another, it is not a declaration calling for the abolition of all oppressive and exploitative relations, specifically not within the country that is declaring its independence. This is more particularly the declaration of the propertied and politically dominant classes within the emerging United States. All this is clearly indicated in the content of what grievances are enumerated – and what evils are glaringly *not* mentioned, most prominent among them slavery.... When the authors of this declaration list among the "abuses and usurpations" that have moved them to break free of the control of the English monarchy the fact that the latter is

---

1. See Avakian, "So Many Lies in So Little Space," part of the series *More Reflections and Sketches,* in *Revolutionary Worker*, No. 197 (18 March 1983).

guilty of "imposing taxes on us without our consent" and "cutting off our trade with all parts of the world," they are giving expression to the outrage of classes which are restricted in their accumulation of wealth and capital by these measures imposed by the ruling classes of a foreign power. Here it should be pointed out that a very significant part of that trade involved the trading in slaves and that even after this was abolished the trade in goods produced with slave labor, in particular cotton, was an integral and indispensable element in building up the economy of the U.S., including in the northern states where for a considerable period before the Civil War a large part of investment in manufacturing came from the profits of the textile industry in England, which in turn utilized to a large degree the cotton grown in the slave states in the southern U.S. And in the manufacturing establishments and manufacturing towns of the north the conditions of the working class attested to the most heartless exploitation and pitiless political oppression.[2]

All this does not demonstrate that there was, after all, no revolution involved in the separation of the United States of America from England, but it does demonstrate that this revolution represented and embodied not some eternal ideals of freedom in conflict with tyranny but the interests of specific class forces of a particular nation in conflict with the ruling classes of another state. The American Revolution was fundamentally a bourgeois revolution (although the further advance of bourgeois production relations in the U.S. would eventually require the abolition of slavery through the Civil War – in a sense the continuation of that bourgeois revolution). That many of the leaders of this Revolution were for some time reluctant to carry it out all the way to the point of actually separating from England and forming a new state, and that they were very concerned to limit the role of the lower classes and keep the contagion of rebellion from spreading without check among their ranks – this too is characteristic of exploiting classes even when they are compelled to seek the overthrow of certain existing social (and international) relations.[3] At the same time, there were, as indicated, certain

2. Avakian, "Declaration of Independence, Equal Opportunity and Bourgeois Right."

3. For some specific analysis of the class position and attitudes of leading figures in this Revolution, see Zinn, *People's History of the U.S.*, in particular chapters 4 and 5. Zinn's account is rich in exposure, although there is a certain tendency to reduce the declaration of ideals and principles by the kind of men

peculiarities to the American Revolution and the nation-state that emerged from it. Both the fundamental features characteristic of bourgeois revolution and bourgeois society generally and the particularities that mark the American Revolution and American society are reflected in their founding documents, in particular the *Declaration of Independence* and the *Constitution* of the United States.

In the well-known opening sentence of the *Declaration of Independence* ("When, in the course of human events. . ."), the basis for the rights of people, and of nations, is set in nothing less than "the laws of nature and of nature's God."[4] As we have seen, this was a view common among the bourgeois political theorists of Jefferson's time (and their predecessors) not only in the U.S. but in Europe as well. On one level this whole concept can be disposed of merely by calling attention to "the fact that there is nothing in 'the laws of nature' that 'entitles' people or nations to anything" and "the fact that there is no god at all"[5]; but a deeper look at this point is also called for. In a letter written in 1787, Thomas Jefferson argued the following, which, not surprisingly, parallels and sheds further light on the passage in question in the *Declaration of Independence:*

> He who made us would have been a pitiful bungler if he had made the rules of our moral conduct a matter of science. For one man of science, there are thousands who are not. What would have become of them? Man was destined for society. His morality therefore was to be formed to this object. He was endowed with a sense of right and wrong merely relative to this. This sense is as much a part of his nature as the sense of hearing, seeing, feeling; it is the true foundation of morality. . . .[6]

---

who led the American Revolution to a mere device or scheme for tricking those they exploited and oppressed into fighting for them against England. While there is some truth to this, what is more fundamental and essential is that at least among many of the "founding fathers" of the USA there was the actual belief that these principles were universal at the same time as they sanctioned class division, an oppressive division of labor, and exploitation (and in the eyes of some, slavery) – a testimony not so much to the hypocrisy as to the class outlook and bias of these people (and representatives of their class generally).

4. *Declaration of Independence*, in Smith, ed., *Constitution of the U.S.*, p. 24.

5. Avakian, "Declaration of Independence, Equal Opportunity and Bourgeois Right."

6. Jefferson, "Reason, the Only Oracle," letter to Peter Carr (10 August 1787), in *The Portable Jefferson*, p. 424.

Notice how in all this Nature is conceived of as some kind of conscious force, whose architect and engineer is "nature's God." But nature is no such thing; insofar as nature means anything as a general description of reality it can only refer to the material world (or universe), and there is not the kind of orderly structure, functioning, and division of labor (everything has its purpose and place) that is attributed to it in the passages quoted above. There is no overall grand design – nor any Grand Designer.

Nor is there a hierarchy inherent in nature that establishes man as its highest creation, destined to rule over the rest of nature by virtue of man's Reason and the Moral Sense with which he is endowed. There is only matter in motion – potentially assuming infinite forms – and human beings are a particular form that matter in motion has assumed, with a certain kind and level of consciousness[7] and capable of increasingly developing the ability to transform other matter in motion. It is this that establishes the general basis for people to enter into and develop through human society, which is characterized by its foundation in the productive forces at hand at any given time and by the ability to further advance these productive forces, thereby calling forth changes in human social organization. "Nature" and "nature's God," as envisioned by Jefferson (and others), do not have any part in all this – they do not exist. And, as for Reason and Moral Sense (again, as conceived of by thinkers like Jefferson), the very fact that different ages and, more particularly, different and opposing classes, have different and conflicting views of these things – that is, of what is in accord with reason and with morality – is itself a refutation of the notion that "He who made us" or man's immutable "nature" has endowed human beings with some inherent and universal reason and morality. To cite again a rather stark – but hardly trivial – example, reason and morality cannot help but mean different and fundamentally opposed things to slaveowners on the one hand and slaves and others favoring the abolition of slavery on the other hand.

The fundamental point involved in all this will become clearer by examining the next (and probably most famous) passage from the *Declaration of Independence:*

---

7. This consciousness is not some nonmaterial attribute of Man but is itself constituted of matter in motion – chemical and electrical transformations in the human brain, in constant interpenetration with the outside world.

We hold these truths to be self-evident, that all men are created equal; that they are endowed by their Creator with certain inalienable rights; that among these, are life, liberty, and the pursuit of happiness. That, to secure these rights, governments are instituted among men, deriving their just powers from the consent of the governed; that, whenever any form of government becomes destructive of these ends, it is the right of the people to alter or to abolish it, and to institute a new government, laying its foundation on such principles, and organizing its powers in such form, as to them shall seem most likely to effect their safety and happiness.[8]

Besides what has already been said concerning the notion of man's being endowed with rights (or anything else) by a supernatural creator; and besides what has been demonstrated concerning the historical context and class content (and conflicting views) of such concepts as equality, life, liberty, and the pursuit of happiness;[9] it should be clear that governments are not "instituted among men" to "secure these rights" for everyone, without regard to class position, and that governments do not as a general rule derive their powers from "the consent of the governed." Even on the most obvious level, how could the government of the newly formed United States, for example, be considered to have derived its powers "from the consent of the governed" when, at the time of the formation of the United States of America, a majority of the people "governed" – including slaves, Indians, women, men who did not meet various property requirements, and others – did not even have the right to vote . . . to say nothing of the real power to govern and determine the direction of society?

More fundamentally, the social contract theory which informs the *Declaration of Independence* (and which is derived in a general sense from the theories of John Locke and also Jean-Jacques Rousseau) does not correspond to the actual basis on which governments have originated. Human beings have always been social, but human society has not always served as a means for individuals to secure private property and the rights attendant to it. In its most essential character, human society has always been

---

8. *Declaration of Independence*, in Smith, ed., *Constitution of the U.S.*, p. 24.

9. It is interesting to note that the idea that the aim of society and its government is to provide for the happiness of the citizens is also found in Aristotle, and that Aristotle was – like many signatories of the *Declaration of Independence* – quite capable of reconciling this notion with the defense of slavery (see chapter 2, n. 7).

a means of collectively confronting and dealing with "outside forces" – first and foremost the rest of nature, and, at times at least, other associations of human beings. Governments did not arise out of a contract among individuals entering into society from a "state of nature" – coming together to form a commonwealth in order to institutionalize and legalize some abstract natural rights, above all the right to property. Governments arose out of the need for some regulation of the common affairs of society. As the productive forces of society developed, establishing the basis for the accumulation of surpluses privately and for a further division of labor, government developed into an apparatus that stood above society and that served and protected the interests of a class of people who were able to monopolize ownership of the important means of production – and could therefore force others to labor for them – while also monopolizing the political and intellectual life of the society. In other words, the *state* emerged – as an expression of the division of society into classes and as an instrument of class dictatorship. And in subsequent changes in society in which one class of private property owners replaced another in the ruling position, what was fundamentally involved was the conflict between the economic interests of the contending classes – and the replacement of one form of exploitation by another – not "the consent of the governed."[10]

All this sheds light on the next passage in the *Declaration of Independence,* which deals with the reasons why separation from England is justified (giving first the general principles said to underlie this right of separation before the document launches into a listing of specific grievances against "the present King of Great Britain"). This passage – including its familiar mention of "a long train of abuses and usurpations, pursuing invariably the same object" that "evinces a design to reduce them under absolute

10. Even in the proletarian revolution, whose goal is the elimination of all forms of exploitation, "consent of the governed" – while it can be said to be actually realized for the first time with the dictatorship of the proletariat, in terms of the majority ruling over the exploiting minority – is not really what is most fundamentally involved: the fundamental question is revolutionizing society, in the superstructure and the economic base, to abolish class distinctions. This will open up whole new vistas for the all-around development of society and its members, materially and in the realm of social relations, as well as culture and ideology in the broadest sense. In this regard, it is helpful to recall the summation by Marx, cited earlier, "Right can never be higher than the economic structure of society and its cultural development conditioned thereby" (see chapter 3, n. 30).

despotism," and therefore establishes the right of the afflicted people "to throw off such government and to provide new guards for their future security"[11] – once again puts forward in general terms the theories of Locke and also of Rousseau, specifically on the right of a people to revolution. Both Locke and Rousseau ground this right in the principle that where the government has violated the rights of the people – has, in effect, violated the terms of the social contract – then there is no longer any legitimate government but only usurpation and despotism, and the people have no recourse other than revolution to restore the rightful relation between government and the people.[12] In the *Declaration of Independence,* as in Locke and Rousseau, this basic principle is clearly an expression of an idealized vision of bourgeois society, where people as commodity owners enter equally into contracts, where the regulation of such contracts is entrusted to government but where government must rule through laws that themselves properly reflect these relations, and not by arbitrary authority – which constitutes despotism – a violation of the terms of the contract. And as with the expression of bourgeois ideals generally, this principle conceals the fundamental relationship in the real world of capitalist society – the relationship between the bourgeoisie and the proletariat – a relationship of exploitation and oppression. It should not surprise us that the fashioners of these bourgeois ideals saw no right of revolution for those they in reality exploited and oppressed.

This, in turn, will become even clearer by focusing on a sentence, among those enumerating the "abuses and usurpations"

---

11. *Declaration of Independence*, in Smith, ed., *Constitution of the U.S.*, p. 24.

12. Note, for example, the echoes in the *Declaration of Independence* of the following passage in Locke's *Second Treatise* concerning the right of revolution:

> *revolutions happen* not upon every little mismanagement in public affairs. *Great mistakes* in the ruling part, many wrong and inconvenient laws, and all the *slips* of human frailty, will be *born by the people* without mutiny or murmur. But if a long train of abuses, prevarications and artifices, all tending the same way, make the design visible to the people, and they cannot but feel what they lie under, and see whither they are going; it is not to be wondered, that they should then rouze themselves, and endeavor to put the rule into such hands which may secure to them the ends for which government was at first erected. . . . (Locke, *Second Treatise*, p. 113; see also pp. 81, 105, and 111 for similar expressions of the right of revolution.)

For the same basic position, as expressed by Rousseau, see *Social Contract*, Book 3, especially chapter 10: "The Abuse of Government and Its Tendency to Degenerate."

committed by the British monarch, which is both striking in what it says and extremely significant in what it points to without full elaboration:

> He has excited domestic insurrections amongst us, and has endeavored to bring on the inhabitants of our frontiers, the merciless Indian savages, whose known rule of warfare is an undistinguished destruction of all ages, sexes, and conditions.[13]

To begin with, it is the case that "it would be hard to imagine a more blatant and complete reversal of truth and falsehood, of right and wrong, of victim and criminal, of just and unjust warfare, than is contained in this description – yes, in the *Declaration of Independence* – of the relations between the Indians and the Europeans who founded the United States of America on territory they stole from the Indians through murder and plunder."[14] But in addition, the "domestic insurrections" that are rather vaguely referred to in this passage were in large part slave revolts, which the King of England had of late been attempting to encourage and make use of in his conflict with the leaders of the American Revolution. Even at that time, a pamphleteer favoring the British monarchy in the conflict was quick to seize on glaring contradictions:

> But how did his Majesty's governors excite domestic insurrections? Did they set father against son, or son against father, or brother against brother? No – they offered freedom to the slaves of these assertors of liberty. . . . It is their boast that they have taken up arms in support of these their own self-evident truths – that all men are created equal, that all men are endowed with the unalienable rights of life, liberty, and the pursuit of happiness. Is it for them to complain of the offer of freedom held out to these wretched beings; of the offer of reinstating them in that equality which, in this very paper, is declared to be the gift of God to all; in those unalienable rights with which, in this very paper, God is declared to have endowed all mankind?[15]

---

13. *Declaration of Independence*, in Smith, ed., *Constitution of the U.S.*, p. 26.

14. Avakian, "Declaration of Independence, Equal Opportunity and Bourgeois Right."

15. John Lind, "An Answer to the Declaration of the American Congress" (1776), cited in Garry Wills, *Inventing America: Jefferson's Declaration of Independence* (New York: Vintage Books, 1979), p. 73.

In addition to the kind of apologia noted and answered earlier – that even if it involved sharp contradictions such as this, the *Declaration of Independence* still expresses an ideal which can stand as a goal to be fought for, a standard to be actually applied to everyone – it is often argued that people such as Thomas Jefferson (principal author of the *Declaration of Independence* and "'The Apostle of Americanism' in the judgment of one biographer"[16]) were actually in favor of the emancipation of the slaves. More particularly, it is not infrequently argued by those familiar with the history of the American Revolution that Jefferson's original draft of the *Declaration of Independence* contained an indictment of slavery itself. In fact, the indictment referred to, contained in Jefferson's draft but taken out by the Congress that adopted the *Declaration,* is worth examining for what it says, what it means, and how it fits into the overall views of Jefferson, apostle of Americanism.

The passage, as written by Jefferson, reads as follows:

> He has waged cruel war against human nature itself, violating it's [sic] most sacred rights of life and liberty in the persons of a distant people who never offended him, captivating & carrying them into slavery in another hemisphere or to incur miserable death in their transportation thither. This piratical warfare, the opprobrium of *infidel* powers, is the warfare of the *Christian* king of Great Britain. Determined to keep open a market where *Men* should be bought & sold, he has prostituted his negative for suppressing every legislative attempt to prohibit or to restrain this execrable commerce. And that this assemblage of horrors might want no fact of distinguished die, he is now exciting those very people to rise in arms among us, and to purchase that liberty of which he has deprived them, by murdering the people on whom he also obtruded them: thus paying off former crimes committed against the *Liberties* of one people, with crimes which he urges them to commit against the *lives* of another.[17]

Not only is there more than a little hypocrisy involved in Jefferson's attempt to portray the slaveowners in America as victims themselves of slavery, as though the slaves had been virtually forced on them by the King of Great Britain, but, as pointed out by Garry Wills in his book *Inventing America,* the Virginia slave-

---

16. Peterson, "Introduction" to *The Portable Jefferson,* p. xii.
17. Cited in Wills, *Inventing America,* p. 377.

holders, of which Jefferson was one, were anxious "to slow the slave trade with a colonial tariff," whose aims were "to limit the volatile slave population, equalize the balance of trade, sustain the price of slaves already arrived, and create revenue."[18] Wills further notes:

> The King's crime is his use of blacks as he has been using Indians and loyalists. That is: The real onus of the charge is that the King has been *freeing* slaves to fight against their American owners—a reference to Governor Dunmore's call, in 1775, for Virginia slaves to attack their masters. The irony of charging the King with manumission as a crime led Jefferson to write his tortuous preamble to this charge. He was trying to erect a shaky moral platform from which to denounce the novel "atrocity" of freeing slaves.[19]

And Wills sums up:

> The slave paragraph deleted from the Declaration has been read by modern commentators through a haze of false assumptions—e.g., the assumption that Congress omitted the grievance (when it included it under an earlier heading), or that Jefferson was attacking the institution of slavery itself (rather than the King's part in first enslavement); the assumption that the basis for the charge was Virginian opposition to further enslavement (rather than control of slave imports); the assumption that Jefferson attacked the King's vetoes for keeping men enslaved (rather than maintaining the traffic where it would devalue slaves). But the main misreading comes from a refusal to look at the paragraph's conclusion and real point—the accusation that the King's real crime is his attempt to *free* Virginia's slaves. *That* was the war atrocity at issue in this part of Jefferson's list.[20]

Wills does argue that Jefferson favored the eventual emancipation of the slaves—which is true, although Jefferson held back from taking any effective action toward the general emancipation of slaves because he was convinced this would be too

---

18. Wills, *Inventing America*, p. 67. Despite his critical analysis of parts of the *Declaration of Independence* and of Jefferson as its principal author, Wills is, to understate the matter, sympathetic to Jefferson, and *Inventing America* is ultimately a celebration of Jefferson "and his Declaration" (p. 362—see especially part 5 and the "Epilogue").

19. Wills, *Inventing America*, p. 72.

20. Wills, *Inventing America*, p. 74.

divisive among the whites (a fact Wills also allows). Wills goes further, however: "It is erroneous to say that Jefferson denied either equality or self-rule to the blacks as a matter of right. But he thought they had, what all men have, the right to self-rule *as a people.*"[21] Wills is dealing with Jefferson's insistence that the future emancipation of the slaves would require their complete separation from the whites. So here Wills asserts that the deportation of the freed slaves "was necessary so they could exercise that right" to self-rule as a people.[22] Wills also knows (and acknowledges) that Jefferson regarded the commingling of Blacks and whites as injurious to the whites and to the new nation-state they had established. Jefferson drew this contrast between slaves in ancient Rome—who, he said, were of the same race as their master—and slaves in Jefferson's America:

> Among the Romans emancipation required but one effort. The slave, when made free, might mix with, without staining the blood of his master. But with us a second is necessary, unknown to history. When freed, he is to be removed beyond the reach of mixture.[23]

And while he could write on one occasion that it would please him to see proof "that nature has given to our black brethren, talents equal to those of the other colors of men, and that the appearance of a want of them is owing merely to the degraded condition of their existence, both in Africa & America,"[24] Jefferson never abandoned his view that Blacks were inferior to whites, and that the Blacks must be separated, when finally emancipated, in order to prevent the "staining of the blood" of the whites through race-mixing.

Thus it may be true that Jefferson did not deny the right of self-rule to Blacks as a people—because, as Wills points out, Jefferson thought that all people possessed the necessary moral sense for a well-founded society, even if they might not all be intellectually equal—but it would be foolish to conclude that Jefferson believed that a nation of Blacks could achieve, or deserve, a

21. Wills, *Inventing America,* p. 306.

22. Wills, *Inventing America,* p. 306.

23. Jefferson, "Notes on the State of Virginia," in *The Portable Jefferson,* p. 193.

24. Jefferson, "Homage to a Black Man," letter to Benjamin Banneker (30 August 1791), in *The Portable Jefferson,* p. 454.

status among nations equal to a nation of whites. As is clear in his writings on education, for example, Jefferson believed not in "an artificial aristocracy, founded on wealth and birth, without either virtue or talents," which characterizes feudal society, but in the bourgeois notion of a "natural aristocracy" based on talent and intelligence, which is "the most precious gift of nature, for the instruction, the trusts, and government of society."[25] And, as we have seen, also entirely consistent with bourgeois principle, Jefferson placed his own nation's interests above all others and considered other nations, as he himself said, only "in proportion as they are more or less friendly to us."[26] Thus, Jefferson's position on the right of Black people to self-rule – in form a stance of "equal but separate" – could only translate in practice into a relation of inequality, of oppressed and oppressor nations – as indeed has been the actual character of the relations between Black people and whites in the USA after the abolition of slavery.

Another important question concerning Jefferson's viewpoint and the *Declaration of Independence* is the matter of the rights of property. Wills argues, "Those who think Jefferson's Declaration is Lockean have been justifiably puzzled by the omission of property from the brief list of 'inalienable rights' in that document."[27] Wills poses the question this way:

> No one can doubt that Jefferson – like all whigs of his time (and all tories too) – recognized a right to private property. The problem is more circumscribed: Did he recognize it as *the* fundamental right, in Locke's sense; and if so, why did he exclude it from the list of basic rights given in the Declaration? Put more precisely: Did he recognize it as an unalienable right?[28]

Wills's answer is that in his thinking on this question, Jefferson was more in line with the eighteenth-century Scottish Enlightenment theorists and political economists, such as Francis Hutcheson and Adam Smith, than with Locke, who lived a century earlier. As Wills summarizes it, the views of Hutcheson in particular – whose influence on Jefferson Wills emphasizes – placed

25. Jefferson, "The Natural Aristocracy," letter to John Adams (28 October 1813), in *The Portable Jefferson*, p. 534.

26. Jefferson, "These . . . are my principles," in *The Portable Jefferson*, p. 479.

27. Wills, *Inventing America*, p. 229.

28. Wills, *Inventing America*, pp. 230-31.

more stress on the process (and rights) of exchange than on the right of retaining property: such views were more fully in accord with a developed system of commodity production and exchange than the earlier ideas of Locke. Further, Wills points to Jefferson's particular conviction that extensive land ownership was crucial for the stability and well-being of the United States of America – extensive both in the sense of spreading over a vast territory and in the sense of involving large numbers of people in land owner-ship. Thus, land must be *alienable* – transferable to new owners through exchange – and not bound by feudal modes of ownership and their legal expressions. It is for these reasons, Wills argues, that Jefferson did not list the right to property among the inalien-able rights. But certainly, for Jefferson as for the "founding fathers" generally, the right to private property – and specifically the right to private ownership of land and other means of produc-tion – was counted among the most essential rights of man: this is clear from their founding documents, including the *Declaration of Independence* as well as the *Constitution* of the United States.

The *Declaration of Independence* also enumerates, of course, a number of grievances which are not directly and explicitly tied to the question of property – for example, the denial of the right of trial by jury, or the stationing of standing armies "without the con-sent of our legislatures" and "quartering large bodies of armed troops among us."[29] And the same basic point applies to the *Con-stitution* of the United States. While it enshrines the right to prop-erty (in this *Constitution* the right – though not the *inalienable* right – to property *is* found, in the familiar litany: life, liberty, prop-erty[30]), the *Constitution*, with its amendments, contains a number of provisions that are aimed at barring the way to despotism. And therein is revealed an essential point: the *Constitution* of the United States, like the *Declaration of Independence,* represents the standpoint of bourgeois democracy in opposition particularly to the principles of monarchy and of feudal society. The *Constitution* is precisely a charter for a specific and historically conditioned society – bourgeois society. That is why – to focus on a simple but nonetheless telling point – there is no provision in this *Constitu-tion* prohibiting anyone from employing someone else for wages

---

29. *Declaration of Independence,* in Smith, ed., *Constitution of the U.S.,* p. 25.

30. See, for example, Smith, ed., *Constitution of the U.S.,* Amendments, Article V, i (The Fifth Amendment).

and profiting from his labor power when thus employed. This is, in essence and at bottom, the very relationship and process that is protected and promoted through all the various provisions of the *Constitution,* even though the exploitation of wage-labor by capital is, of course, never directly mentioned and even though there is nothing in this *Constitution* that explicitly limits rights to the capitalists and excludes the workers from the exercise of these rights.

The most fundamental point is that even with the exercise of these rights, by everyone in society, to the fullest degree possible, capitalist exploitation and bourgeois dictatorship will still be the inevitable result. The underlying reason for this is what was summarized earlier in terms of how the superstructure, including politics and the laws, must reflect and serve the economic base, or else society cannot function. So long as society remains founded on economic relations of wage-labor and the accumulation of wealth as capital; so long as it is marked by a division of labor corresponding to this; then, even if everyone is allowed to vote for political representatives, to make political speeches, organize political meetings and rallies, circulate petitions to government, and so on, it will still be the case that those who employ others as workers and thereby accumulate capital will occupy the dominant position in society and will ensure that the political system, the laws and legal structure – the whole superstructure – keep this system functioning and keep them in the ruling position. If they do not do so, someone else will – and, as a matter of fact, someone *must* – unless there is a revolution to completely overturn and uproot the capitalist order and its basic production and other social relations. And while a Constitution that declares equal political rights for everyone can very well serve the bourgeoisie and capitalist society – by covering over the basic relations of exploitation and class antagonisms – such a Constitution cannot serve a socialist revolution and a socialist state that aims at abolishing class divisions. Such a revolution and such a state require not the granting of rights to everyone equally (on paper, at least) but the *explicit restriction* of the rights of some – former exploiters, any would-be exploiters, and those who actively oppose the revolutionization of society – and the specific *elimination* of the right for anyone to exploit others.

Thus, it is in no way accidental (or coincidental) that the U.S. *Constitution* in its application has been a tool of bourgeois dictatorship serving capitalist exploitation. Of its very nature, this *Constitution,* with its opposition to monarchal despotism and aristocratic privilege and including the rights it upholds, is in the service of and is aimed at furthering the fundamental production relations and the underlying accumulation process of capitalism −though this is a capitalism with the peculiar historical admixture of slavery[31] (and with the "shadow" of slavery even after slavery itself was abolished). In sum:

> It is not that the Declaration of Independence (and the U.S. Constitution along with it) represent the interests and outlook of the bourgeoisie (with the historical influence of the southern slaveowning aristocracy) only in the most narrow sense. These documents do contain grievances and provisions that are not directly and immediately reducible to how the members of the ruling classes can accumulate more wealth and power for themselves. Rather they represent these class interests in the broadest sense − and it is precisely in this way that their class content and historical limitations are most profoundly demonstrated.[32]

The Civil War

The Civil War in the U.S. in the 1860s was not a "terrible tragedy," nor was it the result of some "great misunderstanding." It was not fought by the southern Confederacy in defense of the principle of "states' rights" − the slaveowners were not in the least in favor of so-called "states' rights" when it came to the question of returning to them runaway slaves captured in the northern states, as happened in the landmark legal decision involving runaway slave Dred Scott in the decade before the Civil War. On the other hand, despite the efforts of abolitionists and the resistance and revolts of the slaves themselves − and their heroic fighting in the Civil War itself − it was not fought by the Union government in the

31. This is reflected in the well-known "compromise" that involved counting slaves as equal to three-fifths of free persons for the purpose of determining the apportionment of representatives (and direct taxation) among the states when the *Constitution* was adopted (see Article I). It is also revealing to note James Madison's defense of this provision in the *Constitution,* which Madison links to the position that "government is instituted no less for protection of the property than of the persons of individuals" (James Madison, "Federalist Paper No. 54," in *The Federalist Papers* [New York: New American Library, 1961], p. 339).

32. Avakian, "Declaration of Independence, Equal Opportunity and Bourgeois Right."

North, and its president, Lincoln, for the purpose of abolishing the atrocity of slavery in some moral sense. None of these reasons—which are still put forth as explanations of the causes and driving forces of the Civil War—gets to the heart of the matter: The Civil War arose out of the conflict between two modes of production, the slave system in the South and the capitalist system centered in the North; this erupted into open antagonism, warfare, when it was no longer possible for these two modes of production to coexist within the same country.

After the invention of the cotton gin in 1793, cotton replaced tobacco as the main product of the slave states and their main export to Europe. By 1859, just before southern secession, cotton exports hit an all-time high of 3.5 million bales, over 60 percent of all exports from the U.S. that year. That the biggest share of this cotton was being shipped to England, and not to New England, was one of the factors contributing to the growing antagonism between the northern industrialists and the southern planters. More important, virtually none of the profits of the slave system went into improvements on the land—slavery in the southern U.S. in the nineteenth century still rested on primitive methods of farming in which the slaves themselves were the most important "tool" for working the land—and the slave states were therefore forced to constantly expand to find new land suitable to primitive slave production. At the same time, as land in particular slave states was exhausted, there was a tendency to turn these states into areas for breeding slaves to be sold into other areas where the land was still more profitably workable. All this exerted a tremendous pressure on the slave system to push west: this was a major factor in the war waged in the 1840s against Mexico which resulted in the conquest by the USA of a large part of Mexican territory (a major part of what is now the southwest of the USA).

During the same period, capitalist machine production made great strides in the North—but not in the South: between 1850 and 1860 the number of factories increased from 120,000 to 140,000 but the value of capital invested doubled (from $.5 billion to $1 billion), as did the value of all manufactured products (from $1 billion to $2 billion). This indicates that concentration of capital, even monopolization, were already beginning to develop. To expand the market for these products, as well as to control the land and rich resources in the West, in particular gold, the capitalists in the North also were compelled to push westward.

The West became a kind of focal point of the conflict between the two sides, and clashes there in the 1850s signalled the approaching collision.

When the war started, however, the predominant view among the ruling class in the North was that what was required was to contain slavery – that the new territories being "opened up" must be preserved for capital (and "free farmers," who would settle the land and provide a base of stability and support for the capitalists) – and that slavery would eventually die out if so contained. Thus, in his first Inaugural Address in March 1861, Lincoln declared:

> I have no purpose, directly or indirectly, to interfere with the institution of slavery in the States where it exists. I believe I have no lawful right to do so, and I have no inclination to do so.[33]

And in 1862, in replying to a letter from Horace Greeley, editor of the *New York Tribune,* who chided Lincoln for being "strangely and disastrously remiss. . . with regard to the emancipating provisions of the new Confiscation Act. . . ," Lincoln wrote:

> My paramount object in this struggle is to save the Union, and is not either to save or destroy Slavery. If I could save the Union without freeing any slave, I would do it; and if I could save it by freeing all the slaves, I would do it; and if I could do it by freeing some and leaving others alone, I would also do that. What I do about Slavery and the colored race, I do because it helps to save this Union. . . . I have here stated my purpose according to my view of official duty, and I intend no modification of my oft-expressed personal wish that all men, everywhere, could be free.[34]

It was to prove impossible, however, to "save the Union" without thoroughly defeating the slave Confederacy – and this in turn proved impossible without emancipating the slaves and enabling them to fight on behalf of that Union (nearly two hundred thousand did so, often fighting on the front lines of the most fiercely contested battles and incurring a death rate of 20 percent, which was 35 percent higher than the rate for white Union soldiers, even while they were only paid about half the wages of

---

33. Cited in Zinn, *People's History of the U.S.,* p. 184.

34. Cited in Zinn, *People's History of the U.S.,* p. 186 (ellipses in statements as cited by Zinn, except the last one).

these white soldiers!). Still, as we have seen, Lincoln at first only extended emancipation to slaves in the states adhering to the Confederacy (and not in other states where there were slaves but which were not part of the Confederacy). Only at war's end was slavery abolished throughout the territory of the U.S. Here, again, we see a Lincoln who was faithful to the interests of capital – despite his "oft-expressed personal wish" to see all men free[35] and his also oft-expressed (and frequently quoted) statements about the rights of labor in relation to capital. The Civil War represented in a sense a completion of the bourgeois-democratic revolution in the U.S., but this did not mean it established, or that the northern capitalists and their political representatives meant to establish, freedom and equality for Black people in relation to white America. Lincoln, like Jefferson and other representatives of the bourgeoisie before and since, considered everything from the point of view of his nation above all, and in the concrete conditions of America in the nineteenth (and twentieth) century that has meant maintaining Black people as a subjugated nation.

By this I don't mean to say that this oppression of Black people had its basis in the thinking of Lincoln (who, after all, was violently removed from the scene in 1865) or of other political leaders of the bourgeois state. It is rather the reverse: their thinking reflected – and their actions served – the underlying material interests of the capitalists for whom the Civil War had brought complete control of the state and a great stimulus to both the development and the monopolization of industry and finance. The only way the complete emancipation of Black people could have been won was if their struggle had been linked up with a class-conscious movement of the working class fighting for this emancipation as part of an all-around struggle whose ultimate

---

35. As a matter of fact, Lincoln had also "oft expressed" his view that Blacks were inferior to whites. For example, in his famous debates with Douglas in 1858, Lincoln insisted: "There is a physical difference between the white and black races which I believe will forever forbid the two races living together on terms of social and political equality. And inasmuch as they cannot so live, while they do remain together there must be the position of superior and inferior, and I as much as any other man am in favor of having the superior position assigned to the white race." And a year later, Lincoln wrote privately: "Negro equality! Fudge! How long, in the Government of a God great enough to make and rule the universe, shall there continue knaves to vend, and fools to quip, so low a piece of demagogism as this." (These statements by Lincoln are cited in Stephen Jay Gould, *The Mismeasure of Man* [New York: W. W. Norton, 1981], p. 35.)

goal was the socialist transformation of society as a whole. But at that time there were not the material or ideological conditions for the development of such a movement of the working class. For one thing, although northern manufacturing was on the ascendancy, much of the industry in the North was barely beyond the handicraft stage in the period leading up to the Civil War, and a large percentage of the workers were craftsmen, or artisans. Further, many of these earned and saved enough money to move West and become landowners, as the Indians were continually driven off their lands and a large territory was stolen from Mexico. And at the time of the Civil War, Marxism had only just been introduced into the political life of the country and the infant workers' movement. Thus, although many workers, especially those influenced by Marxism, fought with determination for the abolition of slavery through the Civil War, they did so overall under the leadership of the bourgeoisie.

And under the leadership of the bourgeoisie, the reorganization of the country, and of the South in particular, that was carried out in the aftermath of the Civil War did not finally result in the development of land ownership among large numbers of Black and white farmers or in their involvement in the political decision-making process. In the period right after the Civil War, partly in response to the mass initiative unleashed through the war and the defeat of the southern slavocracy, but also in order to consolidate its own position, the victorious bourgeoisie was compelled to allow not only poor whites but Blacks as well to own some land, to vote, and in other ways to participate in politics, even to hold office. But from the beginning of this Reconstruction period, the U.S. government was guided – as Lincoln had been throughout the Civil War – by the concern for advancing the interests of the capitalists; where the demands of Black people (or poor whites) came into conflict with those interests, such demands were sacrificed – indeed violent repression, including by federal troops, was often used to put down struggles to realize these demands. It was for the same reason that Reconstruction was reversed, only a decade after it had been initiated . . . and Black people, along with any who would ally with them, were subjected to systematic terror whose purpose was to force Blacks back onto the old plantations, but now in serflike conditions rather than as outright slaves.

Reconstruction did not "fail," as is generally claimed by bourgeois historians. It was abandoned by the northern bourgeoisie which, especially after the financial panic and depression of 1873, "stabilized" the South by turning back the democratic movement of Black, and white, farmers and urban middle classes that arose after the Civil War. The Federal Army was withdrawn from the South in 1877 (to be used immediately against the railroad strike of white workers in the North, part of a rising wave of strikes there; significant parts of the Federal Army were also engaged in battles to suppress Indian resistance in this period). The dominant northern capitalists, who were making further strides in concentrating capital and developing monopolies, had achieved what they needed in the South: the opportunity for expansion and investment (beginning with the railroads) and for new markets. So, with the South, and the southern planters, safely under the domination of northern capital, the southern region of the U.S. was maintained as an underdeveloped preserve for northern capital: industrial development in the South, to the extent that it went on, was controlled by the bourgeoisie centered in the North, and semifeudal agriculture, with Black peonage as its base, was enforced throughout the South. This was profitable not only to the planters but to the developing commercial interests in the South and, most especially, to the northern bankers and manufacturers who made loans to the planters, bought into the plantations themselves, and used the enforced poverty of the farmers, particularly the Black tenant-farmers and share-croppers, to hold down wages in industry. It would not be until three-quarters of a century later – when the interests of the ruling bourgeoisie in the context of World War 2 and its aftermath demanded it – that the plantation system in the southern U.S., with its legalized segregation enforced through open and systematic terror, would be finally broken up. . . and Black people subjected to new forms of exploitation and oppression.

All this is the concrete realization of the ideals and principles proclaimed by Jefferson and the "founding fathers" in the *Declaration of Independence* and reaffirmed by Lincoln in his famous "Gettysburg Address." The Civil War was historically progressive: it did result in the abolition of literal chattel slavery, however hesitatingly this was undertaken by the bourgeoisie, and it did "clear the ground" for the class antagonism between the proletariat and the bourgeoisie to develop more fully. But it was fought on the basis of bourgeois democracy and the result remained within the confines of capitalism – with its exploitation of the proletariat and, in the actual situation within the U.S., the oppression of the Black nation rooted in the southern U.S. – all enforced through bourgeois dictatorship.[36]

The "Special Situation" of the USA Historically

We have seen that the extensive territory to be conquered in the West played a prominent role in the historical development of the USA. Besides the ways in which this figured into the conflict between the slaveowning and capitalist classes, this "open frontier," all the way to the Pacific Ocean, played a major part in the eventual emergence of the USA as a world power. Of course, this vast area to the West was "open" only in a relative – and national-chauvinist – sense. To conquer this territory involved, above all, not some romantic battle to tame the wilderness (as it is still frequently portrayed), but dirty wars of aggression and extermination against Mexico and the Indian peoples. The rulers of the USA were able, from the beginning, to concentrate great attention on such conquest because they were favorably situated in North America, removed by great expanses of ocean from the European continent and its relatively powerful nation-states. Many of these European powers – notably England, France, and Spain – had a presence in America, but maintaining an extensive empire there was to prove to be beyond their reach, partly because they were continually embroiled in conflicts with each other.

The more farsighted of the "founding fathers" of the USA recognized and seized on this situation from the first. For example, Alexander Hamilton, in polemicizing in favor of a strong federal government, warned – prophetically – that "a vast tract of unsettled territory within the boundaries of the United States" could become the focus of conflicting interests.[37] And he stressed that with only a weak union the different states would "be gradually entangled in all the pernicious labyrinths of European politics and wars; and by the destructive contentions of the parts into which she was divided, would be likely to become a prey to the artifices and machinations of powers equally the

36. In this section on the Civil War I have drawn extensively from an article, "National Liberation and Proletarian Revolution in the U.S.," published in *Red Papers 5* by the Revolutionary Union in the early 1970s, which is now out of print.

37. Hamilton, "Federalist Paper No. 7," in *The Federalist Papers*, p. 60.

enemies of them all."[38] Similarly, in what de Tocqueville would describe as an "admirable Farewell Address which he made to his fellow citizens, and which may be regarded as his political testament," George Washington set forth this view:

> The great rule of conduct for us in regard to foreign nations is, in extending our commercial relations, to have with them as little *political* connection as possible. So far as we have already formed engagements, let them be fulfilled with perfect good faith. Here let us stop.
>
> Europe has a set of primary interests, which to us have none, or a very remote relation. Hence she must be engaged in frequent controversies, the causes of which are essentially foreign to our concerns. Hence, therefore, it must be unwise in us to implicate ourselves, by artificial ties, in the ordinary vicissitudes of her politics, or the ordinary combinations and collisions of her friendships or enmities.
>
> Our detached and distant situation invites and enables us to pursue a different course. If we remain one people, under an efficient government, the period is not far off when we may defy material injury from external annoyance; when we may take such an attitude as will cause the neutrality we may at any time resolve upon to be scrupulously respected; when belligerent nations, under the impossibility of making acquisitions upon us, will not lightly hazard the giving us provocation; when we may choose peace or war, as our interest, guided by justice, shall counsel.
>
> Why forego the advantages of so peculiar a situation?[39]

And some years later, Thomas Jefferson struck a still more "positive" and "optimistic" note—from the point of view of American conquest—in writing to James Monroe, then president of the United States:

> Our first and fundamental maxim should be, never to entangle ourselves in the broils of Europe. Our second, never to suffer Europe to intermeddle with cis-Atlantic affairs. . . .
>
> But we have first to ask ourselves a question. Do we wish to acquire to our own confederacy any one or more of the Spanish provinces? I candidly confess, that I have ever looked on Cuba as the most interesting addition which could ever be made to our system of States. The control which, with Florida Point, this

38. Hamilton, "Federalist Paper No. 8," pp. 65-66.

39. Cited in de Tocqueville, *Democracy in America*, 1, p. 241.

island would give us over the Gulf of Mexico, and the countries and isthmus bordering on it, as well as all those whose waters flow into it, would fill up the measure of our political well-being. Yet, as I am sensible that this can never be obtained, even with her own consent, but by war; and its independence, which is our second interest, (and especially its independence of England,) can be secured without it, I have no hesitation in abandoning my first wish to future chances, and accepting its independence, with peace and the friendship of England, rather than its association, at the expense of war and her enmity.[40]

All of this has had a great deal to do with the development of the "American character" and with the peculiarities of the views of democracy and freedom common in the U.S. As far back as 150 years ago, de Tocqueville already noted how extreme self-interest and a mania for money-making were so quintessentially a part of this "American character" and so integral to the meaning of democracy and equality in the USA – how the American sense of democracy, self-government, and equality are completely bound up with the restless quest for property and wealth. De Tocqueville was, it should be remembered, praising this and holding it up as a model. Hence de Tocqueville could write:

> The chief circumstance which has favored the establishment and maintenance of a democratic republic in the United States is the nature of the territory that the Americans inhabit. Their ancestors gave them the love of equality and of freedom; but God himself gave them the means of remaining equal and free, by placing them upon a boundless continent. . . .
> In what part of human history can be found anything similar to what is passing before our eyes in North America? The celebrated communities of antiquity were all founded in the midst of hostile nations, which they were obliged to subjugate before they could flourish in their place. Even the moderns have found, in some parts of South America, vast regions inhabited by a people of inferior civilization, who nevertheless had already occupied and cultivated the soil. To found their new states it was necessary to extirpate or subdue a numerous population, and they made civilization blush for its own success. But North America was inhabited only by wandering tribes, who had no thought of profiting by the natural riches of the soil; that vast country was still,

---

40. Jefferson, "An American System – the Monroe Doctrine," letter to U.S. President James Monroe (24 October 1823), in *The Portable Jefferson*, pp. 574-76.

properly speaking, an empty continent, a desert land awaiting its inhabitants.[41]

And on the basis of such chauvinist distortion (to cite only one such distortion, there were of course Indian peoples in North America who were cultivating the soil before the Europeans arrived), de Tocqueville could go on to paint this picture of the "push westward":

> At this very time thirteen millions of civilized Europeans are peaceably spreading over those fertile plains, with whose resources and extent they are not yet themselves accurately acquainted. Three or four thousand soldiers drive before them the wandering races of the aborigines; these are followed by the pioneers, who pierce the woods, scare off the beasts of prey, explore the courses of the inland streams, and make ready the triumphal march of civilization across the desert.[42]

To call this "romanticized" or even "prettified" does not come close to capturing what de Tocqueville's description represents: literal genocide, with repeated massacres of whole villages, the deliberate selling of smallpox-infested blankets, and other equally vicious atrocities committed against the Indians, is transformed into "peaceably spreading over those fertile plains" – and for that matter, the fierce resistance of the Indian peoples is replaced by references to the "wandering races of the aborigines" who are almost effortlessly "driven before" three or four thousand soldiers. But what is important to emphasize here is how de

41. De Tocqueville, *Democracy in America*, 1, p. 301.
The influence of certain peculiarities of the development of the USA – including the "open frontier" – on popular American conceptions of freedom and democracy has also been noted and analyzed in various aspects by Marxist-Leninists. A noteworthy article in this regard, which specifically focuses on how these peculiarities have fostered and reinforced bourgeois-democratic prejudices within the U.S. working class, is J. Werner, "Some Preliminary Thoughts on Bourgeois Democracy and the U.S. Working Class," in *The Communist*, Vol. 1, No. 1 (October 1976).

42. De Tocqueville, *Democracy in America*, p. 302. De Tocqueville's view of slavery in America was equally deformed by white-chauvinist bias: he not only asserted the inferiority of Blacks to whites but claimed that the Black slaves passively accepted their lot...though he stated – prophetically – that if a revolution ever happened in the USA in the future it "will be brought about by the presence of the black race on the soil of the United States" (Vol. 2, p. 270; see also Vol. 1, chapter 18: "The Present and Probable Future Condition of the Three Races that Inhabit the Territory of the United States").

Tocqueville links this continuing conquest and expansion in the West to the notions of equality and opportunity in the United States:

> The European emigrant always lands, therefore, in a country that is but half full, and where hands are in demand; he becomes a workman in easy circumstances, his son goes to seek his fortune in unpeopled regions and becomes a rich landowner. The former amasses the capital which the latter invests; and the stranger as well as the native [meaning the white person born in America – B.A.] is unacquainted with want.[43]

This, of course, is actually a romanticized picture, but there was an aspect of reality to it: everyone could not thus prosper, many would remain quite poor, but, for the whites in America, there was a possibility of becoming rich to a significant enough degree that it could be conceived of as equal opportunity to do so. Howard Zinn speaks to basically the same point in terms of the base of support for the new government emerging out of the American Revolution:

> Jackson Main found that one-third of the population in the Revolutionary period were small farmers, while only 3 percent of the population had truly large holdings and could be considered wealthy.
>
> Still, one-third was a considerable number of people who felt they had something at stake in the stability of a new government.[44]

Drawing on the United States of America as his model, de Tocqueville thus contrasted a democratic society with an aristocratic one:

> We do not find there, as among an aristocratic people, one class that keeps quiet because it is well off; and another that does not venture to stir because it despairs of improving its condition. Everyone is in motion, some in quest of power, others of gain.[45]

De Tocqueville does pose the question, "In the midst of this uni-

---

43. De Tocqueville, *Democracy in America*, 1, p. 303.

44. Zinn, *People's History of the U.S.*, p. 98.

45. De Tocqueville, *Democracy in America*, 2, p. 43.

versal tumult, this incessant conflict of jarring interests, this continual striving of men after fortune, where is that calm to be
found which is necessary for the deeper combinations of the
intellect?"[46] But "the deeper combinations of the intellect" without
a rather direct connection to wealth and power have never been a
distinguishing feature of the "American character." What de
Tocqueville is describing is what has come to be known as that
pragmatism that is a particularly American variant of bourgeois
ideology. And while certain aspects of this may disturb de
Tocqueville, overall he finds in it something to be emulated. He
insists that selfishness in America is "enlightened" and that
"Everybody I see about me seems bent on teaching his contem-
poraries, by precept and example, that what is useful is never
wrong."[47] What is useful is, of course, what serves self-
interest – and "Each American knows when to sacrifice some of
his private interests to save the rest."[48] Here, then, is the
American approach to the questions of freedom and the purpose
of government:

> [T]he men of democratic times require to be free in order to pro-
> cure more readily those physical enjoyments for which they are
> always longing. . . . And indeed the Americans believe their
> freedom to be the best instrument and surest safeguard of their
> welfare; they are attached to the one by the other. They by no
> means think that they are not called upon to take a part in public
> affairs; they believe, on the contrary, that their chief business is to
> secure for themselves a government which will allow them to ac-
> quire the things they covet and which will not debar them from
> the peaceful enjoyment of those possessions which they have
> already acquired.[49]

The whole point is perfectly summed up in the very fitting
heading to the chapter from which the above statements are
quoted: "How the Taste for Physical Gratifications is United in
America to Love of Freedom and Attention to Public Affairs."

At one point in this discussion, de Tocqueville poses what he
sees as a perplexing contradiction: an American, he says, at one

46. De Tocqueville, *Democracy in America*, 2, p. 43.

47. De Tocqueville, *Democracy in America*, 2, p. 131.

48. De Tocqueville, *Democracy in America*, 2, p. 131.

49. De Tocqueville, *Democracy in America*, 2, pp. 148, 151.

time "seems animated by the most selfish cupidity; at another, by the most lively patriotism. The human heart cannot be thus divided."[50] While there is an aspect in which these two come into contradiction, and at times this conflict can become acute (and, as a matter of fact, this very contradiction is being given great attention by the ruling imperialists of the USA right now, as they seek to rally people to the higher national interest of confronting and defeating the Soviet bloc in all-out warfare), yet it is a fact of capitalist society that there is a fundamental unity between "the most selfish cupidity" and "the most lively patriotism." If the history of the United States of America has demonstrated anything, it is that.

By the close of the nineteenth century, the vast territory to the West had been basically conquered and those peoples who stood in the way of this had been largely subjugated, where not exterminated. The emergence of U.S. imperialism coincided with this "closing of the frontier" – and with the development of capitalism into monopoly capitalism–imperialism in a number of European countries (and Japan) as well. The initial role of the U.S. in the great imperialist contest to carve up the world – and in particular to seize those parts of what is now called the Third World that had not yet been colonized – was somewhat limited but was nonetheless dramatic. Through the Spanish-American War, the U.S. "announced its arrival at the imperialist banquet table by displacing Spain, the last of the old feudal-based colonizers, as overlord of colonial subjects from Puerto Rico to the Philippines."[51] But the U.S.

> was not yet in a position to partake of the African depredations nor to enter many of the other contests among the European imperialists. Rather, it aimed at vying with these powers in Latin America, the Pacific rim, and China, as well as scooping up colonies from the crumbling Spanish empire.
>
> Despite its self-serving anticolonial fables, the U.S. opposed Spanish colonialism, only to replace it with its own brand of imperialist domination. In the Philippines, after the U.S. defeat of the Spanish in a brief naval encounter in Manila Bay, the entire thrust of U.S. operations in that country was directed toward the bloody suppression of the Filipino people (the U.S. imperialists

50. De Tocqueville, *Democracy in America*, 2, p. 150.

51. Lotta, *America in Decline*, 1, p. 174.

even turned on the moderate leader Aguinaldo who had previously been brought back from China in a U.S. warship to oppose the
Spanish). . . .

The Philippine insurgency was quelled with the aid of concentration camps and water torture. Before it was over, hundreds of
thousands of people, the overwhelming number of them Filipino,
had been killed. As a result of the Spanish-American War, the U.S.
also acquired Guam and Puerto Rico, along with the other territories "freed" from Spanish colonialism. . . . During this period, the
U.S. imperialists also annexed the Hawaiian Islands, occupied
Wake Island, divided the Somoan Islands with Germany and Britain, continued to struggle with the other imperialist powers over
the partition of China, and expanded their influence in Latin
America and the Caribbean.[52]

And Thomas Jefferson's "wish," which he had "abandoned to
future chances," was finally realized: "Cuba was also effectively
brought under U.S. domination with the same duplicity and
violence."[53] The meaning of the much-lauded "American values"
was given graphic illustration at that time by Theodore Roosevelt
(American hero of the Spanish-American War, who was to
become president of the U.S.): castigating the hesitation in some
quarters to annex Hawaii, Roosevelt called this "a crime against
white civilization."[54] And the American meaning of freedom and
equality, particularly as applied to international relations, was
reflected in the pages of the New York *Journal of Commerce:*

> This paper, which has been heretofore characterized as
> pacifist, anti-imperialist, and devoted to the development of com-
> merce in a free-trade world, saw the foundation of its faith crum-
> bling as a result of the threatened partition of China. Declaring
> that free access to the markets of China, with its 400,000,000 peo-
> ple, would largely solve the problem of the disposal of our surplus
> manufactures, the *Journal* came out not only for a stern insistence
> upon complete equality of rights in China but unreservedly also
> for an isthmian canal, the acquisition of Hawaii, and a material in-
> crease in the navy—three measures which it had hitherto
> strenuously opposed. Nothing could be more significant than the

---

52. Lotta, *America in Decline*, 1, p. 176-77.
53. Lotta, *America in Decline*, 1, p. 177.
54. Cited in Zinn, *People's History of the U.S.*, p. 293.

manner in which this paper was converted in a few weeks. . . .[55]

In one sense, demands of this kind for U.S. imperialism's "equality of right" to partake in the partition and plunder of China reflected that the U.S. was not then in a position to enter in a major way into a battle with other imperialists for direct domination in China and many other parts of the world. But, more significantly overall, the U.S. imperialists did not then need to involve themselves in many of these contests in the same way the European imperialists did. In fact, U.S. imperialism enjoyed important strategic advantages as a result of its continuing relative "isolation" from the other centers of imperial power and because of its history of being able to expand for a long period "internally." These advantages were utilized by the U.S. ruling class when the conflicts among the imperialists erupted into World War 1: the U.S. sat out most of the war, making loans and sales, especially but not exclusively to the Anglo-French side, and then, when the opportunity as well as the necessity presented itself (the latter particularly because of the 1917 Revolution in Russia and the strengthened position of Germany as a result), the U.S. entered the war itself, making possible the victory of the Anglo-French-American alliance and the seizing of considerable spoils by the U.S.

Although it was not yet able to take the "high ground" as undisputed chieftain among the imperialists—as it was to do after World War 2—the U.S. emerged from World War 1 in a greatly strengthened position, both absolutely and specifically in relation to the other imperialists. Yet, while its sphere of influence expanded and its role in imperialist world affairs increased, U.S. imperialism still did not have the same necessity as the other world powers to embroil itself deeply in many of the inter-imperialist conflicts that took place between World Wars 1 and 2. To a large degree, the U.S. concentrated on tightening its hold and thwarting the designs of its rivals in Latin America. Thus, in the 1920s, along with continuing military occupation in Haiti and landings, invasions, and occupations in Mexico and other parts of Latin America and the Caribbean, U.S.

naval forays into Central America continued to be commonplace.

55. From Julius Pratt, "American Business and the Spanish-American War," *Hispanic-American Historical Review*, 1934, as cited in Zinn, *People's History of the U.S.*, p. 295.

All this was carried out in the "fraternal" spirit of the Monroe Doctrine. In 1920, the U.S. "fraternally aided" the people of Guatemala with U.S. naval armed force. The U.S. launched similar attacks on Honduras in 1924. Nicaragua was invaded, for the second time, in 1926. Such gunboat diplomacy produced a situation in which, at one point, U.S. officials directed the financial policies of eleven of the twenty Latin American countries – and U.S. banking agents in six of them were backed on the spot by U.S. troops.[56]

And in the 1930s, under the "good neighbor" policy of Franklin D. Roosevelt, U.S. imperialism continued to exploit its favorable position and intensify its robbery in Latin America, in the context of the sharpening interimperialist rivalry that would lead to the Second World War:

> With the important exception of the Philippines, most of the oppressed nations controlled by U.S. imperialism were not to become the ground on which the ensuing world war was fought. The most bitterly contested colonial preserves were in Asia, where both the United States and Japan sought to carve out new empires, and in the arc formed by North Africa and the Middle East, which occupied a strategic position with respect to the European theater.
>
> Only in some areas of Latin America, most notably Argentina, did the imperialists of the German bloc gain significant influence through comprador elements and "fifth column" political factions. In these cases, the U.S. imperialists paid special attention to employing the deception of "good neighborliness" in "assisting" the resistance against the political influence of the rival bloc. In Brazil, for instance, they helped thwart an attempt by the Hitler-inspired Integralists to infiltrate the U.S. lackey government of President Vargas. Needless to say, the U.S. first had to pave the way by making the country safe from revolution, backing Vargas in arresting and torturing thousands and in killing hundreds of national liberation fighters, among whom numbered many members of the Brazilian Communist Party. On the whole, the new tactics of the U.S. were incapable of eliminating the resistance to its brand of imperialism during these years, yet it had an altogether easier go of it than the other imperialists.[57]

Once again, at the start of World War 2, the U.S. was able to hold back from direct involvement; after it did enter the war it

---

56. Lotta, *America in Decline,* 1, p. 189.
57. Lotta, *America in Decline,* 1, pp. 200-201.

was able to concentrate for some time on defeating the Japanese challenge (and undercutting the British) in the Pacific, gaining complete dominance there, while also maintaining a firm hold on Latin America. It was in a position to hold back from a major commitment in Europe until the Soviet Union had absorbed and defeated the great bulk of Germany's forces – then the U.S. moved in at the head of an Allied sweep across war-ravaged Western Europe, establishing its top-dog position there, and scooping up most of the colonies formerly held by the various European (and Japanese) imperialists (neocolonialism was to become the form of American colonial domination in most places). It was on this basis, and through the reorganization and restructuring of imperialist economic and political relations under its control in the aftermath of the war, that U.S. imperialism was to enjoy a position of unparalleled power and the imperialist countries with which it was allied (now including Japan and West Germany) were also to enjoy a rather extended period of relative stability and prosperity at home. But the "American Century" that spokesmen for U.S. imperialism triumphantly proclaimed at the end of World War 2 was not to be realized. The Western imperialist alliance has been battered by an unprecedented storm of national liberation struggle in the Third World – reaching its highest peak so far in the 1960s – and today it is wracked by severe crisis and is facing the challenge of a powerful imperialist rival in the Soviet bloc. A global showdown between these two imperialist blocs is looming directly ahead at the same time as the prospects for revolutionary struggle against imperialism are being heightened, in the Third World and even within the imperialist citadels themselves, the U.S. included. Today the U.S. is not "isolated" or "insulated"; U.S. imperialism is deeply involved, and exposed, in all parts of the world.

This whole history – leading to the rise of U.S. imperialism and its present position in the world, and involving exploitation and depredation that has taken the lives, literally, of tens of millions of people – is of a scope far too great to be encompassed within this book.[58] What is important to stress is not only that,

---

58. A basic analysis of this is presented in Lotta, *America in Decline*, Vol. 1, in particular chapter 2; some chronicling of the crimes of the U.S. ruling class, particularly in Latin America but also in other parts of the world, is found in "Invasions in the 'Neighborhood,'" *Revolutionary Worker*, No. 281 (16 November 1984), and "Terrorists, Forty Years of Dirty Work," *Revolutionary Worker*, No. 277 (19 October 1984).

along with leading to the situation where the U.S. has assumed the role of leader of the Western imperialist pack, all this has fostered and reinforced democratic illusions and bourgeois-democratic – together with outright national-chauvinist – prejudices. At the same time it is important to stress that, through the unprecedented historic conjuncture now shaping up, with its intensified developments toward world war/nuclear devastation on one side and revolutionary struggle and potential revolutionary breakthroughs on the other, these illusions and prejudices will – and must – be challenged and shattered as never before.

5
Imperialism, Democracy, and Dictatorship

Throughout this book the word "imperialism" is used to describe the present-day USA and its major allies – and the rival Soviet bloc as well. "Imperialism" is not just a convenient way to portray the international bullying and robbery carried out by a small number of powerful states; it is not simply a catchword or a part of some ponderous Leninist litany. In recent times the world has witnessed, in such places as Mexico, India, and Ethiopia, a graphic demonstration of the grisly reality that imperialism represents: in an explosion and fire in Mexico City, hundreds are burned alive and thousands more injured, while still more lose what semblance of a home they had; in Bhopal, thousands are murdered – yes, murdered – outright, while tens of thousands more are poisoned, with many facing a more drawn-out, agonizing death (and experts, particularly military strategists, from the "advanced" countries rush in to study the effects of chemical poisoning for future application); meanwhile in Ethiopia, millions, literally millions in one country, many of them small children, stare starvation in the face.[1] And scenes like this – or

1. For concrete exposure of how these events are products of imperialist domination and are part of a larger web of imperialist relations, see "The Mexico

129

even the torture and murder of masses of people in an El Salvador – are only dramatic expressions of the essential relations on which the imperialist world rests and the continual horror that life under imperialism is for the great majority of the world's people. This, it cannot be said too many times, "is no exaggeration but a profound, searing truth commonly overlooked in the preserves of privilege and comfort that exist for broad strata much of the time in the imperialist citadels."[2]

Statistics can tell a part of the story. Whether it is in terms of life expectancy, infant mortality, numbers of hospitals and doctors per capita, amount of food consumed, or any other statistical measure of the quality of life, there is a tremendous gulf between the handful of imperialist countries and the great majority of countries and people on the globe. Take gross national product per person per year, for example: in the U.S., it is over $12,000; in France, over $10,000; Australia, $11,000; and Sweden, over $13,000; whereas in Mexico, one of the least poor Third World countries, it is just over $3,000; in South Korea, $1,600; in Peru, $1,200; Egypt, $620; and Afghanistan (which, it should be remembered, is a Soviet colony now, and was a colony of Western imperialism for a long period before that), $200. For over half of the countries of the Third World it is below $1,000, in many cases well below. Or another way of looking at the same basic phenomenon: the gross national product in relation to every person in Great Britain is more than 35 times greater than in India; it is more than 25 times greater in France than in Senegal; more than 40 times greater in the U.S. than in Haiti; 9 times greater in West Germany than in Turkey; it is also over 25 times greater in East Germany than in Mozambique, and almost 30 times greater in the Soviet Union than in Afghanistan.[3]

City Fire: What Lit the Match" and "Mexico City Explosion: The Fire and the Fire Below," *Revolutionary Worker*, Nos. 282 and 283 (23 and 30 November 1984); "Bhopal: An American Gas Chamber," *Revolutionary Worker*, No. 284 (7 December 1984), and also articles in subsequent issues; and "The Politics of Famine and the Utter Poverty of Imperialism," *Revolutionary Worker*, No. 282 (23 November 1984). The Mexican inferno referred to here occurred before the devastating earthquake of 1985 and its bringing to the surface of yet more horrendous aspects and results of imperialist domination there.

2. Avakian, *Horrible End or End to Horror?*, p. 13.

3. Figures from U.S. Bureau of the Census, *Statistical Abstract of the United States: 1985* (Washington, D.C., 1984), Table 1481, p. 846; and World Bank, *World Development Report 1983* (New York: Oxford University Press, 1983), Table 1,

And, chauvinist mythology notwithstanding, these great disparities cannot be attributed to the fact that the people in these "advanced" countries have worked hard! A miner in Bolivia or South Africa (or an autoworker, an electronics worker, and so on, throughout the Third World) works much longer hours, in far more difficult and more dangerous conditions, than his/her counterpart in an imperialist country; today, in many, many parts of the Third World, the length of the work week, the intensity of the work, and the oppressiveness of the relations between the working people and their overlords and overseers is considerably more onerous than what is described of early nineteenth-century England in the novels of Dickens. But the countries of the Third World are not "centuries behind the advanced countries, on the same course" (to use the terms of another chauvinist myth): they are ensnared in the whole network of imperialist economic and political relations, on the oppressed side of an oppressive division of labor within a world political-economic system; and they are an integral and indispensable source of superprofits and a link in the whole machinery of capital accumulation for the economies founded and centered in the imperialist nations. The statistics cited – while they cannot begin to reveal the real depth of exploitation, suffering, anguish, and anger involved – do reflect something very important: not merely a great, in fact a qualitative, difference between the standards of living in the imperialist countries on the one hand and the nations they oppress on the other, but a relationship of exploitation and plunder in which the high standard of living of the one depends on and requires the low standard of living of the other. As it was so aptly

---

pp. 148-49.

Another obscene manifestation of the gulf, and the oppressive relations, between the imperialist countries and the masses of people and the nations they oppress in the Third World might be pondered: the military budgets of the USA and the USSR are every year greater than the total gross national products of the majority of countries in the Third World. And this stands out as all the more monstrous when it is recalled that the military spending of these imperialist great powers is precisely for the purpose of *maintaining just these oppressive relations* (as well as exploitation and oppression "at home") and of carrying on the contention between such great powers for the right to hold the top-dog position in all this. (For a graphic breakdown of these and similarly revealing and condemning statistics, see Michael Kidron and Dan Smith, *The War Atlas, Armed Conflict – Armed Peace: A Pluto Press Project* [New York: Simon & Schuster, 1983]; and Michael Kidron and Ronald Segal, *The New State of the World Atlas: A Pluto Press Project* [New York: Simon & Schuster, 1984].)

expressed in an article in the *Revolutionary Worker* on Bhopal: "to those that do revel in the privileges of life in the imperialist heartland, we say take a good look at the blinded kids in Bhopal, good Germans, this is what your privileges are made of."[4]

There is also a clear political expression of all this: while in the imperialist countries the form of bourgeois rule is generally a democratic one and, particularly since World War 2, it has been possible to a considerable extent for the bourgeoisie to avoid utilizing its repressive apparatus to openly intimidate and suppress rebellion amongst a large part of the population,[5] in the countries oppressed by imperialism, dictatorship is exercised much more openly and ruthlessly, and bloody suppression of the masses is resorted to quickly and repeatedly, as a general rule. Just as in the economic sphere, here too there is not only a great difference but a direct relationship: the relative lack of open terror and brutal repression, at least much of the time, in these imperialist countries is dependent on the pitiless repression of the literally billions of colonial (or neocolonial) victims of imperialism. This, too, is an integral and indispensable part of securing the necessary conditions for the extraction of super-profits in the Third World, for the overall process of imperialist accumulation (as well as for the "protection" of the empire and its colonies from the challenge of other, rival imperialists) – and for maintaining a relatively stable home base, at least for a time, perhaps even a fairly extended period of time. This fundamental point could not be put in more clear, and stark, terms than are found in the following summation:

> The platform of democracy in the imperialist countries (worm-eaten as it is) rests on fascist terror in the oppressed nations: the real guarantors of bourgeois democracy in the U.S. are not the constitutional scholar and Supreme Court justice, but the Brazilian torturer, the South African cop, and the Israeli pilot; the *true* defenders of the democratic tradition are not on the portraits

4. "How Much Longer?" *Revolutionary Worker*, No. 284 (7 December 1984). Again, for a basic analysis of the crucial role of the Third World in the overall imperialist accumulation process – and more particularly of its role in relation to the relative stability and prosperity in the imperialist countries for an extended period after the Second World War – see Lotta, *America in Decline*, Vol. 1, in particular chapter 1.

5. Here I am speaking especially of the U.S.-led Western imperialist alliance, although the same point basically applies to the Soviet bloc as well.

in the halls of the Western capitols, but are Marcos, Mobutu, and the dozens of generals from Turkey to Taiwan, from South Korea to South America, all put and maintained in power and backed up by the military force of the U.S. and its imperialist partners.[6]

At times the truth of the above statement forces its way to the surface – for example in the ugly, pogromist reaction among fairly broad (and mainly privileged) strata in the USA when the Iranian students took over the U.S. embassy there and "held America hostage" (and, just for the record, proved with documents captured in the embassy itself that it was exactly what they said it was: a "spy den" and center for plotting and conspiring to reestablish a firm U.S. grip on Iran). But more generally, the lopsidedness in the world and the division of labor within the overall structure of imperialist world relations – where there is a great gulf between the economic and political conditions in the imperialist countries on the one hand and in the countries dominated by imperialism on the other – all this is accompanied by corresponding ideological distortions. In particular, democratic illusions and prejudices are fostered and reinforced. This is especially so in the imperialist countries, where these inclinations are frequently linked with the most virulent – or in some cases a more subtle but still grotesque – imperialistic chauvinism. Even in the oppressed nations, however, there is the fairly widespread tendency to believe that the imperialist countries – even the ones directly oppressing you – are somehow democratic (at home at least) and that the goal is to win for your country the same kind of democracy (and the corresponding economic conditions) that seem to pertain there. Speaking to this general phenomenon in terms of a peculiar "shell game" that the imperialists play, I noted:

> A favorite tactic of the imperialists these days, particularly the U.S. imperialists, is the tactic of letting others do the dirty work of murder and massacre while they stay in the background posing as the benevolent patriarch seeking (or able, if it so pleases him) to restrain the "extreme elements" among his "friends." The U.S. in relation to Israel in Lebanon (and the Middle East generally) or in relation to the death squads in El Salvador (along with whatever government is in power there) are examples of this. This is a tactic the U.S. imperialists have found useful and necessary in a number

6. Wolff, *Science of Revolution*, p. 184.

of situations, especially as a result of their defeat and exposure in
Vietnam but also because of the imminence of world war, which
means they can't get that deeply involved again – until it's time to
go all the way.

The fact that they have the ability as well as the necessity to
use this tactic has very much to do with the lopsidedness in the
world. . . .

. . . On this very basis these imperialists seek to run a game,
effecting a certain division of labor (or terror), to "skin the ox
twice" politically (to use Lenin's phrase): achieving the brutal suppression in the colonies (or neocolonies) so necessary and essential to the functioning of their whole system – including for the
bribing and pacifying of broad layers of the people in the "home
country" – and at the same time acting as if they have nothing to do
with all this terror, that they are surprised and horrified when it is
brought to their attention, and if everyone will just leave everything to them they will try to see if they can influence those
leaders "down there" (or "over there") to act more in accordance
with American democracy, as soon as those troublesome rebels,
commies, and so on have been dealt with. To no small degree this
game is played for the benefit of the more privileged strata in the
imperialist countries – most of whom have never really felt the
iron fist of bourgeois dictatorship – and those who are or aspire to
be in a similar position within the oppressed countries themselves. Unfortunately, however, it also takes in more than a few
people genuinely opposed to oppression, including some of the
basic masses themselves.[7]

In light of all this – and to shed further light – it is worthwhile
to consider briefly an exchange found in the book *Beyond the Cold
War* by E.P. Thompson. Thompson is a leading figure in the
British (and more generally the European) peace movement; his
politics are generally social-democratic. In one of the essays in
this book, Thompson replies to a Czechoslovakian "dissident"
who suggests that Thompson is a dupe of the Soviets. In the
course of his reply, Thompson argues that there may be some connection between the freedoms allowed in England and the colonial empire England has historically enjoyed, with the resultant
prosperity: "A prosperous empire may possibly be able to 'afford,'
in its metropolis, a little more space for liberty and dissent
amongst its own citizens."[8] But, Thompson hastens to add, "I do

7. Avakian, *Horrible End or End to Horror?,* pp. 147-49.

8. E.P. Thompson, *Beyond the Cold War* (New York: Pantheon Books, 1982),
p. 93.

not discount the significance of these internal freedoms, or dismiss them as 'phoney': they were ardently fought for, stubbornly maintained, and remain exemplary for us today."[9]

Notice how Thompson giveth with the one hand while with the other he taketh away: he admits that these "internal freedoms" rest on a foundation of colonialism, but then he turns around and argues that they exist because the people in the mother country have "ardently fought for" and "stubbornly maintained" them. Does Thompson mean to imply that the vast majority of people in the world – living under openly repressive neocolonial regimes that repeatedly resort to vicious terror to suppress resistance – find themselves in such conditions because they have *not* fought "ardently" and "stubbornly" against these conditions? Or is it that they live in the colonies while Thompson resides in the mother country, and the one enjoys these "internal freedoms" to a significant degree because the others do not? And, as a matter of fact, such "internal freedoms" will be allowed in the mother country itself only so long as they are not utilized in any way to seriously threaten the established order and the interests of the ruling class – and particularly so long as the people in the mother country do not break with their own ruling class and side with its colonial victims in rebelling against it.

If one is conscious of the reality that the world is dominated by imperialism, and if one has any inkling of the consequences of this for the great majority of the world's people, then one should feel compelled to help shatter the whole imperialist system and its entire framework, to remake social relations on an international scale. The question of "internal freedoms" in the imperialist mother countries should then be looked at in this light. Such "internal freedoms" exist, to the degree that they do, not because they "were ardently fought for" and are "stubbornly maintained" by the people of the imperialist countries, but mainly because the imperialists prefer to rule at home in a way that blunts rather than intensifies class contradictions and allows them to advertise these home countries as bastions of freedom. They prefer to do so – and they often have the ability to do so exactly because of their worldwide exploitation and plunder – but they have repeatedly shown that, where necessary to uphold their interests and preserve their rule, they will subject the people, particularly the lower classes, at home to some of the same

9. Thompson, *Cold War*, p. 93.

murderous repression they more regularly mete out (in some cases directly, but more often today through their dependent regimes) in their colonies or neocolonies.

It is not that the people in the imperialist countries should willingly submit to vicious repression and state terror because people in the Third World are regularly subjected to it – they should take advantage of the openings that do exist for political activity – but they should take advantage of them to build a revolutionary movement, in unity with the people in the oppressed nations of the world, toward the overthrow of imperialism and all exploitative relations. And they should recognize and be prepared for the eventuality that if they do this – and unless they are willing to play by the rules established by the imperialists and to support them whenever there is any serious crisis or challenge to their basic interests – they will be met with ruthless repression, most especially at times of serious crisis and social upheaval. In the aftermath of World War 1, and on the basis of witnessing the collapse of the opportunist Second (socialist) International and its leviathan party, the German Social-Democratic Party, Lenin made the point that it was necessary to tell the German workers that a revolution might bring a drop, at least temporarily, in their wages! Similarly, it is necessary to tell the workers and others in the imperialist countries today that making a revolution will almost certainly involve incurring – and advancing in the face of – much more severe repression than is normally meted out to broad masses in the imperialist countries, but such a revolution is infinitely preferable to the continuation of imperialism and its consequences. Anyone who is unwilling to tell them this is obviously no revolutionary and does not even deserve the name of socialist, though he may make a fitting social democrat.

As for Thompson's claim that the "internal freedoms" in the imperialist countries are "exemplary," it can be seen that they are indeed exemplary of a bourgeois dictatorship as it functions in an imperialist country where and when it can rely on international exploitation and colonial depredation – and the service of a significant bourgeois labor movement – to help retard the development of a revolutionary struggle on the part of the working class at home. Along with summarizing the main and essential features of imperialism as a special stage of capitalism (the dominance of monopolies, the merging of banking and industrial capital to form finance capital, the export of capital as more significant than the export of goods, the formation of international cartels, and the struggle among the imperialists for the redivision of the world),[10] Lenin specifically noted, "The export of capital, one of the most essential economic bases of imperialism, still more completely isolates the rentiers from production and sets the seal of parasitism on the whole country that lives by exploiting the labor of several overseas countries and colonies."[11] At the time Lenin wrote this, England provided the paramount example of this phenomenon; and, although it no longer occupies the preeminent imperialist position it once did, England continues to be a salient example of a country on which the "seal of parasitism" is set. One of the main consequences of this, Lenin pointed out, was that a section of the working class in such a country receives significant bribes – a share, even if only a small share, relatively speaking, of the colonial spoils – and becomes an aristocracy of labor acting as a social base for imperialism and for a chauvinist and reformist labor movement.[12] E.P. Thompson is a representative of precisely this trend.

Opposed to this are not only the billions of exploited and oppressed people in the Third World but also millions of exploited and oppressed people in the imperialist countries themselves, particularly the lower and more thoroughly dispossessed sections of the proletariat, who constitute a social base for a revolutionary communist movement. While, of course, not spontaneously free of any democratic illusions or bourgeois-democratic inclinations, these sections of the basic masses do see and experience daily the iron fist of bourgeois dictatorship. For there is vicious repression and state terror carried out continually – and not only in times of serious crisis or social upheaval – in the imperialist countries; it is carried out specifically against those who do not support but oppose the established order, or who simply cannot be counted on to be pacified by the normal workings of the imperialist system – those whose conditions are desperate and whose life situation is explosive anyway.

In the U.S. the hundreds of police shootings of oppressed people, particularly Blacks and other minority nationalities, every

10. See Lenin, "Imperialism, the Highest Stage of Capitalism," *LCW*, 22, chapter 7.

11. Lenin, "Imperialism," *LCW*, 22, p. 277.

12. See, for example, in addition to "Imperialism, the Highest Stage of Capitalism," Lenin's article "Imperialism and the Split in Socialism," *LCW*, 23.

year; the fact that jails are overwhelmingly filled with poor people, the greatest number again being Black and other minority nationalities – it is an amazing but true statistic that one out of every thirteen Black people in the U.S. will be arrested each year (and Blacks are incarcerated eight and one-half times as frequently as whites)![13] – and the widespread use of drugs, surgical techniques, and other means to repress and terrorize prisoners (as well as an astounding number of people not in jail, including allegedly recalcitrant children); the use of welfare and other so-called social service agencies to harass and control poor people down to the most intimate details of their personal lives; this, and much more, is part of the daily life experience of millions of people in the major imperialist countries. Along with all this, of course, is the use of the state apparatus for direct political repression: in the U.S. since the 1960s, for example, there have been thousands of people sent to jail (and tens, indeed hundreds of thousands arrested) for political activity opposed to the ruling interests; scores of political activists have been murdered by the state in this period, while the political police (FBI, CIA, etc.) have carried out (with the cooperation of the media) campaigns of the vilest personal slander and harassment to discredit people taking political stands opposed to the government, even prominent people on some occasions.[14]

In times of severe crisis and social strain, of course, all this is carried out more intensively and extensively. The 1960s were

---

13. These statistics are cited in "A Nation of Prisonhouses," *Revolutionary Worker*, No. 236 (30 December 1983). It is also worthwhile noting the obviously related fact that, while certain middle- and upper-class Blacks in the U.S. have benefited from a share, however unequal, in the spoils of imperialism, in many communities of Black people such things as the unemployment rate and the infant mortality rate are higher than in many Third World countries.

14. Many among the relatively better-off (but nonruling-class) strata actually do have some sense of the real nature of the state – or at least some sense that it carries out extensive repression – even while they have many illusions and prejudices and consider the kind of position outlined here to be "paranoid." This is indicated in a story recounted to me of an argument a comrade had with some people in this category. After detailing numerous examples of repression in the U.S., especially that directed against revolutionaries, this comrade was told by these people that he was greatly exaggerating all this. "Okay," he replied, "I'll tell you what: I'll buy you a subscription to the *Revolutionary Worker* and have it mailed to your house – you don't even have to pay for it." "No, don't do that!" was their immediate response, expressing genuine horror at the thought of what government lists they might get put on, and with what consequences, merely for receiving this newspaper.

dramatic proof of this – in the U.S. and the imperialist countries generally (whether in Paris or in Prague) – and the present period of far more fundamental crisis and looming world war will witness this on a much greater scale. Already, right now in the U.S., to cite one important aspect of this, hundreds of thousands of immigrants, "illegal" and "legal," are being subjected to a campaign of terror – including raids at their places of work and homes, the sudden and forcible separation of parents from children, and the deportation of large numbers of refugees back to the waiting arms of death squads and other government assassins in countries like El Salvador. The same kind of thing is also being directed against immigrants in France, West Germany, England, and other imperialist democracies.

Through all this, while overt political repression by the state is in one sense the clearest indication of the class content of democracy – in the imperialist countries as well as elsewhere – in another sense the daily, and often seemingly arbitrary, terror carried out against the lower strata in these imperialist countries concentrates the connection between the normal workings of the system and the political (that is, class) nature of the state. This is well captured in a review of the book *Not In Our Genes*, in particular the following paragraph of that review, dealing with one especially stark aspect of the overall picture:

The list of horrifying tales of theories of mental illness serving reactionary political and ideological ends goes on and on: here a young black in England is diagnosed as schizophrenic because he "uses the religious language of Rastafarianism"; there undercover researchers get admitted to California mental hospitals by pretending to hear voices and then find it almost impossible to get released even after their "symptoms" stop and they explain that they are healthy. The sheer scale of statistics gives one pause for reflection: ". . . one in twelve men and one in eight women in the United Kingdom – the proportions are similar in the United States – will now go to a hospital at some point in their lives to be treated for mental illness" (p. 197). What a tremendous indictment of the nature of these societies! These figures of course encompass not just the victims of political persecutions (of direct nature) but also all those who at one time or another become unhinged because they are simply unable or unwilling to go along with the current state of life in this supposed "best of all possible worlds." The authors point out that while there are such things as real mental illnesses, one has to wonder about whether one could deem sick a woman who was terrified that she might be raped, or someone who might fall into "apathetic despair about the likelihood of the world surviving nuclear holocaust through the eighties" for instance (p. 199).[15]

Out of this overall picture, what is most essential to grasp is not only that imperialist domination in most of the world means brutal repression as well as life-stealing poverty for the masses of people; nor that the reality of life in the imperialist countries themselves involves a genuinely horrifying pattern of repression and terror for significant numbers of people, particularly among the nonbourgeoisified proletariat, oppressed nationalities, and immigrants — what is most essential is how all this fits together. When the political leaders and statesmen of the "advanced" countries insist, as they have been known to do, that all this is necessary to preserve their vaunted democracy and way of life, they are not telling a damnable lie: they are telling a profound and damning truth.

Imperialist Rivalry and the Demagoguery of Democracy

The "free world," as advertised by the leaders of the West, is a very peculiar place. It is said by them to represent those areas where freedom and democracy reign, yet by far the greatest number of states which they include within it do not meet their own definition of democracy: many are military dictatorships, and in the majority, repression by the state is so obvious and brutal that few would bother to deny it. South Africa, South Korea, and Chile come to mind as examples — and the point is that they are more typical of the "free world," in terms of how intensive and extensive repression is, than, say, Sweden. But all this is beside the point: these countries are legitimately part of the "free world" not because the state does not repress the people but because they are *not* part of that "other world" — the world of totalitarian communism centered in the Soviet Union.[16] In other

15. Skybreak, *"Not In Our Genes*: A Breath of Fresh Air in the Scientific Sphere," in *Revolutionary Worker*, No. 284 (7 December 1984); passages in quotes and page numbers from *Not In Our Genes* are as cited by Skybreak.

16. The theory of totalitarianism and its political role will be discussed in the next chapter.

words, as more than one newspaper in the U.S. editorialized about the Shah of Iran as his regime was tottering under the blows of mass rebellion a few years back: he may be a dictator, but he is our dictator.[17]

What's more, the very same dictator can change his whole nature – from bad to good, from free to totalitarian, or vice versa – merely by switching sides. The military dictatorship in Somalia is a classic example. Not too long ago it was allied with the Soviet Union and, in the eyes of the Western imperialists, was a clear-cut example of a totalitarian state. But then it exchanged its neocolonial relationship with Soviet social-imperialism for a neocolonial relationship with Western imperialism – and, presto, totalitarianism has vanished from Somalia. At the same time, the regime in Ethiopia underwent the very opposite transformation. Of course, for its part, the Soviet bloc is quick to point to the glaring contradictions in all this to ridicule the notion of the "free world," to discredit the claims of the Western powers to be the great upholders of freedom and democracy, and to portray the Soviet Union and its allies as the true defenders of the fullest democracy, attaining its highest expression in the "realistic socialism" (i.e., social-imperialism) found in the Soviet Union (and wherever else the Soviet rulers say it exists at any given time).[18]

That the essence and most fundamental aspect of the conflict between the Western and Soviet blocs is not an ideological battle between freedom and totalitarianism – or between communism

17. This calls to mind the distinction drawn by Alexander Haig a few years back, when he was Secretary of State – a distinction between authoritarian regimes (those are the ones allied with the West and therefore part of the "free world") and totalitarian regimes (it is obvious what puts a state in this category).

18. Ethiopia and Somalia also provide a classic example of the Soviet twist to all this. As I've already had occasion to note, there

> has been the increasing spectacle of bourgeois and reactionary forces that are aligned with the Soviet bloc in the Third World donning the mantle of Marxism-Leninism. The essence of this was starkly and somewhat comically exposed in recent years with the game of "musical Marxist-Leninist" that was played by the Soviet social-imperialists in the Horn of Africa (when the music stops – when the alignments change – change the Marxist-Leninist label from one head to another). For a while the military dictatorship in Somalia was aligned with the Soviet bloc so it got to be called "Marxist-Leninist"; then there was a changing of partners (blocs), with Somalia going over to the U.S. bloc and Ethiopia, Somalia's adversary, switching to the Soviet side, so now the Dergue in Ethiopia gets to be called "Marxist-Leninist." (*Harvest of Dragons*, p. 149)

and capitalism – can be gleaned from the alliance of the Western imperialists with China against the Soviet Union (both of which these Western imperialists call "communist-run countries" – but neither of which *is* any longer). But posing a few pointed questions to the imperialists, on both sides, can also help to make clear that this conflict arises from the underlying logic – the basic dynamic of accumulation – of the capitalist system itself.

You, Messrs. "democrats of the free world," excuse what crimes you cannot deny commiting and justify what cannot be concealed about this "free world" by insisting that such things are necessary to defeat the real source of evil – Soviet totalitarian imperialism. But when England first began plundering Egypt and India, when France began looting Africa, when the USA slaughtered tens of thousands of Filipinos in betrayal of the promise of national independence...when all this and an almost endless list of similar depredations was being carried out, all the way up to the first of your international slaughterfests, the First World War – how could the Soviet Union be blamed, when it did not yet exist? When, even earlier, genocide against the native peoples in America (and Australia) was begun, when the trading in human flesh and the cruel exploitation of slave labor was first utilized to enrich Europe and America, how could this somehow be justified by the need to combat communist ideology when the *Communist Manifesto* had not yet been written – and in fact Karl Marx had not yet been born?

And you, Soviet masters of "socialist productivity" and "natural allies" of the anti-imperialist struggles in the world, attempt to explain many features of the Soviet Union and its actions in the world by pointing to the Western imperialists as the reason why such things are unavoidable. There is, of course, truth to the assertion that world imperialism has had a great deal to do with what has gone on inside the Soviet Union and with its role internationally – going back to the military invasion involving every major imperialist state in the Soviet Republic at its very inception. But since when does one fight against and defeat imperialism by emulating it? By restoring capitalism in the Soviet Union and transforming it into an imperialist state? Since when does one apply the lessons of Lenin's analysis of imperialism by adopting all the essential features of this system that Lenin outlined, as has happened with the Soviet Union since the mid-1950s?

Imperialism means the division of the world among the imperialist powers and the repeated struggle among them to redivide it. The rape and exploitation of the colonies is tightly interwoven with fierce rivalry among the imperialists. In this contest, different imperialist states tend to group together in alliances and blocs according to their particular interests. But a specific feature of the interimperialist rivalry of the last three decades has been that one imperialist bloc claims the mantle of socialism. Thus the struggle in the ideological realm between these two blocs – taking the appearance of a conflict between communism and imperialism, or democracy and totalitarianism (depending on which side is defining it) – has assumed some new and more complex features as an important, if overall secondary, aspect of the confrontation between them.

On the one hand, there is obviously a farcical aspect to the use of the labels "freedom" and "democracy" (to say nothing of "socialism" and "communism") as weapons in interimperialist rivalry. But it should be no less obvious that this is part of a deadly serious contest now approaching an Armageddian showdown. And, especially in the face of calls – and demands – to line up with one side or the other, it is crucial to grasp that when both sides speak of freedom and democracy (with whatever particular twists the one or the other gives to this), the reality they are upholding and preparing to defend at all costs is the reality of the horrors that have been spoken to here.

Monopoly and "Violations" or "Corruptions" of Democracy

As Lenin pointed out, the growth of monopolies and their dominant role in the economy – "the displacement of capitalist free competition by capitalist monopoly" – is one of the most essential features of imperialism.[19] Lenin also pointed out, however, that "At the same time the monopolies, which have grown out of free competition, do not eliminate the latter, but exist above it and alongside it, and thereby give rise to a number of very acute, intense antagonisms, frictions and conflicts."[20] One of the main political and ideological manifestations of this is the tendency,

19. Lenin, "Imperialism," *LCW*, 22, p. 265.
20. Lenin, "Imperialism," *LCW*, 22, p. 266.

basically reflecting the viewpoint of smaller-scale capitalists and propertyholders (or those aspiring to this position), to see the concentration of tremendous wealth and power among a very small circle as a departure from the basic principles of the system, as a "violation" or a "corruption" of democracy as they believe it once was – or at least was intended to be – practiced. In saying this I do not mean to imply that all, or even most, of those who articulate this view in some systematic way are themselves small businessmen or propertyholders and that their expression of this view is marked by the most narrow calculations of personal business fortunes. Often that is far from the case, and what is involved is the musing, and not infrequently the agonizing, of intellectuals over what they perceive as the almost inevitable abuse of wealth and power when it is concentrated in too few hands. Here it is very helpful to recall Marx's statement that one must not imagine

> that the democratic representatives are indeed all shopkeepers or enthusiastic champions of shopkeepers. According to their education and their individual position they may be as far apart as heaven from earth. What makes them representatives of the petty bourgeoisie is the fact that in their minds they do not get beyond the limits which the latter do not get beyond in life, that they are consequently driven, theoretically, to the same problems and solutions to which material interest and social position drive the latter practically. This is, in general, the relationship between the *political* and *literary representatives* of a class and the class they represent.[21]

An illustration of the basic point here is provided in the book *Media Monopoly,* whose author, Ben Bagdikian, after describing in considerable detail, over the course of the book as a whole, many of the ways in which large corporations exert control over the media, attempts to point toward a remedy in his concluding chapter, "To Undo Excess" – itself a revealing title. Bagdikian poses the problem this way: "If a nation has narrowly controlled information it will soon have narrowly controlled politics."[22] And as for where hope for a solution may lie, Bagdikian argues:

> Each generation has to establish its own priorities and reinvigorate the best principles of the society. This generation is no

21. Marx, "The Eighteenth Brumaire of Louis Bonaparte," *MESW*, 1, p. 424.
22. Bagdikian, *Media Monopoly,* p. 226.

different. By raising small, minority voices today, this generation, like the Jeffersonians 180 years ago, can produce a change that will strengthen American democracy and validate the principle of a truly informed consent as the basis for a free society.[23]

Fundamentally speaking, what has already been gone into in this book, not only on Jeffersonian democracy in particular but on the ideal and reality of democracy in general, should make clear what is wrong with the above view. But it is also important to recall here that, even at the time of the founding of the USA, there were very great class divisions within the country and, as Howard Zinn has pointed out, it was overwhelmingly representatives of the upper classes—"men of wealth, in land, slaves, manufacturing, or shipping"[24]—who led the American Revolution and framed the *Constitution* of the new state; it was these upper classes that, above all, benefited from that Revolution and that ruled the new state. To argue now that a monopoly of wealth and power constitutes a "violation" or "corruption" of the democratic principles on which countries like the USA are founded is, in reality, to come right up to the point of having to recognize that from the beginning and of necessity the actual content given to these principles has been rule by the rich, with real democracy among its ranks only and dictatorship exercised over the poor and exploited classes.[25] If a small group of monopolists effectively dominates the political — as well as the economic — life of the USA in this era, then what must be said of the situation 200 years ago, keeping in mind not only what has just been pointed out concerning the class position and interests of the "founding fathers" but also the fact, pointed out earlier, that at the time a majority of the people "governed" in the USA were, literally, disenfranchised? But it is precisely from drawing the necessary conclusion from all this that antimonopoly democrats pull back.

My point here is not that there is no significant difference be-

---

23. Bagdikian, *Media Monopoly*, p. 238.

24. Zinn, *People's History of the U.S.*, p. 89.

25. In this light it is both interesting and somewhat ironic that de Tocqueville, who romanticized early U.S. society and glossed over its great inequalities of wealth and power, actually expressed the concern that in the future what he called "an aristocracy created by manufactures" might arise and constitute a serious threat to democracy. (See de Tocqueville, *Democracy in America*, Vol. 2, Second Book, chapter 20: "How an Aristocracy May Be Created by Manufactures.")

tween the USA of 200 years ago and the USA of this era, that there is no qualitative difference between capitalism and monopoly capitalism (imperialism). The point is exactly that what is urgently required is not to seek to go back to an idealized past where bourgeois society was, supposedly, not riddled with class antagonism and not ruled by an oppressive minority – it is to go forward, utilizing the conditions brought into being by capitalism, and, yes, by monopoly, to overthrow this system and advance to a whole new era in world history. Lenin noted how with the development of capitalism into monopoly capitalism–imperialism around the turn of the century,

> a petty-bourgeois-democratic opposition to imperialism arose . . . in nearly all imperialist countries. . . .
>
> In the United States, the imperialist war waged against Spain in 1898 stirred up the opposition of the "anti-imperialists", the last of the Mohicans of bourgeois democracy, who declared this war to be "criminal", regarded the annexation of foreign territories as a violation of the Constitution, declared that the treatment of Aguinaldo, leader of the Filipinos (the Americans promised him the independence of his country, but later landed troops and annexed it) was "Jingo treachery", and quoted the words of Lincoln: "When the white man governs himself, that is self-government; but when he governs himself and also governs others, it is no longer self-government; it is despotism." But as long as all this criticism shrank from recognizing the inseverable bond between imperialism and the trusts, and, therefore, between imperialism and the foundations of capitalism, while it shrank from joining the forces engendered by large-scale capitalism and its development [i.e., the proletariat – B.A.] – it remained a "pious wish".[26]

26. Lenin, "Imperialism," *LCW*, 22, p. 287.

6

Bourgeois Socialism
and Bourgeois Democracy

*A frail old man with hair swirling above his head in an incongruous
white pompadour stands alone under a spotlight in the center of the
stage and shrugs his shoulders with infinite weariness.*

*"Oh, maybe it's not worth it," he says. "Maybe we should just keep
silent tonight. We're all so good at keeping silent, and they say silence is
golden. I could, for instance, just keep my mouth shut tonight for three
hours plus the intermission. That way, we won't take any risks."*

*Another shrug. A supreme effort. "Or maybe we could just talk
about . . . no, better not to talk about that," he says. "Or, let's say, about,
about. . . . No, about that people are keeping silent these days on every
street corner."*

*By this time the audience is laughing in recognition, and, of course,
the old man does not keep silent.*

The above are the opening paragraphs from an article in the *New
York Times*. The *Times* apparently finds this story "fit to print"
because the comedian described is a *Soviet* comedian, Arkady
Raikin. The *Times* reports, with an appropriate tone of wonder-
ment, that

Mr. Raikin, who is a Jew, is not only popular with audiences, he
has been honored by the authorities. In 1968 he was given the

coveted title of People's Artist of the U.S.S.R. In 1980 he won a
Lenin Prize, and three years ago he was made a Hero of Socialist
Labor, the nation's highest civilian award.

His programs of skits and monologues play to full houses that
sometimes include members of the ruling Politburo, and his role
has broadened from that of stand-up comic to that of a leading
social critic in a country where social criticism is not an easy or
politically safe pastime.[1]

This last line is the punch line: the "angle" of this article is that
routines like Raikin's about "keeping silent" would meet with
laughter (a sort of nervous laughter at first) only in a place like the
Soviet Union, where people are hesitant – not to say terrified – to
voice dissenting opinions or make remarks critical of the government, especially in public. But is it not striking that the opening
paragraphs quoted above could easily be describing a scene in the
U.S. or any of the other "industrial democracies" of the West?

In actuality, the picture that is monotonously painted in the
West of the Soviet Union (and its "satellite states") – that what
exists there is a grey monolith where no one dare complain about
anything and where there is not even any significant semblance
of democracy – is a crude distortion. As another, perhaps more
dramatic, illustration of this, consider the following:

Imagine for a moment that a top U.S. nuclear scientist, a "father of
the H-bomb"-type like Edward Teller, suddenly came out for the
Soviet Union. Suppose that this scientist took to publicly encouraging the Soviets, in order to "correct the strategic balance," to
deploy SS-20 missiles all over Eastern Europe and to build a new
first-strike-capable ICBM as soon as possible. Imagine that this
scientist greets Soviet chief of state Chernenko, praising the
economic and military power of the Soviet Union and exhorting
the Soviets to "carry with honor the burden that history has placed
on her citizens and leaders." Imagine that this scientist became a
hero in all the Soviet-bloc countries, with the Soviet government
officially warning the U.S. to keep its hands off of him. Then imagine, if you can, the treatment that this scientist would have suffered in this country, assuming of course that he survived.

Reverse this tale, make the scientist a Soviet citizen, father of
the Soviet bomb, and a current hero-of-the-West, and you have the

1. "Comic's Wicked Wit Keeps Russians Tickled Pink," *New York Times,* 11
October 1984.

true story of the Soviet Union's best-known dissident, physicist Andrei D. Sakharov.[2]

Bourgeois Dictatorship, Revisionist Democracy

This is not to say that the Soviet Union (or any of the other Eastern European countries) is exactly like the Western imperialist democracies, including in how repression is carried out and dissent dealt with. There are differences, some of them significant. But what is the same is what is most fundamental: in both cases, the state is a bourgeois dictatorship while there are forms of democracy that play an important part in "legitimizing" and maintaining a base of support for the regime, and the class in power claims that its state represents the highest possible expression of democracy. As for the differences, besides the most obvious one—that the Soviet Union and its bloc still claim the mantle of socialism, while in fact capitalism has been restored in the Soviet Union and state capitalism characterizes the Soviet bloc—these are well outlined, in basic terms, in the following summation:

> Despite the convergences, the Soviet state is not a bourgeois democracy out of the Western imperialist mold. In a nutshell, we could say that Soviet democracy lacks any institutionalized decision making by the masses, even in the sham sense of U.S.-style elections. There are far less civil liberties and dissent is much more constricted—though the greater liberalism in the West may be due at least as much to its greater share of the plunder in the Third World, and consequent higher living standards, as it is to the historically given shape of the bourgeois-democratic institutions. On the other hand, the Soviet masses are drawn into participation in administration of social and economic life to a much more extensive degree than are workers in the West.
>
> The particular form of bourgeois dictatorship in the Soviet Union, then, does manifest a number of distinctive differences from the typical bourgeois-democratic forms of the West. We will call the Soviet form "revisionist democracy."[3]

2. "The Darling of the Western World," *Revolutionary Worker*, No. 273 (21 September 1984).

3. Lenny Wolff and Aaron Davis, "Notes Toward an Analysis of the Soviet Bourgeoisie," *Revolution*, No. 52 (Summer 1984), p. 20. For an all-around analysis of the bourgeois and imperialist nature of the Soviet Union and its bloc (and debate with defenders of the Soviet Union), see *The Soviet Union: Socialist or Social-Imperialist?*, Parts I and II (Chicago: RCP Publications, 1983).

The distinctions pointed to here are important to keep in mind in order to see beyond appearance and to the essence of the state and its relation to the nonruling classes in both blocs. It is not accidental—nor merely the result of a peculiar and petty obtuseness—that, in response to the raising of the "Sakharov issue" by Western leaders (including very directly by President Mitterrand of France, during a visit to the Soviet Union not long ago), one of the main tacks of the Soviet leaders has been to point to the large numbers of unemployed in the Western countries and smugly declare: there is the real violation of human rights. The Soviet revisionist bourgeoisie (Marxist-Leninist in word, capitalist-imperialist in fact), in order to maintain its "socialist" cover and deal with its particular present-day exigencies, is especially concerned to pose as the champion of—or the paternalistic "deliverer" to—"The Workers." And its vision of the quintessential Worker is one who is remarkably like those imperialist-fattened, hidebound kulaks-on-concrete who have been seen, hard-hats on head, American flags in hand, lumbering and bellowing after anti-establishment demonstrators in the U.S. (for example, during the Vietnam War), attacking them in the name of apple-pie Americanism—in other words, remarkably like those thoroughly bourgeoisified Blue Collars glorified by the ruling class in the U.S. these days.[4] While they may not be able to grant Soviet Archie Bunkers the same wage level as their counterparts in the U.S., the Soviet rulers are concerned to insure that they receive many benefits—housing subsidies, medical treatment, and not the least, job security—that equal or even exceed what the bourgeoisified strata of workers in the West get. And more generally, the Soviet state pays more attention than even the social-democratic imperialist regimes in the West to such questions as employment and the basic life requirements of the workers, even the non-bourgeoisified workers, and to workers' "involvement" in the func-

---

4. It may be ironic that one of the groups that is most strongly anti-Soviet in the U.S. (and some other Western countries)—the more hard-core aristocrats of labor—would, if they were living in a Soviet-style regime, be among the groups whose position might well improve and who might then be more inclined to support such a regime.

But where such a prospect fails to move such people to be more pro- (or at least less anti-) Soviet, this is largely explainable by the fact that the question of what benefits they might receive if the Soviet imperialist bloc, instead of the Western imperialist bloc, had the dominant position in the world and they were living under its rule, is an abstraction difficult for them to conceive of and not exercising the same attraction as the concrete privileges they are granted by virtue of living in the actually dominant Western bloc.

tioning of economic and social life, especially through the trade union apparatus, which itself functions as part of the state machinery, keeping the workers in line.

All this provides the context for the statement cited earlier – on the similarities and differences in the use of psychiatry and "drug therapy" for repressive purposes in the West and the Soviet bloc – a statement worth citing again here for its broad implications:

> It is important to see that it was not so much that the Soviet pro-testers were being punished for their protest, although they them-selves clearly believed that they were. Rather, the state seemed concerned to *invalidate* a social and political protest by declaring the protesters to be *invalids,* sick, in need of care and protection to cure them of their delusions that there were any blemishes on the features of the Soviet state. But we would argue that the forensic and other psychiatrists who are asked to diagnose the disease of the Soviet protesters are not behaving very differently from their counterparts in the West. Perhaps the chief difference lies in that while the most common candidates for psychiatric hospitalization in the West are drawn from among the working class, women, or ethnic minority people who find it hard to locate a megaphone to speak their troubles to the waiting media world, the Soviet intelli-gentsia who have been hospitalized are neither inarticulate nor dispossessed.[5]

As a general characterization, while (as shown in the story on the Soviet comedian) the Soviet revisionist bourgeoisie is also capable of co-opting some criticism and dissent among the intelli-gentsia in the Soviet bloc, there is less room for departure from the official line – less *laissez faire* in relation to the intelligentsia – and much less room for the freedom of the small entrepreneur than in the West. But there is more relative weight given to the employment, health, and welfare of the workers, and there is considerably more institutionalized "grass roots" involvement in enterprises and other spheres of economic and social life.

With the above as a general background, let's turn to the theoretical formulations of the Soviet revisionists on the ques-tions of democracy, the state, and revolution. In *For a Harvest of Dragons,* while focusing to a considerable extent on other aspects

5. Lewontin, Rose, and Kamin, *Not In Our Genes,* p. 166.

of Soviet revisionist theory, I also emphasized—and illustrated through examining some representative passages in major Soviet works of political theory and philosophy—how these so-called "Marxist-Leninists" have revised, repudiated in fact, the basic Marxist-Leninist understanding of the nature of the state and the need for a violent revolution to overthrow the dictatorship of the bourgeoisie and establish the dictatorship of the proletariat as the necessary form of state through which to carry forward the struggle, worldwide, for communism. Further, I emphasized how, along with this, instead of pointing and leading the way beyond the confines of the bourgeois ideals of democracy and equality, they have sought to act as the true champions of these ideals.[6] Here I will return specifically to the question of the state and revolution, and in particular to the views of the Soviet revisionists on the transition from capitalism to socialism and whether or not this transition can be made peacefully. In many ways, this concentrates extremely important and essential differences between revolutionary communism and Soviet revisionism, including on the decisive question of democracy and its relation to the struggle to advance beyond the capitalist to the communist epoch.

As a general guideline, it is helpful to turn to a statement made by Lenin in the course of polemicizing against the revisionists of his time on this touchstone question of the state and revolution: "Dialectics are replaced by eclecticism—this is the most usual, the most widespread practice to be met with in present-day official Social-Democratic literature in relation to Marxism."[7] And as a focus for examining modern-day revisionist eclectics (the attempt to mix together and reconcile things that are in contradiction with each other) and the overall line which they serve on the state and revolution, we can turn to a major Soviet study, *The Political Economy of*

---

6. This can be seen, for example, in the statement by M. A. Suslov (see chapter 1, n. 4) as well as in the treatment of the question of equality in a major book by two other leading Soviet theoreticians. After stating, correctly, that "Marxism has never insisted on the possibility and the need for the individual equality," they then twist this around, turning it back on itself, so that the conclusion is that Marxism is the same as bourgeois democracy—that it "has always stood only for equal opportunities of development for all" (V. Kelle and M. Kovalson, *Historical Materialism: An Outline of Marxist Theory of Society* [Moscow: Progress Publishers, 1973], p. 119). Here it seems unnecessary to repeat all that has been said about how equality in general and "equal opportunity" in particular are categories of bourgeois right.

7. Lenin, "The State and Revolution," *LCW,* 25, p. 405.

Revolution, in particular its fourth chapter, "Democracy."[8]

The author of this study, K. Zarodov, is at great pains to answer the accusation that the line of the Communist Party of the Soviet Union (CPSU) and its "fraternal parties" represents the negation of democracy and that the coming to power of a Soviet-style

---

8. Not surprisingly, the same kind of eclectics will be found to characterize the statements of the Communist Party, USA on the questions of the state and revolution, of democracy, and of the possibility of constitutional – that is, peaceful – transition to socialism. For example, in its 1970 *New Program of the Communist Party,* it says that socialism in the U.S.

> will extend democracy to its fullest, taking as its starting point the democratic traditions and institutions of the American people. We believe and advocate that within the framework of building and defending socialism, a socialist society in our country will guarantee all the liberties defined in the Bill of Rights but never adequately realized in life....
>
> Indeed, the freedoms in the Bill of Rights will take on far greater meaning for the great majority, who will now own the meeting halls, press, radio and television, and will be able to exercise that freedom effectively. But socialism does not provide freedom for everybody and everything. It is not anarchism. It provides no freedom for racist or anti-Semitic practices and advocacy. Nor does it provide freedom for advocacy of a return to capitalist exploitation and class society (*New Program of the Communist Party* [New York: New Outlook Publishers, 1970], pp. 103-104).

Note that the ideas that the framers of this document fear may be controversial, such as not allowing freedom to advocate a return to capitalism, are "sweetened" and "set up" by making a reference first to a more "acceptable" bourgeois-democratic article of faith among those to whom the document is addressed. But, along with this, it should be pointed out that this statement is full of assertions that contradict each other: above all, it is impossible to uphold the U.S. *Constitution's* "Bill of Rights" and to take as a starting point "the democratic traditions and institutions of the American people" and proceed to build socialism and prevent people from advocating – and in fact carrying out – a return to capitalist exploitation. As discussed earlier, this "Bill of Rights" and these "democratic traditions and institutions" are expressions of and can only serve capitalism and bourgeois class dictatorship; to abolish capitalist exploitation, and to formulate laws and develop policies that restrict the right to advocate (and prevent counterrevolutionaries from carrying out) capitalist restoration, it is necessary to criticize and move beyond these bourgeois-democratic principles, conventions, and institutions.

Further, in this 1970 *New Program,* the CPUSA goes to great lengths to stress the possibility of peaceful transition (though it does not rule out violence altogether; violent resistance might be put up by big capitalists as a people's government moves to institute socialism after having curbed the monopolies, this *New Program* explains, and this violence would have to be forcibly suppressed). But as for the *necessity* of a violent *revolution* to *overthrow* the *bourgeois dictatorship* – this is not to be found in this *New Program.* And a year after this *New Program* came out, the CPUSA published a pamphlet entitled "How Socialism Will Come to the United States, the Viewpoint of the Communist Party," which never once mentioned the "possibility" of armed revolution. Even more striking is the argument that was actually contained in the 1968 "Draft" of the CPUSA's *New Pro-*

regime represents the death-knell of democracy. He replies:

> Communist parties in Italy, France, Spain, Japan and other
> developed capitalist countries, like those in the former colonies
> and semicolonies, hold democracy to be of paramount impor-
> tance. Prominent communist activists and scholars elaborate the
> question in a score of books and pamphlets.

All of which exonerates the revolutionary communist [sic]

---

gram – that peaceful transition to socialism in the USA has a precedent: "the Constitutional Amendment abolishing slave property, which in its day was just as
sacrosanct as capitalist property is today" ("Draft" of the *New Program* of the
CPUSA [1968], p. 97). Here these revisionists have not only forgotten the Civil
War and the hundreds of preceding slave revolts that were necessary before
slavery was abolished – an abolition that was *formalized* in a Constitutional
Amendment. They have also "forgotten" that even this abolition of slave property
represented the replacement of one system of exploitation by another and not the
complete abolition of all exploitation that is achieved through the socialist revolution – a revolution that obviously must be much more deepgoing than all previous
ones – a revolution that must involve the two radical ruptures spoken of by Marx
and Engels in the *Communist Manifesto* (the radical rupture with all traditional
property relations and with all traditional ideas).

While this particular formulation was eventually dropped and did not appear
when the CPUSA's *New Program* was published in 1970, this was not out of any
summation that the notion of peaceful transition to socialism is, after all, opportunist. The dropping of this perhaps embarrassing formulation (*perhaps* embarrassing for the *CPUSA*) was itself part of an overall opportunism, above all the attempt to peddle the "possibility" of peaceful transition. Indeed, the CPUSA, which
has an almost unblemished record (and I don't know of any blemishes at all on it)
for slavishly tailing whatever line comes out of the Soviet Union, had first openly
trumpeted the notion of peaceful transition as far back as the mid-'50s, following
the lead of Khrushchev (then head of the Soviet party and state), with his "three
peacefuls" (peaceful coexistence with the imperialist states, peaceful competition
with capitalism, and peaceful transition to socialism). Thus, in a "Draft
Resolution" prepared for its 16th National Convention in 1957, we read that "the
new world situation and its impact on all countries" had led to "profoundly important and qualitatively new elements" being introduced "into the body of Marxist
theory by Marxists of many countries." Examples?

> For example, we as well as other Marxist parties have already discarded as
> obsolete Lenin's thesis that war is inevitable under imperialism. We have
> long since rejected as incorrect Stalin's thesis of the alleged law of in-
> evitable violent proletarian revolution. Likewise, we are making impor-
> tant modifications in the theory of the state, as evidenced in our advocacy
> of the peaceful, constitutional path to socialism." ("Draft Resolution," p. 56)

Although since that time – and particularly in the last ten years or so – some of the
more blatant language of revisionism contained in resolutions such as this has
been toned down, and some of the formulations eclectically "modified," to leave
more opening for the "possibility" of having to use some violence to achieve
socialism, this too has only been a tactical adjustment in the service of a
thoroughly opportunist, counterrevolutionary line set by the leaders of the

movement of the charge, laid by its opponents, of "contempt" for democracy. For Communists, as we have seen, the problems, role and future of democracy in the struggle for the new, socialist society carry great weight indeed.[9]

And in returning to and reemphasizing this point, he polemicizes against the argument he characterizes as follows:

> Bourgeois ideologists claim that socialist reconstruction is nothing more than the antithesis to democracy. By fair means and foul, they belittle and even discount the role played by the revolutionary forces of the working class, the Communists' fight to assert and extend the people's democratic rights and freedoms. With their reformist colleagues, they chant variations on one and the same theme: revolutionary Communists believe society is transformed through armed force alone, ergo communist parties can have no vested interest in consistently defending democracy and its institutions. No sooner does the revolutionary vanguard of the working people come to power, concludes the chorus, than democracy is doomed. By way of proof, they twist the policies pursued by the victorious socialist revolutions into "antidemocratic repressive" measures.[10]

The key phrases in the passage above are "assert and extend the people's democratic rights and freedoms" and "consistently defending democracy and its institutions." For this author – like Soviet theoreticians generally – attempts to portray democracy

---

CPUSA in pursuit of their own bourgeois aims – and those of their Soviet patrons. Thus it is that the latest *New Program* of the CPUSA continues to put emphasis on the possibility of peaceful transition to socialism. (See *New Program of the Communist Party, USA* [New York: New Outlook Publishers, 1982], especially pp. 55-56.)

9. K. Zarodov, *The Political Economy of Revolution* (Moscow: Progress Publishers, 1981), p. 172. It is not possible here to thoroughly discuss the far-reaching implications of the phrase *"former* colonies and semicolonies" in the statement quoted above (emphasis added here). The use of such a formulation is part of the broader Soviet line that effectively negates colonialism in the form of *neo*colonialism – a negation that is convenient, not to say necessary, for the Soviet socialimperialists, who are the latest neocolonialists themselves, having perhaps learned some of the tactics of this from the USA, which has widely implemented neocolonialism in place of old-line, open colonialism in the period after World War 2 (though it continues to enforce old-line colonialism in such places as Puerto Rico). This basic Soviet line is examined at greater length in *For a Harvest of Dragons,* in particular in the first section of chapter 3, pp. 122-24.

10. Zarodov, *Political Economy of Revolution,* p. 184.

under socialism as simply the full assertion and extension of democracy under capitalism, while at the same time he attempts to pose it as the opposite of bourgeois democracy. Thus, Zarodov writes that

> the radical reshaping of socio-economic relations begun by the October Revolution provided a material base for consummating the working people's democratic rights proclaimed by law. Furthermore, it instituted social freedoms unknown to capitalism, including, first and foremost, the freedom from man's exploitation by man. Thus, the October Revolution did more than assert genuine political democracy; it led the world in democratizing the very foundation of society, its system of socio-economic relations.[11]

Here is a classic example of what, in China when it was led by the revolutionary line of Mao Tsetung, was called "two-into-one": the attempt to merge together two things that are in fact locked in struggle with each other. In the above statement by Zarodov, there is no sense that, while there is a unity between socialist democracy and the advance to communism, this is a *unity of opposites,* and there is also—and in the final analysis most importantly—*conflict, struggle* between them. As Lenin explained, not only is it the case that democracy under socialism means democracy among the masses and dictatorship over the exploiters; but beyond that it means a struggle to uproot the conditions—material, political, ideological—that make exploitation and class division possible; and finally, the very advance and the ultimate victory of this struggle will lead to the elimination of democracy itself, its "withering away."[12] In opposition to this, to present things as Zarodov does—and even to reduce the fundamental question of transforming the entire economic base of society to eliminate classes to a question of "democratizing" the foundation of society—is to try to confine things strictly within the limits of bourgeois right, however much one pokes jabs at bourgeois democracy and claims to uphold socialist democracy. Thus, what Zarodov presents us is truly an example of the substitution of eclectics for dialectics, especially the substitution of reformist gradualism for the recognition of, and the orientation of

11. Zarodov, *Political Economy of Revolution,* p. 188.
12. See Lenin, "State and Revolution," *LCW,* 25, p. 460; see also chapter 5 of this book.

the whole revolutionary strategy toward, sudden upheavals and radical ruptures. To refer again to Lenin's *The State and Revolution,* what the Soviet revisionists present is only "a vague notion of a slow, even, gradual change, of absence of leaps and storms, of absence of revolution."[13]

The fundamental point here will become even clearer by turning more directly to how the question of achieving the transition from capitalism to socialism is dealt with. Zarodov weaves back and forth on the question of peaceful versus violent "socialist revolution," but through it all he puts the main emphasis on the notion that, as he phrases it, there is in contemporary capitalist societies "unprecedented scope for working through established democratic institutions" in seeking to make the transition to socialism. Zarodov thus feels compelled to write the following highly revealing passage:

> At this point, the reader may ask: where do we take issue with the proponents of some "special" democratic route to socialism? On the use of parliamentary means? No. On the inadmissibility of civil war? No again. We object to the tendency to put absolute value into the form (this applies especially to parliamentary democracy), to make it, that is, an end-in-itself, eclipsing the main issue, the essence of the transformation sought. We disagree with those who declare that peaceful revolutionary development is not merely the most desirable, but the *only* democratic, the *only* acceptable, route to socialism. We dispute the all but total identification of democratism in revolution with legality, the notion that a nation can achieve revolutionary progress within the bourgeois legal set-up, at both the democratic and the socialist stages.[14]

It might be tempting to merely point to and dismiss the obfuscating double-talk and eclectics here by repeating the remark Marx made about a point in another opportunist document: "let him understand who can."[15] But several specific assertions and formulations in the above statement are very valuable "teachers by negative example" (to use another important concept popularized in China when it was under Mao's leadership).

First, it should be noted that Zarodov states his agreement

---

13. Lenin, "State and Revolution," *LCW,* 25, p. 401.

14. Zarodov, *Political Economy of Revolution,* p. 190.

15. Marx, *Critique of the Gotha Programme,* p. 19.

with those who insist on the "inadmissibility of civil war." But then he says that the Soviet revisionists cannot agree with those who argue that peaceful transition is "not merely the most desirable" (with this Zarodov indicates agreement) but also the "only acceptable route to socialism." We will try to achieve our ends through adhering to bourgeois legality, Zarodov is saying, but we will not be bound by it. By "the inadmissibility of civil war," Zarodov specifically means that it is "inadmissible" for revolutionary forces to initiate a revolutionary civil war against the ruling bourgeois interests (and its supporters among the population); rather all efforts must be focused, according to this revisionist variant of bourgeois logic, on winning a majority through peaceful means and on using such peaceful means to get government positions and move (or nudge) society in the direction of socialism. But if the ruling bourgeois interests do not peacefully accede to this, if *they* initiate violence to resist such progress toward "socialism," then it is legitimate, even necessary, for the popular forces to use violence to resist this reactionary violence. So runs the revisionist scenario. Nowhere here, of course, does Zarodov even hint that the peaceful transition to socialism is "merely" an impossible illusion—actually he vigorously argues to the contrary throughout. Before pursuing this point in further depth, however, it is important to call attention to the fact that in the above passage the whole standard and framework that is presented—the criterion by which to judge things—is that of democracy. The argument is over what is true "democratism" and the target of the polemic is those who insist on identifying "democratism in revolution with legality." Legality is not the only true "democratism"—Zarodov is very firm on this. Yet one will search in vain for any statement that "democratism" is not the only true socialism—or that socialism is not, in its essence and end point, the only true "democratism"—that socialism is a transition to communism, to the abolition of classes and the withering away of...not only the state but, with it, democracy.

It may be argued—and it is generally argued by bourgeois-democratic apologists of Western imperialism, and some others—that the rulers of the Soviet Union are not, in any case, sincere in their professions of "democratism." But the truth is that in the ruling circles in Soviet society there is every bit as much belief in democratic principles, as they conceive of them, as there is belief in democratic principles, differently conceived of, in the ruling circles in the Western imperialist countries. In both cases, there is a mixture of cynical hypocrisy and sincere conviction – all conditioned by and corresponding to the same fundamental bourgeois class outlook and bias. If what is meant by this argument is that, in insisting on their adherence to – and their vision of – democracy, the Soviet revisionists and those who follow them are aiming at attracting social movements and forces to their banner and using these as leverage to pursue the objective of gaining power, this is certainly true (though it must also be pointed out at the same time that this is the purpose for which all bourgeois representatives have always raised the banners of freedom, democracy, equality, and so on – again, with a mixture of calculating realpolitik and of actual adherence to principle . . . bourgeois principle). How "democratism" fits into the overall strategy of the Soviet Union (and its followers) can be seen more clearly by focusing on what Zarodov chooses as a major case study: Chile under the Popular Unity Government of Salvador Allende, in which the Communist Party of Chile played a very influential role.

During its three-year existence, from the time of Allende's election in 1970 until the reactionary coup d'état in 1973, this Popular Unity Government was held up as a paramount example of the possibility of peaceful transition to socialism by the Soviet-line revisionist parties. And, amazing as it may seem, it is *still* upheld as such by these people. Zarodov writes, "As the Chilean Revolution demonstrates, under the mounting tension of the class struggle, bourgeois legality serves both the revolution and reaction."[16] This is truly an astounding assertion, given that it was precisely, from the beginning and throughout, the Popular Unity Government's attempt to carry out its program within the confines of bourgeois legality that handcuffed it and set it up for a coup. As a matter of fact, this program contained certain anti-imperialist measures and other reforms but did not represent a radical break with the whole imperialist framework, and certainly did not represent the socialist transformation of society. This may have represented, on the part of Allende, his actual belief in what was the extent of possible and desirable change, but on the part of the Communist Party of Chile it was linked to a strategy of using the Popular Unity Government as a means of putting pressure on the staunchly pro-U.S. Christian Democratic Party,

16. Zarodov, *Political Economy of Revolution*, p. 192.

with the aim of drawing it into an alliance with the Communist Party in a restructured state in which these revisionists (and ultimately their Soviet backers) would share power, for a period, with the Christian Democrats – backed, for their part, by the U.S. As explained in the book *Chile: An Attempt at "Historic Compromise,"* this is a part of a broader strategic orientation of the Soviet bloc:

> Even though the goal is always the same (regimes of state exploitation of the people with Soviet social-imperialism pulling the strings), the methods differ according to time and place. Where there is direct domination by the USSR, social-imperialism resorts to armed intervention (as in Czechoslovakia) to crush any attempt at independence or at subversion of state capitalism. In the regions where the domination of the other superpower, U.S. imperialism, is relatively weak, as in Africa and certain regions of Asia, state power is also seized through violence, even though the USSR acts in an underhanded manner. On the other hand, in Western Europe and in America, where U.S. influence predominates, it seems that the strategy is to avoid open challenge (for the time being) with U.S. imperialism and with the forces that are close to it and not to establish a "socialist" model of the Eastern European type. Instead, an alliance is forced with the populist sectors under United States' influence in order to infiltrate the government and state apparatus and engage in joint exploitation of the people together with the ruling circles or a section of them at the expense of the others. This is the precise mission the pro-Soviet so-called communists had (and still have) to accomplish in Chile. From there stems their active promotion of the line of "peaceful road", preventing any mobilization of the people aimed at blocking the road to the reactionary offensive.[17]

It is for these reasons that, from the beginning and even in the face of the mounting offensive by the reactionary forces (with the full backing of U.S. imperialism) during the latter days of the Allende government, the Soviet-camp revisionists continued to insist on the "peaceful road" in Chile – and to hold Chile up as a "model" of this "road." Thus:

> In 1970, on the eve of the election of the Popular Unity government in Chile, headed by Salvador Allende, Castro wrote an arti-

---

17. Jorge Palacios, "Introduction" to *Chile: An Attempt at "Historic Compromise,"* translated with permission of the author, U.S. edition (Chicago: Banner Press, 1979), p. 21.

cle in a revisionist journal in Chile citing that country as an example of the possibility of the electoral path to socialism. Later, during the Allende government and specifically when its reformist "peaceful road to socialism" was increasingly showing itself incapable of really carrying out a radical transformation of society, the Cuban leaders emphatically stated that there was no alternative to this "road" in Chile.

This stand was not determined by loyalty to Allende – nor certainly to the advance to socialism, by peaceful or any other means – but served the aims of the revisionist Communist Party of Chile, which was using its extensive, even dominant, influence in the Popular Unity government as leverage to seek an "agreement" with the Christian Democratic Party that would bring about not socialism but a form of state capitalism in which the Communist Party, and the Soviet Union behind it, would gain a significant stronghold. It is this which explains why these revisionists consistently restrained the struggle of the masses, even supporting the armed forces in disarming the masses and calling on the masses not to resist with arms the reactionary coup d'etat that brought a bloody end to the Allende period. It was the aims of the Chilean Communist Party and the Soviet social-imperialists behind them – who did not want a direct confrontation with U.S. imperialism and its henchmen in this situation – that the Cuban leaders, who by now had become unapologetic apologists for Soviet social-imperialism and its bloc, were consistently supporting and promoting. All this is a very important negative experience whose profound lessons must be fully grasped.[18]

But, of course, any lessons for revolution that can be derived from this experience will have to be grasped by someone other than the Soviet-camp revisionists. For their part, and in accordance with their counterrevolutionary nature and objectives, they are still insisting – and for the reasons indicated above will continue to insist, at least until they are involved in an all-out confrontation with Western imperialism – that "the most important lesson to be learned from the Chilean events is that neither road to revolution – through force of arms or peaceful means – should be raised to an absolute value."[19]

18. *Basic Principles for the Unity of Marxist-Leninists and for the Line of the International Communist Movement* (a draft position paper for discussion prepared by the Revolutionary Communist Party of Chile and the Revolutionary Communist Party, USA, 1981), paragraphs 97-98. (Distributed by RCP Publications, Chicago; also available in French and Spanish editions.)

19. Zarodov, *Political Economy of Revolution*, p. 195.

[margin text, rotated: METHODOLOGY OF U.S. COURTS]

Nor are these revisionists deterred by the fact that their line runs counter to the fundamental principles of Marxism-Leninism and the whole of historical experience. Faced with this, they resort to two main devices: first they search through Lenin's works to find passages here and there that can be pieced together as a justification for their line (that can act as a thread holding together a threadbare rationalization); but then they argue that, in any case, there is new historical experience since Lenin's time that modifies or invalidates certain previously held theses, that "the substantial socio-economic structural changes now observed in many capitalist countries, together with massive realignments among the national and international class forces, offer revolutionaries unprecedented scope for working through established democratic institutions,"[20] even though the use of violence cannot be ruled out – and certainly has not been by the Soviet camp.

One of the main aspects of this, which involves the combining of the above-mentioned devices, is the notion that the development of monopoly capital has provided the basis both for a broad front of forces, uniting to defend democracy against the anti-democratic power of the monopolies, and for a greater possibility of peaceful transition to socialism. Thus, while stating that "the democratic movement and the socialist movement have different social bases – nothing can change this cold hard fact," and while warning against the illusion of the limitless possibilities offered by capitalist democracy, Zarodov hastens to make clear:

> This is not to say that economic and social shifts in the capitalist structure have no impact on democracy's potential in the socialist struggle. On the contrary, a broader democratic front, which is what monopoly economic tyranny leads to, can tip the balance towards socialist reconstruction. A democratic struggle involving a wide cross-section of society is an excellent and much-needed political training ground for the masses; here they become conscious of their true class interests and find their proper bearings in the fundamental conflict between labor and capital.
>
> On the other hand – and this is especially significant – the rising proportion of workers in the economically active population, the proletariat's key role in social production, its concentration in the leading branches of the economy, improved organization and greater influence, advance the democratic movement all the closer to the struggle for socialism. Marxist-Leninist parties now

20. Zarodov, *Political Economy of Revolution*, p. 189.

include these new avenues to socialism in their anti-monopoly strategy.[21]

And:

[E]xamples, drawn from real life and not some predetermined schema, illustrate democracy's potential for rallying the majority of the people to fight against the monopolies and for socialism. Indeed, nothing cements a broad people's alliance so well as democratic aspirations.[22]

Indeed, nothing makes clearer the nature of the aspirations these revisionists are attempting to appeal to and the nature of the "socialism" they are striving to bring people under – they are fundamentally, thoroughly bourgeois.

In the effort to justify (or, perhaps, sanctify) this line, Zarodov cites some statements by Lenin on how monopoly capital-imperialism represents the negation of democracy. In the very opening of this chapter on "Democracy," Zarodov begins with the bald assertion, "In the twentieth-century revolutionary process, the struggle for democracy and the struggle for socialism are indissolubly linked. This, indeed, is its salient feature."[23] And this is quickly followed by a quote from Lenin: "Imperialism is indisputably the 'negation' of *democracy in general*, of all democracy...."[24] It is true that Lenin did make such an analysis, particularly in his struggle against socialists who were altogether negating the importance of democratic demands – including but not limited to the right of nations to self-determination – and their relation to the struggle for socialism. It is also true that, in making the flat statement that imperialism represents the negation of democracy – and that democracy corresponds to free competition while political reaction corresponds to monopoly[25] – Lenin went overboard and was guilty of some exaggeration and one-sidedness. But people such as the Soviet revisionists, who claim to be (and in fact are) conversant with the works of Lenin as a

21. Zarodov, *Political Economy of Revolution,* p. 183.

22. Zarodov, *Political Economy of Revolution,* p. 177.

23. Zarodov, *Political Economy of Revolution,* p. 165.

24. Cited in Zarodov, *Political Economy of Revolution,* p. 165-66.

25. See, for example, Lenin, "A Caricature of Marxism and Imperialist Economism," *LCW,* 23, in particular p. 43, which is where the statement cited in Zarodov is found (see n. 24).

whole, cannot be excused as merely ignorant when they pretend that Lenin meant to argue for some kind of merging of the democratic and socialist struggles that might somehow make possible a safe "slide" into socialism, without the need for violent revolution. Not only did Lenin not make such ridiculous (and calculatingly eclectic) arguments as are embodied in the Soviet revisionist notion of a broad democratic front "tipping the balance towards socialist reconstruction"; he emphatically insisted, over and over, on the necessity of violent revolution to overthrow capitalism and establish socialism. Indeed, in the same time period that he made the statement quoted above, about monopoly capital representing the negation of democracy, Lenin wrote that "the liberation of the oppressed class is impossible not only without a violent revolution, *but also without the destruction* of the apparatus of state power which was created by the ruling class. . . . As we shall see later, Marx very explicitly drew this theoretically self-evident conclusion on the strength of a concrete historical analysis of the tasks of the revolution."[26] This is hardly an isolated statement by Lenin: not only is this same position repeatedly stressed throughout *The State and Revolution* — including, in one key passage, the hardly ambiguous observation that "the necessity of systematically imbuing the masses with *this* and precisely this view of violent revolution lies at the root of the *entire* theory of Marx and Engels"[27] — but it is also emphasized in many other works by Lenin, before and after the October Revolution, especially in his polemics against the revisionists of his day on this question.[28]

It is thus the crassest opportunism for the Soviet revisionists to raise, as an argument for the possibility of peaceful transition, the experience of the period between the February and October 1917 Revolutions in Russia, when there were circumstances in which the Bolsheviks "campaigned for 'peaceful revolutionary advance,'"[29] as Zarodov puts it. First of all, it is obvious that even the possibility of such "peaceful revolutionary advance" was based on the Tsar's regime having been overthrown through a violent uprising in February 1917. But beyond that, what did actual experience

26. Lenin, "State and Revolution," *LCW*, 25, p. 393.

27. Lenin, "State and Revolution," *LCW*, 25, p. 405.

28. See, for example, Lenin, "The Proletarian Revolution and the Renegade Kautsky," *LCW*, 28.

29. Zarodov, *Political Economy of Revolution*, p. 181.

demonstrate? It made undeniably clear once again what Lenin (and Marx and Engels before him) had concluded from previous historical experience: that a violent revolution is absolutely necessary to achieve the transition from capitalism to socialism (in Russia this meant not only armed insurrections in October 1917, but after that several years of warfare against "home-grown" counterrevolutionaries and imperialist armies in league with them).

Finally on this point, contrary to the claims of the Soviet revisionists, there is also no historical experience since Lenin's time – nor, more specifically, since World War 2 – which suggests that a peaceful transition to socialism is possible. In fact, not only has no genuine socialist revolution ever occurred except through the most arduous revolutionary warfare – as exemplified especially by the Chinese Revolution, as well as the Russian Revolution before it – but there are not even any governments in power that the Soviet revisionists themselves call "socialist" that have been able to seize and retain power without armed conflict[30] – except

30. As for the argument – which is made, at times at least, by the Soviet revisionists – that regimes in Eastern Europe (other than the Soviet Union itself) came to power peacefully in the aftermath of World War 2 and on the basis of the new international alignment of forces established through that war, two things must be said: first, these regimes were in fact established as a result of armed conflict on a massive level – they were established precisely through the victory of the Soviet Red Army in Eastern Europe (even if the actual coming to power of the new regimes took place a few years after the war); and second:

> The socialist camp that emerged from the Second World War was never solid. Little revolutionary transformation was carried out in most of the Eastern European Peoples' Democracies. In the Soviet Union itself powerful revisionist forces unleashed going into, in the course of, and in the aftermath of the Second World War grew in strength and influence. In 1956, following the death of Stalin, these revisionist forces led by Khrushchev succeeded in capturing political power, attacked Marxism-Leninism on all fronts and restored capitalism in that country. (*Declaration of the Revolutionary Internationalist Movement,* * p. 21)

Thus, there is certainly nothing in this experience which would indicate that the peaceful transition to socialism is possible.

*This *Declaration* was "adopted by the delegates and observers at the Second International Conference of Marxist-Leninist Parties and Organizations which formed the Revolutionary Internationalist Movement." The following are the participating parties and organizations of the RIM: Central Reorganisation Committee, Communist Party of India (Marxist-Leninist); Ceylon Communist Party; Communist Collective of Agit/Prop [Italy]; Communist Committee of Trento [Italy]; Communist Party of Bangladesh (Marxist-Leninist) [BSD(ML)]; Communist Party of Colombia (Marxist-Leninist), Mao Tsetung Regional Committee; Communist

perhaps the present regime in the Soviet Union itself, which came to power through a relatively bloodless coup in the mid-1950s and has since used only the "normal" repressive force of an established state to remain in power – all of which shows that, while it may be possible for revisionism to rise to power in certain circumstances without a major armed conflict (and certainly without revolutionary warfare), even this is not always possible, while the coming to power of a truly socialist regime is impossible without a violent revolution.

This brings us back to the essential point. The Soviet revisionists do not insist on the possibility of peaceful transition to socialism because they are opposed to violence – in principle or in practice. They do so because this line – leaving open the use of both peaceful and violent means to gain power, and often the combination of the two simultaneously – is a very important part of their overall drive to expand their sphere of influence and contend with the rival (and openly capitalist) imperialist bloc. On the other hand, these revisionists' professions of "democratism" – their insistence that Soviet democracy is the only true realization, and the highest possible expression, of democracy – are not merely a cynical deception: the bourgeoisie in the East is no less (and no more) a true believer in democracy than is its counterpart and rival in the West, but it believes in and seeks to implement a different form of the same bourgeois essence; its ideal is revisionist democracy, which is the particular form appropriate to the exercise of its bourgeois dictatorship.[31]

Party of Peru; Communist Party of Turkey/Marxist-Leninist; Haitian International Revolutionary Group; Nepal Communist Party [Mashal]; New Zealand Red Flag Group; Proletarian Communist Organization, Marxist-Leninist [Italy]; Proletarian Party of Purba Bangla (PBSP) [Bangladesh]; Revolutionary Communist Group of Colombia; Revolutionary Communist Party, USA; Revolutionary Communist Union [Dominican Republic]; Revolutionary Internationalist Contingent [Britain]; Union of Iranian Communists (Sarbedaran).

31. There is a kind of ironic twist to the claims of the Soviet revisionists (and in this they are joined by their Chinese counterparts and revisionists generally) that they are the true bearers of what are in actuality the bourgeois ideals of democracy, equality, and so on: in a sense these revisionists can also be said to be inheritors and present-day practitioners of the mechanical materialism of the early, rising bourgeoisie, complete with a worship of the machine, of perfect order and "clockwork-like efficiency." Of course, it is wrong – and the revisionists are wrong – to take the position that the traditional bourgeoisie found in the Western

The Theory of Totalitarianism and Its Political Role

The notion – or accusation – of totalitarianism is, as everybody knows, one of the main weapons in the ideological arsenal of Western imperialism in its conflict with the Soviet bloc. In recent times, with the ever-increasing intensity of the rivalry between these two imperialist blocs, and with the revival of some of the more virulent denunciations of the Soviet system as part of this – not as a reversion to the Cold War but as ideological preparation for literal, all-out confrontation between the two sides in what would be the most devastating of all wars in human history – the theme of Soviet totalitarianism has become much more prominent in the West. Like all ideological weapons, of course, this requires its theoretical justification; and while it is the more open – and often the more openly reactionary – spokesmen for Western imperialism who broadcast this denunciation for the broadest public consumption, it would be remiss not to recognize the important role of social-democratic (and generally bourgeois socialist) apologists of Western imperialism as purveyors of the concept of Soviet totalitarianism. Indeed, perhaps the two most influential works on the theme of totalitarianism are by people of this general political persuasion: *1984*, a popularly written novel by George Orwell, and *The Origins of Totalitarianism*, an abstruse attempt at scholarly dissertation by Hannah Arendt.

Before examining a number of the main arguments in these works – and in particular Arendt's, which, as its title implies, is an attempt to provide a theoretical analysis of the origins and nature of totalitarianism – it is worthwhile to briefly summarize what seem to be the basic premises of the theory of totalitarianism and to point to the origins and nature, that is, the political role, of this theory. This is not a scientific theory (at least not a scientifically correct one) but is a distortion of reality in the service of definite class interests and specific political objectives; it lacks even internal, logical consistency in the final analysis and is therefore difficult to summarize systematically. But a few major themes are

---

imperialist countries has abandoned, or is no longer capable of upholding, the banners of democracy and equality (and, for that matter, the efficient utilization of technology and organization of production); the revisionists are not the only upholders of bourgeois ideals and practitioners of bourgeois principles, but they certainly have as much claim to this as anyone else.

identifiable. The totalitarian state is just that—the total state—which means that the division between the state and private society (or the world of individuals) is obliterated. The totalitarian state reaches into and seeks to—it must—control every sphere, even the most personal. There can be no room for personal initiative, or even personal inclinations that are not manipulated by the state. The totalitarian state is not merely a one-party dictatorship, but the party itself is personified in the Leader, who is infallible. Terror, even terror utilized when there is no real threat to the regime, is an integral part of the totalitarian state; but equally important (and equally, if not more, terrifying to the antitotalitarian theorists) is ideology—that is, the systematic indoctrination of the populace with the official ideology and the absolute impermissibility of deviation from that ideology (at least among those groups in society that are considered worthy of concern). World domination and an apocalyptic vision of remaking not just society but people themselves, in their very nature, is seen as the ultimate goal of the totalitarians.

A few passages from Arendt's *Totalitarianism* should help to illustrate this:

> Totalitarianism is never content to rule by external means, namely, through the state and a machinery of violence; thanks to its peculiar ideology and the role assigned to it in this apparatus of coercion, totalitarianism has discovered a means of dominating and terrorizing human beings from within.

> Total domination does not allow for free initiative in any field of life, for any activity that is not entirely predictable. Totalitarianism in power invariably replaces all first-rate talents, regardless of their sympathies, with those crackpots and fools whose lack of intelligence and creativity is still the best guarantee of their loyalty.

> The chief qualification of a mass leader has become unending infallibility; he can never admit an error.

> Totalitarian domination, however, aims at abolishing freedom, even at eliminating human spontaneity in general, and by no means at a restriction of freedom no matter how tyrannical.

> The fanaticism of the elite cadres, absolutely essential for the functioning of the [totalitarian] movement, abolishes systematically all genuine interest in specific jobs and produces a mentality

which sees every conceivable action as an instrument for something entirely different. And this mentality is not confined to the elite but gradually pervades the entire population, the most intimate details of whose life and death depend upon political decisions—that is, upon causes and ulterior motives which have nothing to do with performance.

Total domination, which strives to organize the infinite plurality and differentiation of human beings as if all of humanity were just one individual, is possible only if each and every person can be reduced to a never-changing identity of reactions, so that each of these bundles of reactions can be exchanged at random for any other.

Total terror is so easily mistaken for a symptom of tyrannical government because totalitarian government in its initial stages must behave like a tyranny and raze the boundaries of man-made law. But total terror leaves no arbitrary lawlessness behind it and does not rage for the sake of some arbitrary will or for the sake of despotic power of one man against all, least of all for the sake of a war of all against all. It substitutes for the boundaries and channels of communication between individual men a band of iron which holds them so tightly together that it is as though their plurality had disappeared into One Man of gigantic dimensions. To abolish the fences of laws between men—as tyranny does—means to take away man's liberties and destroy freedom as a living political reality; for the space between men as it is hedged in by laws, is the living space of freedom. Total terror uses this old instrument of tyranny but destroys at the same time also the lawless, fenceless wilderness of fear and suspicion which tyranny leaves behind. This desert, to be sure, is no longer a living space of freedom, but it still provides some room for the fear-guided movements and suspicion-ridden actions of its inhabitants.

The struggle for total domination of the total population of the earth, the elimination of every competing nontotalitarian reality, is inherent in the totalitarian regimes themselves; if they do not pursue global rule as their ultimate goal, they are only too likely to lose whatever power they have already seized. Even a single individual can be absolutely and reliably dominated only under global totalitarian conditions.[32]

And so on.

32. Hannah Arendt, *The Origins of Totalitarianism* (New York: Harcourt Brace Jovanovich, 1973), pp. 325, 339, 348-49, 405, 409, 438, 465-66, and 392.

As will become clear, central to the whole outlook and methodology of the antitotalitarian theorists is the recasting and reinterpretation of events according to the a priori notions of their theory. This is a Procrustean outlook and methodology: anything which does not fit the theory, any event of world history which does not conform to and confirm its assumptions, is bent and mutilated to make it fit. These theorists are every bit as fanatical about this as the totalitarians portrayed in their writings. Perhaps a petty example will, ironically, help to give an inkling of this. You may think that the gimmicks and deceptions practiced by advertisers are explained by what they appear to be – the effort to promote the sale of products to realize profit (and to promote certain ideological objectives). But to the theoretician obsessed with totalitarianism, there is something far more sinister involved – a totalitarian urge – "there is a certain element of violence in the imaginative exaggerations of publicity men, that behind the assertion that girls who do not use this particular brand of soap may go through life with pimples and without a husband, lies the wild dream of monopoly, the dream that one day the manufacturer of the 'only soap that prevents pimples' may have the power to deprive of husbands all girls who do not use his soap."[33]

There is, however, a method to such madness, as Arendt displays here, and a deeper design. These antitotalitarians claim on the surface that traditional political distinctions of Left and Right are pushed into the background – indeed basically rendered irrelevant – by totalitarianism: "Practically speaking, it will make little difference whether totalitarian movements adopt the pattern of Nazism or Bolshevism, organize the masses in the name of race or class, pretend to follow the laws of life and nature or of dialectics and economics."[34] But when we look at the historical circumstances in which this theory has arisen and examine its main tenets in that light, it becomes clear that the target is really not Nazism (or Bolshevism, for that matter) but the Soviet bloc. This theory was developed in the context of World War 2, including the events of the late 1930s leading up to it and above all the situation that arose in its aftermath. It was not widely promoted (or the Soviet Union was not targeted in the same way it is now) during the period 1941-45, when the Soviet Union was allied

33. Arendt, *Totalitarianism*, p. 345.
34. Arendt, *Totalitarianism*, p. 313.

with the "Western democracies" against the fascist Axis (that is, German, Italian, and Japanese imperialism and their allies).[35] It was after the war that this theory was fully fertilized and blossomed forth. For the Soviet Union – and what was then a large and potentially very powerful socialist camp under its leadership – had emerged as the direct antagonist to imperialism in the West. (This became all the more the case, and this socialist camp was seen as all the more dangerous, after the victory of the Chinese Revolution in 1949.)

Thus, although theoretically the analysis of totalitarianism focused on the Soviet Union on the one hand, and Nazi Germany on the other, as the two embodiments of a whole new kind of state, posing an unprecedented threat to democracy, in reality the Soviet Union (and its bloc) were the targets of this analysis for the simple reason that Nazi Germany no longer existed – it had been defeated and had been born again, in the western part of Germany, as a democracy. It is in this light that one can understand the significance of Arendt's insistence on strictly distinguishing totalitarianism from other regimes that she generally describes as tyrannical or despotic dictatorships.

According to Arendt, fascist Italy was never really fully totalitarian.[36] Even in the case of Nazi Germany – and Arendt contrasts this with the Soviet Union – she says that at the start of World War 2 it "was not yet completely totalitarianized" and that "only if Germany had won the war would she have known a fully developed totalitarian rulership."[37] It is in this light as well that the significance of the following central argument by Arendt can be fully grasped: "Thus the fear of concentration camps and the resulting insight into the nature of total domination might serve to invalidate all obsolete political differentiations from right to left

35. There was, of course, a period when the imperialists of the USA, England, and France were trying to create a situation in which Germany would attack the Soviet Union and the two of them would fight it out while the "democratic states" sat it out – and then move in to clean up at the appropriate time (and this, by the way, was the real intent, and is the real lesson, of the Munich Pact entered into by England and France with Germany in 1938). In the U.S. such a strategy had adherents even after England (and, before its early defeat, France) were at war with Germany, beginning in the fall of 1939, but before the U.S. entered the war. Had it been possible for such a strategy to be fully and openly implemented throughout World War 2, then the totalitarianism theories would very likely have been given much greater promotion throughout that war.

36. See Arendt, *Totalitarianism*, pp. 308-309.

37. Arendt, *Totalitarianism*, pp. 409, 310.

and to introduce beside and above them the *politically most impor-*
tant yardstick for judging events in our time, namely: whether they
serve totalitarian domination or not."[38] Given that this statement
was made in 1950 – and keeping in mind Arendt's precise distinctions, as indicated just above – this "yardstick" serves as the basis
to single out the Soviet Union: it is "the focus of evil in the modern
world," to use the contemporary phrase. At the same time, this
"yardstick" serves to apologize for the many not-so-democratic
regimes that make up such a big part of the "free world," and, of
course, it also serves to prettify, and distract attention from, the
criminal nature of the Western imperialist democracies
themselves. This is the real content and political role of this
theory of "totalitarianism."

Let's turn, then, to some of the major pillars of this theory.
Right off, it must be observed that they are grounded in air: this
theory is based on idealist assumptions that ignore, deny, and/or
distort objective reality, and in particular the material foundation
of society and the state. To take the question of the state first, it is
important to recall what was discussed at some length earlier:
that the state is never some neutral force, nor can it ever insure
democracy for everyone – the state always represents one kind of
dictatorship or another. But it represents the dictatorship of a
class, not of a particular individual, group, party, or movement
that stands aside from – or above – class interest or is somehow
detached from the economic basis of society in which class relations are rooted. To quote again from Raymond Lotta's concise
summation on this point (made, significantly, in the course of a
debate on the nature of Soviet society today),

> the state is not some neutral instrument up for grabs, which can be
> forced or pressured to act in the interests of this or that class....
> The state is an objective structure of society whose character is
> determined not by the class origins of its leading personnel but *by*
> *the specific social division of labor of which it is an extension and the*
> *production relations which it must ultimately serve and reproduce.*[39]

It is precisely the point underlined above that the theory of
totalitarianism is (or pretends to be) ignorant of. Thus, certain formal similarities between Germany under Hitler and the Soviet

---

38. Arendt, *Totalitarianism,* p. 442, emphasis added.
39. Lotta, "Realities of Social-Imperialism," pp. 40-41, emphasis added.

Union in the period of Stalin's leadership are seized on to concoct a theory of a whole new kind of state, profoundly different not only from democracy but even from heretofore known kinds of open dictatorships (tyrannies, despotisms, autocracies, and so on). As we have seen, it is not merely the open declaration of authority by one party, nor even just the personification of party rule in the infallible Leader, nor yet the open suppression of enemies in the name of the ideals of the party and the will of the Leader, that is the essence of totalitarianism, as defined by these antitotalitarian theorists; it is above all the openly proclaimed and seriously intended objective of controlling and remaking the whole world, but more than that the people who make up human society – to change them in their very essence – not only in their social relations but also in their thinking, values, morals. . . even in their feelings and emotions.

Before speaking to the profound differences between "Hitler Germany" and "Stalinist Russia," it first seems necessary to indicate what of real substance was similar between them, in opposition to other world powers, in the crucial period in world history in which these two states existed – and which forms the world-historical matrix for the theory of totalitarianism: the period leading up to and extending through World War 2. This essential similarity is not just that both were in extremely difficult situations and driven to extreme measures – this was, or would become during this period, true of every world power – but that both were in a position to drastically alter the whole structure of power relations involving the European states (and the USA) – power relations in which Anglo-French (and American) interests dominated – and thereby to drastically alter the whole structure of power relations in the world in a way highly detrimental to Anglo-French-American interests. But there the similarity ends. Throughout this period, Germany was and remained nothing other than a bourgeois imperialist state, though it ruled at home not in the "classical" form of bourgeois democracy but through a fascist – an openly terroristic – form of bourgeois dictatorship. And, on the other hand, throughout this period the Soviet Union was and remained a socialist state, a dictatorship of the proletariat, although serious errors – it is not an exaggeration (or gratuitous) to say grievous errors – were made in how this dictatorship was carried out and the socialist system defended and extended.

This takes us back to the fundamental point underscored

(margin handwritten notes: "from 1917 & 1950s, USSR was a socialist state" and "MAO STALIN & the internal action/Boundary")

earlier: with all the peculiarities of Nazi Germany (including the "deviations" from "classical" capitalist economic policies), the underlying production relations, the division of labor, and the dynamics of accumulation were all those of capitalism, particularly capitalism in its imperialist stage; whereas in the Soviet Union in this same period, with all the difficulties encountered and mistakes made in carrying out and carrying forward the socialist transformation of society, the underlying production relations, the division of labor, and the accumulation process were those of socialism. While it must be stressed that socialism is a society *in transition to* communism and is still marked by many remnants and "defects" inherited from the old society, and, moreover, is a society fighting for its life against the forces of capitalist restoration, in the socialist country itself and internationally – all of which found very acute expression in the Soviet Union in the period leading up to and during World War 2 – this in no way eliminates the fundamental, qualitative difference between socialism and capitalism. Nor should certain secondary similarities obscure the fundamental, qualitative difference between the socialist Soviet Union under Stalin on the one hand and imperialist Nazi Germany (and, for that matter, England, France, and the United States, as well as other imperialist states – including the Soviet Union itself, after Stalin) on the other hand.

And this, in turn, takes us to another decisive dimension in which the antitotalitarians fly in the face of a scientific, materialist method and analysis of society. One of the most striking things about their concept of totalitarianism is how it almost entirely (if not literally and completely) eliminates any sense of contradiction and dynamic tension in the economic base in the alleged totalitarian society (whether it is capitalist or socialist, on the Right or the Left). This is very clear in Orwell's *1984,* where the ruling party elite (headed by or personified as Big Brother) has everything absolutely in hand and under control, including in the economic sphere. The wars it carries on (or the appearance of these wars – it is never completely clear whether these wars really take place or not, or whether it really matters) do not stem from any underlying contradictions in the economic system – as in fact all wars ultimately do in the real world – but are merely manufactured as part of manipulating and controlling the populace, down to their very emotions. In a certain sense, Orwell may perhaps be excused in this, because he does not claim to be presenting a scientific analysis but is writing literary fiction.

However, no such excuse can be made for Arendt, who declares in all seriousness that, with the rise of totalitarianism,

> we are indeed at the end of the bourgeois era of profits and power, as well as at the end of imperialism and expansion. The aggressiveness of totalitarianism springs not from lust for power, and if it feverishly seeks to expand, it does so neither for expansion's sake nor for profit, but only for ideological reasons: to make the world consistent, to prove that its respective supersense has been right.[40]

It is not possible here to thoroughly dissect and refute such a statement or to thoroughly examine Arendt's political economy, as it can be gleaned from *Totalitarianism*. But, fortunately, that is not really necessary here either: an extensive analysis of the actual dynamics and compulsions of the imperialist states in today's world – including the Soviet Union – has been made elsewhere[41]; and, moreover, life itself – and an examination of events occurring right around us these days – provides a rich source of refutation of Arendt's argument. But it is relevant, and revealing, to note that Arendt's analysis of imperialism is heavily influenced by the theories of Rosa Luxemburg, as can be seen in the following passage, in which Arendt quotes from Luxemburg:

> The ensuing crises and depressions during the decades preceding the era of imperialism had impressed upon the capitalists the thought that their whole economic system of production depended upon a supply and demand that from now on must come from "outside of capitalist society." Such supply and demand came from inside the nation, so long as the capitalist system did not control all its classes together with its entire productive capacity. When capitalism had pervaded the entire economic structure and all social strata had come into the orbit of its production and consumption system, capitalists clearly had to decide either to see the whole system collapse or to find new markets, that is, to penetrate new countries which were not yet subject to capitalism and therefore could provide a new noncapitalistic supply and demand.[42]

Luxemburg was a revolutionary, "a founder of the Communist

---

40. Arendt, *Totalitarianism,* p. 458.

41. For such an analysis the reader is again strongly urged to study *America in Decline* and Parts I and II of *The Soviet Union: Socialist or Social-Imperialist?*

42. Arendt, *Totalitarianism,* p. 148; Arendt's citation for the statement from Luxemburg is *Die Akkumulation des Kapitals* (Berlin: 1923), p. 273.

Party of Germany, who was murdered in 1919 by the military authorities acting under the auspices of the Social Democratic Party."[43] But her outlook and political line were also characterized by reformist tendencies. And the basis for this can be seen in her erroneous political-economic theory.

As explained in *America in Decline,*

> Luxemburg failed to comprehend the specificity of the imperialist stage of capitalist development, in particular the contradiction between monopoly and competition. For Luxemburg, capitalism's international thrust was mainly a question of increasing and extending the scope of its trade with the rest of the world....
>
> In 1913, Luxemburg published her major theoretical work, *The Accumulation of Capital.* There and in her subsequent *Anti-Critique* she put forward a schema based on a chronic shortfall in demand.... Closing this demand gap required, according to Luxemburg, a class of buyers outside of capitalist society who could absorb this output without adding to it – and these consumers were to be found in pre- or non-capitalist sectors, mainly in the colonies. Eventually, however, these layers would be incorporated into the process of capitalist production and no one would be left to realize this commodity product. Hence, the capitalists would not be able to realize surplus value and underwrite further expansion.[44]

It is not difficult to see how such an analysis – with its implications that capitalism will, out of its own dynamic, reach its final limits – could be accompanied by gradualist political tendencies, by the resistance to attempts to accelerate the proletarian revolution through "pushing on" the workers from "outside" or "above" their ranks – which, of course, is what Lenin essentially, and very correctly, urged (as can be seen especially in *What Is To Be Done?*).[45] And it is also not difficult to see how such Luxemburgist analysis, when taken up by Arendt (who was a Social Democrat and, to put it extremely mildly, a counterrevolutionary), could be

43. Lotta, *America in Decline,* 1, p. 259.

44. Lotta, *America in Decline,* 1, pp. 259-60.

45. Luxemburg herself was critical of Lenin on this point; and attacking *What Is To Be Done?* has become a *sine qua non* and a veritable *profession de foi* of all good antitotalitarians. Arendt makes her obligatory attack (though she somewhat "moderates" it) in a footnote of *Totalitarianism* (p. 365). For a fuller discussion of the questions concentrated in *What Is To Be Done?* and the controversy surrounding it, see Avakian, *For a Harvest of Dragons,* pp. 74-84.

incorporated into a line that said that capitalism and imperialism have basically run their limits and have been superseded by totalitarianism. On one level, this is another instance of first time, tragedy; second time, farce. But in this case, the farcical theories of totalitarianism, particularly in their thrust against genuine communism and against Soviet social-imperialism today, play a deadly serious role as weapons in the hands of the Western imperialists.

Hence, it becomes especially necessary to answer some of the main slanders against Stalin and distortions of events in "Stalinist Russia" that are found in Arendt's *Totalitarianism.* Stalin, in his positive aspect (which, overall, was his principal aspect) represents the firm exercise of the dictatorship of the proletariat and the first profound steps in carrying out socialist transformation; in his secondary (though not insignificant) negative aspect, he shared certain features with the revisionists who rose to power after his death and who restored capitalism in the Soviet Union, turning the world's first socialist state into a social-imperialist world predator. It is in both aspects – distorted almost beyond recognition and then combined and magnified in distorted form into a grotesque monstrosity – that Stalin constitutes the object of antitotalitarian attack.[46]

In her attack on Stalin, Arendt does not content herself with seizing on certain real errors committed in "the Stalin period": a too extensive reliance on the secret police, rather than primary reliance on the conscious activism of the masses, to identify and suppress counterrevolutionaries; the mixing up of two fundamentally different types of contradictions (those between the people and the enemy and those among the people themselves),

---

46. An extensive analysis of Stalin's role as leader of the Soviet Union over three decisive decades is beyond the scope of this book. I have elsewhere undertaken analysis of some important aspects of this, focusing in particular on Stalin's mistakes – in the context of upholding Stalin overall, as the leader of the world's first socialist state who, despite his mistakes, made important contributions to the international communist movement – viewing these mistakes from the standpoint of how to draw the appropriate lessons for carrying forward the struggle to overthrow the bourgeoisie, establish and exercise the dictatorship of the proletariat, and continue the advance to world communism. See, for example, *Conquer the World,* pp. 3-28; and "Outline of Views on the Historical Experience of the International Communist Movement and the Lessons for Today," in *Revolution,* No. 49 (June 1981), pp. 4-9. Analysis of important aspects of this question is also contained in *The Declaration of the Revolutionary Internationalist Movement,* particularly pp. 15-21.

so that the target of repression became too broad and a certain "chill" set in among the people, actually undermining their ability to carry forward the class struggle against the old, and particularly against newborn, exploiters; some excesses in the struggle for the collectivization of agriculture; and, along with this – and particularly as part of the inner-party struggles that were a crucial aspect of the overall struggle in society – some rather crude re-writing of history. Nor is Arendt satisfied with inventing, or repeating, horror stories of millions upon millions of entirely innocent people subjected to terror and/or executed. Still less, of course, does she criticize Stalin – where criticism can and should be made – for covering over, to a considerable extent, the imperialist and reactionary nature of the Western democracies that were in conflict with Germany and with which Stalin sought alliance, in the late 1930s and again after the Soviet Union was attacked by Germany and entered World War 2. Rather, Arendt exaggerates and refashions not only real errors but slanderous fabrications, so that everything that was done (along with much that was never done) is ripped away from any real material basis or actual political context and is reinterpreted as the expression of a transcendental totalitarian will. Put more simply, it is all a plot by the totalitarians – with Stalin the totalitarian supreme. There is no real class struggle, no imperialist encirclement of the Soviet Union, no danger to the socialist system from within or without, indeed no socialism – or to whatever degree these things do exist, they are only convenient pretexts or covers for the real motive: the totalitarian drive for complete domination. A few examples will help make this clear.

Many people have long recognized the fact that after Lenin's death there was a real struggle, involving Stalin, Trotsky, and others in the leadership of the Soviet Communist Party, over what direction Soviet society must take in the context of an international situation dominated by Britain, the USA, and France, with Germany crushed as a result of World War 1 but the attempts at revolution in Germany also crushed and the prospects for successful revolution elsewhere not immediate. But this is mere illusion, Arendt would have us believe. According to her, the whole thing – and specifically the whole conflict between Stalin's line on the possibility of socialism in one country and Trotsky's theory of "permanent revolution," which denied the possibility of socialism in one country – was merely an invention, a device utilized by Stalin as part of his totalitarian urge for absolute power. I'm not joking – this is actually what she says: "Stalin likewise reckoned with both Russian public opinion and the non-Russian world when he invented his theory of 'socialism in one country' and threw the onus of world revolution on Trotsky."[47]

And so it was, Arendt tells us, with the collectivization of agriculture in the Soviet Union. Arendt treats the whole thing as an unmitigated disaster. She seems to suggest that the New Economic Policy, initiated by Lenin, after the Civil War in the early 1920s, as a temporary measure – which he openly called a retreat – should have been continued, more or less indefinitely. Stalin, however, broke with this and brought on forced collectivization with its calamitous results, according to Arendt, not because of the desperate struggle between socialism and capitalism in the Soviet Union at that time – a struggle in which the countryside was a concentration point and decisive arena – but because of... (do I have to say it again?)... his totalitarian urge for absolute power. Thus Arendt can write that when, in the early 1930s, Stalin's regime "proceeded to the liquidation of classes," it began,

> *for ideological and propaganda reasons,* with the property-owning classes, the new middle class in the cities, and the peasants in the country. Because of the combination of numbers and property, the peasants up to then had been potentially the most powerful class in the Union; their liquidation, *consequently,* was more thorough and more cruel than that of any other group and was carried through by artificial famine and deportation *under the pretext of expropriation of the kulaks and collectivization.*[48]

It is difficult to know whether to feel more anger or amazement at statements such as this. One gets absolutely no sense from Arendt of the sharp class polarization among the peasantry at that time in the Soviet Union, nor specifically that these kulaks (rich peasants) repeatedly and ruthlessly took advantage of the difficult, often extremely desperate, conditions in the countryside to profiteer and generally to further enrich themselves, even withholding grain to jack up the price while many people were starving or on the edge of starvation. (Arendt almost treats the kulaks as mythical creatures invented by the Stalinist Ministry of

47. Arendt, *Totalitarianism,* p. 413.
48. Arendt, *Totalitarianism,* p. 320, emphasis added.

Totalitarian Propaganda – the Ministry of Truth in Orwell's *1984.*)
Yes, mistakes were made in the struggle against the kulaks and
for collectivization of agriculture in the late 1920s to early 1930s –
the pace of collectivization was sometimes too fast, force was
used in some situations where persuasion should have been
relied on, middle peasants were sometimes made the target of
attack along with the kulaks themselves, and other mistakes
were made (and Stalin himself called attention to and worked to
correct many of these errors[49]). But, really, Arendt and other
"anti-Stalinists" notwithstanding, the kulaks were not heroic
fighters for some pristine agrarian way of life – they were grasping, profiteering exploiters.

But the most outrageous, and at the same time most essential,
aspect of Arendt's rewriting of history in accordance with antitotalitarian mythology is her attempt to deny that there was any
fundamental antagonism between "Stalinist Russia" and "Nazi
Germany" or between the Soviet communists and the Nazis. In
fact, these two parties, and Hitler and Stalin personally, actually
had the greatest respect and mutual admiration for each other,
Arendt says, because after all they could recognize a kindred
soul. In the attempt to substantiate this – and carry it to its fullest
extreme – Arendt not only cites statements of respect by each side
for the other (which can be as readily dismissed as they can be
supplied, for what serious adversaries have not, in one way or
another, expressed respect for each other?); she even goes so far
as to claim that "contrary to certain postwar legends, Hitler never
intended to defend 'the West' against Bolshevism but always remained ready to join 'the Reds' for the destruction of the West,
even in the middle of the struggle against Soviet Russia."[50] While
it is obviously true that Hitler never intended to defend the West
against Bolshevism, in the sense that he always did intend to
defeat other powers in the West himself, the idea that Hitler had
nothing against Bolshevism, that his rabid anticommunism was
merely a charade, is ridiculous; that someone could actually
argue this in a book that is taken seriously by many people is

---

49. This can be seen in a number of articles and speeches by Stalin in this
period, including "Dizzy With Success," written in 1930 (in *Problems of Leninism*
[Peking: Foreign Languages Press, 1976], pp. 483-91), although, of course, this will
be dismissed as merely more deception and falsification by those, like Arendt,
who are obsessed with totalitarian Stalinist demons.

50. Arendt, *Totalitarianism*, p. 309.

remarkable. And as for the assertion that Hitler was always ready to make common cause with "the Reds" for the destruction of the West, even during the bitter, grinding war (notice how Arendt refers to it here merely as a "struggle") with the Soviet Union – well, that only serves to illustrate again the old adage that paper will put up with whatever is written on it. What are we supposed to believe – that the whole war between Germany and the Soviet Union, lasting over four years and constituting the decisive front of the overall war in Europe, on which Hitler staked everything, ultimately, and lost, while the Soviet people underwent tremendous sacrifice to vanquish the powerful military machine under Hitler's command – that this whole war was the result of some whim on the part of Hitler, or Stalin, that for some silly reason, or perhaps because of the clash of totalitarian wills, they just couldn't get together, despite Hitler's inclinations, as Arendt alleges them (was it Stalin's "fault")? This, it seems, is how such antitotalitarian theorists write (or rewrite) history.

The real history of these crucial events, together with a basic analysis of their underlying causes and motive forces, is summarized very concisely in *America in Decline,* and given the depths of fabrication and obfuscation Arendt descends to in distorting all this – and a great deal of confusion and misinformation generally concerning it – it is worthwhile quoting at length from this summary in *America in Decline*:

> The roots of the Second World War lay in the redivision of the world in 1918. The interwar period was just that – a truce which would, of necessity, be broken. Britain had defeated its rivals, but found its international position greatly weakened. The U.S. emerged stronger, consolidating its position in Latin America where the most developed colonies were located. But dislodging the other imperialist powers from their most profitable or strategically key positions in Asia and Africa still required arduous struggle. The U.S. had designs on Britain's Far East colonies and spheres of influence – designs which became imperative with the onset and continuation of profound crisis throughout the 1930s. Japan's need to expand its empire had been met only partially as a result of the first interimperialist war and reasserted itself more powerfully. The German bourgeoisie could not break out of the strangling vise of defeat in the last war and gain new spheres of influence without coming into direct confrontation with both Britain and, especially, France.
>
> On its western border, Germany faced France and Belgium; in

the east it faced a set of defense alliances among smaller states, most of which were backed by France; at sea in the European theater, Germany faced a still-dominant British navy. The opening stages of the war saw Germany attack Poland in order to smash one flank of the Anglo-French imperialist front and turn it to their advantage in the larger contest to follow. British and French aid to Poland was extended to fortify that flank as part of their contention with Germany....

. . . The British strategy for dealing with Germany found initial expression in Prime Minister Neville Chamberlain's "appeasement" policy. The purpose of Chamberlain's 1938 Munich agreement to give the Sudetenland to Germany was, in fact, to push the Germans to the east and into confrontation with the Soviet Union.... There was, however, never any question, either on the part of Britain or the U.S., of letting the German imperialists swallow the Soviet Union: they wanted the Germans to choke on it. The Soviet Union, quite rightly, was determined neither to be swallowed nor to be shattered. Owing to the Soviet need to buy time and the German need to first establish a tenable western periphery before it lay siege to the Soviet Union, the two countries signed a mutual nonaggression pact in August 1939....

For its part, Germany recognized that bursting through the confines of the existing division of the world and displacing Britain as the dominant imperialist power (and ultimately absorbing its colonial empire) could not be accomplished without obtaining overwhelming political and military superiority over Britain. As far as the German imperialists were concerned, the key to forcing Britain to its knees was the defeat of the Soviet Union. The plunder of the USSR's industry, agriculture, and abundant mineral resources, such as its southern oil fields, while valuable in itself, was essential in order to prepare Germany for further battle. Germany could then once again shift the bulk of its military weight toward the West, now backed by the resources of all of continental Europe....

. . . As it turned out, the main way that the U.S. and British allies worked to defeat Germany was through the Soviet Red Army. Military history here is very clear. Even Winston Churchill admitted in March 1943 that for the next six months Great Britain and the United States would be "playing about" with half a dozen German divisions while Stalin was facing 185 divisions. Overall, the Soviet Union suffered 20 million war-related deaths, including 7.5 million who died directly in battle. By contrast, the combined British, French, and U.S. battle deaths totalled under 750,000 – less than 10 percent of the Soviet figure. Simply put, the Soviet Union was responsible for the defeat of Germany. What neither the Germans nor, for that matter, the U.S. imperialists banked on was the force and tenacity with which, once the initial German advance was halted at Stalingrad, the Soviet army would push back the German invaders; nor, of course, had they anticipated the political reverberations this would have.[51]

One of the most glaring things in Arendt's *Totalitarianism* is how she glosses over (even virtually ignores) the whole attempt by Stalin, from the mid-'30s until the end of the decade, to get the "Western democracies" to enter into an alliance with the Soviet Union against Germany—a policy whose rebuff by these "Western democracies" was signified by the 1938 Munich Pact referred to earlier, among other things. Now, as indicated before, criticism can and should be made of this policy of Stalin's, from the standpoint that it was accompanied by a certain covering over of the imperialist and reactionary nature of these "Western democracies," a blurring over of the class content of democracy itself, and a skewing of the international communist movement in accordance with the exigencies of this attempted alliance. But the important point here is that the pact between the Soviet Union and Germany in 1939 was entered into by Stalin only after his repeated attempts to draw the "Western democracies" into an alliance against Germany were just as repeatedly rebuffed; and, as explained in *America in Decline,* this pact with Germany was then signed "owing to the Soviet need to buy time and the German need to first establish a tenable western periphery before it lay siege to the Soviet Union." But, of course, Arendt deals with none of this—or none of it in its true light (she makes a number of references to sudden and dramatic turns in Soviet foreign policy, but she never comes close to examining the real basis for these, treating them instead as...yet other examples of totalitarian chicanery).

Arendt cannot recognize the real dynamics involved in all this—in particular the real necessity faced by the Soviet Union, and its policies in response to that necessity (with the mistakes that can and must be identified from a scientific, revolutionary communist standpoint). She cannot recognize this because it is a central tenet of her whole antitotalitarian theory and convictions —a central tenet without which the whole thing falls to the ground—that totalitarianism has a logic and dynamic all of its own, which transcends and supersedes distinctions of Left and

51. Lotta, *America in Decline,* pp. 208–212.

Right. Everything, all reality, must be observed through the prism of this theory and these convictions, however much reality may be bent in the process. Thus, in Arendt's eyes, Marx's scientific methodology – the dialectical and historical materialism with which he penetrated beneath the superficial, and often inverted, appearance of things to reveal the real mainsprings of human social organization and its historical development – becomes "Marx's great attempt to rewrite world history in terms of class struggles."[52] For if it is true – and a scientific truth of central and far-reaching significance – that "class struggle is the immediate driving power of history,"[53] then how can one hope to substantiate such interpretations as the following by Arendt:

> Underlying the Nazis' belief in race laws as the expression of the law of nature in man, is Darwin's idea of man as the product of a natural development which does not necessarily stop with the present species of human beings, *just as* under the Bolsheviks' belief in class-struggle as the expression of the law of history lies Marx's notion of society as the product of a gigantic historical movement which races according to its own law of motion to the end of historical times when it will abolish itself.[54]

What is noteworthy here is not only Arendt's obscurantist distortion of Marxism (and her obscurantist attitude toward Darwinism) but the notion that the Marxist theory of class struggle is of the same nature as the Nazi theory of race, with its genocidal conclusions. Thus, she can, without embarrassment, write such things as this:

> it cannot be doubted either that the Nazi leadership actually believed in, and did not merely use as propaganda, such doctrines as the following: "The more accurately we recognize and observe the laws of nature and life,. . . so much the more do we conform to the will of the Almighty. The more insight we have into the will of the Almighty, the greater will be our successes." It is quite apparent that very few changes are needed to express Stalin's creed in two sentences which might run as follows: "The more accurately we recognize and observe the laws of history and class struggle,

52. Arendt, *Totalitarianism*, p. 333.

53. Marx and Engels, "Letter to August Bebel, Wilhelm Liebknecht, Wilhelm Bracke and Others" (17-18 September 1879), in *Selected Letters [MESL]* (Peking: Foreign Languages Press, 1977), p. 69.

54. Arendt, *Totalitarianism*, p. 463, emphasis added.

so much the more do we conform to dialectic materialism. The more insight we have into dialectic materialism, the greater will be our success." Stalin's notion of "correct leadership," at any rate, could hardly be better illustrated.[55]

Even if we allow that there were certain tendencies under Stalin's leadership to treat aspects of Marxism-Leninism somewhat mechanically and to reduce certain of its tenets to dogma, can any person in his/her right mind – or whose outlook and vision have not been totally obscured by antitotalitarian apriorism and class bias – really not recognize the profound difference between even Arendt's "paraphrase" of "Stalin's creed" and the words of the Nazi leader Martin Bormann which Arendt quotes just before this "paraphrase"? Just because two people profess their adherence to a comprehensive worldview, and insist moreover that adherence to this worldview is directly relevant to changing the world in a desired way, does that make their worldviews essentially the same, or render irrelevant any differences between them? Is there really no difference between dialectical materialism and reactionary idealism, between belief in the "will of the Almighty" – especially as conceived of by a Nazi – and an understanding of the "laws of history and class struggle"?

By now it should be clear that what guides Arendt – and this is generally true, it seems, of especially the social-democratic anti-totalitarians – is not so much a theory as an obsession.[56] And it should be noted that there is, along with a maniacal anti-

---

55. Arendt, *Totalitarianism*, pp. 345-46, ellipses in original.

56. At times the dimensions of this obsession become almost comical. For instance, Arendt seriously – and approvingly – cites a comment by Boris Souvarine (contemporary, and adversary, of Lenin as well as Stalin) that Stalin "took care always" – he literally says *always* – "to say the opposite of what he did, and to do the opposite of what he said" (cited in *Totalitarianism*, p. 362). Can anyone really imagine a person, let alone a whole society, actually functioning while being governed by the principle of always saying the opposite of what you did and doing the opposite of what you said? Such a statement goes beyond the boundaries of the zany and approaches the limits of the lunatic.

Or another example: In seeking to portray to his readers the sense of the outrages committed by wealthy and powerful interests against poor people in Appalachia, Michael Harrington, an American social democrat, begins with these words: "Fantasize a neo-Stalinist regime in an advanced Western country" (Michael Harrington, *Decade of Decision* [New York: Simon & Schuster, 1980], p. 178). Further comment here seems unnecessary – except to observe again that while such people include Hitler and Nazism in their denunciations, the real obsession is with Stalin and "Stalinism."

communism (conceived of and presented as "anti-Stalinism"), a very definite reactionary, obscurantist streak in Arendt. This comes out, for example, in her treatment of Darwin. It is one thing to expose and denounce the distortion and misuse of Darwin's theories to justify such things as eugenics – to say nothing of Nazi extermination policies – but it is quite another to make remarks such as the following: "Almost a century before evolutionism had *donned the cloak of science,* warning voices foretold the inherent consequences of a madness that was then merely in the stage of pure imagination."[57] Similarly, the understanding that the human species is capable of great flexibility, that it possesses great plasticity in terms of its response to the rest of nature, and that with the change in their circumstances – above all their social system – people are capable of great changes in their outlook and beliefs. . .yes, even their feelings. . .all this is tremendously liberating to those without a vested interest in the present order of things. Of course, it is as necessary as it is difficult to correctly handle the dialectic between changing people's circumstances and changing their outlook and values – and it is extremely important to sum up errors, and positive experience as well, in this regard – but to people like Arendt the mere attempt to do this is itself horrifying. Hence we hear the following dark existential ruminations: "Since the Greeks, we have known that highly developed political life breeds a deep-rooted suspicion of this private sphere, a deep resentment against the disturbing miracle contained in the fact that each of us is made as he is – *single, unique, unchangeable.*"[58] And, she says, "Nineteenth-century positivism and progressivism perverted this purpose of human equality when they set out to demonstrate what cannot be demonstrated, namely, that men are equal by nature and different only by history and circumstances, so that they can be equalized not by rights, but by circumstances and education."[59] Here Arendt reveals both the bourgeois – and more specifically, bourgeois-democratic – essence of her outlook, and at the same time the reactionary essence of the bourgeois-democratic ideal in this era: the notion, and insistence, that on the one hand equality is the highest principle but that on the other hand human "equal-

57. Arendt, *Totalitarianism,* p. 179, emphasis added.

58. Arendt, *Totalitarianism,* p. 301, emphasis added.

59. Arendt, *Totalitarianism,* p. 234.

ity is an equality of rights only."[60]

It should not surprise us, then, that although she obviously regarded Nazism (and other variants of fascism) as anathema and worked actively against them,[61] Arendt's overriding obsession is with "Stalinism." When she insists that the driving force of totalitarianism – beyond any state or territory it controls at any given time, beyond even the party or the Leader – is the movement of totalitarianism towards its ultimate goal of world conquest and absolute domination over everyone,[62] Arendt has in mind, above all, "Stalinist" totalitarianism. Keeping in focus the context in which *The Origins of Totalitarianism* appeared (it was first published in 1951), as well as the distinction Arendt drew even between Nazi Germany and "Stalinist Russia" (that the former was never fully totalitarianized, while the latter definitely was), then not only her general political orientation but a more

---

60. Arendt, *Totalitarianism*, p. 234.

61. Arendt, a German Jew, became an active Zionist in 1930 and helped Jews escape from Germany. She was, however, a social-democratic Zionist, and while she regarded the creation of the state of Israel as necessary for the restoration of the national and moreover the human rights of the Jewish people (see *Totalitarianism*, p. 299), she raised appropriately liberal objections to some of the more outrageous ways in which the national (and human) rights of the Palestinian people were trampled on in the process.

Having fled to Paris in 1933, Arendt came to the U.S. and lived there until she died in 1975. Generally speaking, she was on the liberal end of the bourgeois political spectrum in the U.S. She was also what has been described as a "cosmopolitan Zionist" – that is, she attacked what she regarded as the false notion of the non-European character of the Jews. Her apologetics for Western imperialism (and its historical development) were often quite remarkable and also quite extensive. For example, she claims that

> even slavery, though actually established on a strict racial basis, did not make the slave-holding peoples race-conscious before the nineteenth century. Throughout the eighteenth century, American slave-holders themselves considered it a temporary institution and wanted to abolish it gradually. Most of them probably would have said with Jefferson: "I tremble when I think that God is just." (*Totalitarianism*, p. 177)

And she can write, apparently with a straight face:

> The happy fact is that although British imperialist rule sank to some level of vulgarity, cruelty played a lesser role between the two World Wars than ever before and a minimum of human rights was always safeguarded. It is this moderation in the midst of plain insanity that paved the way for what Churchill has called "the liquidation of His Majesty's Empire" and that eventually may turn out to mean the transformation of the English nation into a Commonwealth of English peoples. (*Totalitarianism*, p. 221)

62. See, for example, Arendt, *Totalitarianism*, pp. 411-12.

specific political purpose becomes very apparent. This is especially so when she insists that among "the most conspicuous" of the "errors of the nontotalitarian world in its diplomatic dealings with totalitarian governments" is not only "the Munich pact with Hitler" but also "the Yalta agreements with Stalin."[63] Again, Arendt is making such a summation at a time when Hitler is long gone and there is only one totalitarian bloc around (you haven't been paying attention if you don't know which one). And it is very significant that today, as part of their intense ideological and political preparation for world war with the Soviet bloc—a war they will cast as the apocalyptic confrontation between democracy, Western civilization, and the Judeo-Christian tradition on one side, and godless atheistic, communistic totalitarianism on the other side—representatives of Western imperialism are now openly calling the Yalta Agreement into question. By the same token, when Arendt says of totalitarianism that the victory of this "concentration-camp system would mean the same inexorable doom for human beings as the use of the hydrogen bomb would mean the doom of the human race,"[64] she is voicing a viewpoint very similar to the rationale of the Western imperialist spokesmen today who insist that, horrible as a nuclear war may be, there is one thing worse. . . and that is enslavement by totalitarianism.

It is perhaps an irony of history that Arendt's attempts, in *The Origins of Totalitarianism*, to provide a theoretical underpinning for the notion—and denunciation—of totalitarianism can play a more important role for Western imperialism now than when the book was originally written. This irony is heightened by the fact that, strictly speaking, the Soviet Union and its bloc today do not fit Arendt's definition of totalitarianism (something more or less acknowledged by Arendt in her 1967 preface to the work).[65] But

63. Arendt, *Totalitarianism*, p. 393.

64. Arendt, *Totalitarianism*, p. 443.

65. See Arendt, *Totalitarianism*, p. XVII-XXII.
In this light the exchange between E. P. Thompson and Václav Racek, a Czechoslovakian "dissident," is interesting and enlightening. For one thing, it brings out once more that as a general rule those who might be called the "mainstream dissidents" in the Soviet bloc—who are more or less unabashedly pro-West—are among the most despicable people in the world. True, the Soviet-bloc revisionist rulers must bear much of the responsibility for this, but this truth does not make these "dissidents" any less despicable. If anyone is inclined to think this is unfair, listen to what Thompson feels compelled to say, in order to instruct such "dissidents" in the need for more sophistication in upholding the Western imperialist alliance against the Soviet bloc. He writes that, in his discussions with

this only underscores, once more, that the concept of totalitarianism is not merely lacking in any scientific validity, nor is it merely bourgeois-democratic mania: it is a weapon in the ideological arsenal of Western imperialism whose function, especially now, is to help prepare for the launching of the actual military weapons that are the only real "argument" of substance of such reactionary forces.

In concluding this specific discussion of the theory of totalitarianism, it is important to recall that the dictatorship of the proletariat – which is what existed under and was upheld by Stalin, notwithstanding his mistakes – does not differ from other forms of the state in that it is a dictatorship: all states are class dictator-

---

such "dissidents,"

> I have been told – to give one example – that Allende was a "Communist dictator," overthrown by a popular general strike. This is not true. Allende was a democratically-elected President, with reformist policies, who was first "de-stabilized" and then murdered in a military coup. The appalling tyranny, executions, tortures, and purging of all intellectual life in Chile in the years which followed this coup out-rival anything to be seen in Eastern Europe in the past decade. (Thompson, *Cold War*, p. 88)

Imagine what kind of people it is – and we are not talking about people without knowledge of politics and world affairs, these are "dissident" intellectuals, overwhelmingly – with whom one has to argue something like this!

Still, through it all, Thompson makes clear that he knows where his bread is buttered. Thus, in responding to Racek's accusations that Thompson has been duped by the Soviet-bloc rulers – accusations that Racek seeks to substantiate by reference to *The Origins of Totalitarianism*, among other things – Thompson not only says that not everything Arendt wrote in that book about the Soviet bloc strictly applies today, but he specifically insists:

> You even suppose that you have to persuade me that the social system you live under is "essentially different" from my own, and you say that it may sound "odd" to me to learn that my public criticism of the British political system is itself a proof of the continuing reality of our democratic process.
>
> And why should I have to be persuaded of these things? I have written about them myself, again and again. Much of my work as a historian has involved me in the examination of the sources, the realities, and the limits of our democratic process. It is because this process is now threatened, under the pressure of militarization, that I write so sharply today. (Thompson, *Cold War*, p. 87)

What is striking in this entire exchange is that, whatever the differences between them, both Thompson and Racek conduct this argument on the classical terms of the bourgeois democrat in the service of Western imperialism, who knows that when push comes to shove and the "pressure of militarization" is supplanted by the reality of outright warfare, there is after all one side which, whatever its faults may be, is "essentially different" and whose triumph is worthy of support – indeed in large part precisely because it can be publicly criticized, from an openly bourgeois-democratic point of view.

WHO WRITES "PERMITTING" THE EDUCATION? WORKING CLASS OR VANGUARD?

ships. It differs fundamentally in that it is the dictatorship of the nonexploiting majority over the exploiting minority; it aims at, and serves as a vehicle for, carrying forward the struggle for the abolition of all systems of exploitation and all bases for class divisions throughout the world. It is as an expression of this that the leaders of this state openly proclaim that it is a dictatorship and what its aims are as such. But it is also important to state here that in "Stalinist Russia" the masses of people experienced far greater freedom and had a far greater understanding of the truth than has ever been the case in any bourgeois-democratic country, without exception. To really grasp the profound truth and significance of this statement, it is necessary to realize not only that all bourgeois-democratic societies rest on a foundation of capitalist exploitation, while in the Soviet Union, until after Stalin's death, relations of exploitation had been overthrown and no longer dominated (though they were not yet completely eliminated). It is also necessary to realize that, however much it may have been marred by mechanical materialist tendencies and pragmatic adulterations, there was a serious attempt under Stalin's leadership to educate people in the scientific standpoint and method of Marxism-Leninism, while in all bourgeois-democratic countries—and this is no exaggeration—from the very earliest age, through the educational system, the mass media and in other ways, *the people are systematically misinformed and lied to about every significant question of current political and world affairs and of world history* and are *systematically indoctrinated and imbued with an upside-down worldview and errant methodology.* And this takes place, not through the kind of extreme, and exotic, measures of the totalitarian state of Orwell's *1984,* but through the "normal," oh-so-democratic functioning of bourgeois-democratic society and its state.

Social Democracy — Bourgeois Democracy

Apart from their particular obsession with "Stalinist totalitarianism," the social democrats (and this is especially true of social democrats in the U.S.) are distinguished to a large degree by the fact that they really have little to say about the question of democracy that is original—that is different from the dominant, established view of democracy among more or less openly bourgeois apologists for Western imperialism. They are also generally distinguished by the triviality of much of what they do say about this question (a look at something like *Dissent* magazine will readily confirm this). These social democrats tend to focus on their various reformist schemes for achieving "economic democracy" – that is, social welfarism – to go along with what they see as the already established (but, of course, always requiring perfecting) political democracy in the West. The essential thrust and role of such people's concern with democracy is to uphold and defend Western bourgeois society and its traditions – in other words, to uphold and defend Western imperialism – against the challenge from Soviet social-imperialism and against real revolution and genuine, revolutionary communism.

There are, however, attempts by people who could be broadly defined as social democrats to give a more radical, even a "Marxist" formulation to their views on democracy, which distinguishes them from the standard (classical) apologetics for Western imperialism. Two such works, significant for their content and/or their influence, will provide the focus for the final part of this chapter: *Democracy and the Rule of Law: Liberal Ideals and Marxist Critiques*, by Bob Fine, and *Marxism and Democracy: Beyond "Real Socialism,"* by Agnes Heller with Ferenc Feher.

Bob Fine's recently published book, *Democracy and the Rule of Law: Liberal Ideals and Marxist Critiques*, is an attempt to reconcile Marxism and bourgeois democracy. Fine is not an influential figure in the way Heller is, and on one level his arguments are readily refuted – in many cases they are almost transparently ridiculous. But he does manage to touch on several questions which are important to address, and it is in this respect that it is worthwhile to examine Fine's basic thesis and some of his main argumentation in support of it.

Fine's book shares with Heller's a fundamental error in how it treats the relation between the base and the superstructure of society. Fine's error on this, however, is the "mirror opposite" of Heller's: while (as will be explored shortly) Heller's tendency is to divorce the superstructure from its foundation in the economic base, in *Democracy and the Rule of Law* Fine merges essential aspects of the superstructure, in particular law, with the base. Fine asserts that law itself is a production relation. This is an important component of what constitutes his pivotal argument – that the state is not an instrument of class dictatorship – and it is an integral part of his general thesis that, as he puts it in his "Conclusion":

> Marx sought to transcend private property, law and the state not because he was skeptical of democracy, but because of the limits which juridic forms impose upon it. . . . Thus when Marx referred to the withering away of private property, law and the state, he had in mind not merely their abolition but also their replacement by *more* democracy and *more* individual liberty than is possible within their confines.[66]

Thus, as we shall see, Fine reduces Marx – if not to a "common liberal" (as Lenin pointed out the renegade Kautsky had done)[67] – to a "Marxist" liberal, and he reduces Marxism from a scientific theory of the complete overthrow of all existing social conditions and relations and the radical rupture with all traditional property relations and ideas into a reformist recipe for gradualist change utilizing and in turn extending the forms of bourgeois democracy and the bourgeois concept of freedom.

Right away, in his "Introduction," Fine begins to unfold his pivotal argument: that Marx "saw the state in general as class-based did not mean that he ignored the importance of distinguishing one bourgeois state from another; the state in his view expresses a relation between classes and is not just an instrument of the ruling class."[68] The eclectic viewpoint and method expressed here (which are, significantly if ironically, similar to those of the Soviet revisionists, in particular on this decisive question of the state) are carried forward throughout the book, but before too long Fine's point begins to come more clearly into focus: the character of the state is dependent on the particular relations between classes at any given point and, more specifically, it changes its character in accordance with the relative strength of the classes locked in struggle. Hence: "The particular form taken by the state is. . .not static: from one period to the next it may become more or less alienated from the people, more or less subject to democratic control, more or less bureaucratic, more or less bound by rules of law, more or less permissive of working-class organization, etc."[69]

---

66. Bob Fine, *Democracy and the Rule of Law: Liberal Ideals and Marxist Critiques* (London: Pluto Press, 1984), p. 210.

67. See Lenin, "The Proletarian Revolution and the Renegade Kautsky," *LCW*, 28, in particular pp. 231-42.

68. Fine, *Democracy and Law*, p. 6.

69. Fine, *Democracy and Law*, p. 93.

Fine attempts to ground his position in an analysis of basic bourgeois property relations. He tells us that

> Marx never overcame his ambivalence between his conception of bourgeois equality and freedom as "only a semblance and a deceptive semblance" and his realization that "this semblance exists nevertheless as an illusion on his [the worker's] part and to a certain degree on the other side, and thus essentially modifies his relation by comparison to that of workers in other modes of production." If this "semblance" has such a palpable reality, then it should no longer be called a semblance.[70]

While merely noting in passing that what Fine describes as Marx's "ambivalence" is actually his application of dialectical and historical materialism (Marx is emphasizing the enslavement of the proletariat in capitalist society on the one hand and contrasting it with open, chattel slavery on the other – Fine has quoted Marx on precisely this point in leading up to this "ambivalence" argument[71]), what is most significant here is how Fine resolves Marx's alleged ambivalence:

> The main point is this. Workers under capitalism are not propertyless. They remain at all times owners of private property, at best in the form of personal possessions (means of subsistence) and at worst in the form of labor-capacity alone. It is this fact which turns ideologies centered around the sanctity of private property into viable means of persuasion rather than alien means of mere oppression. Marxists should relate to this rather than simply denounce private property as something entirely oppressive and bad, from which workers are entirely expropriated and in which they have no interest.[72]

Fine is not without a point here. It is true that in their aspect of possessors and sellers of their commodity, labor power, workers can be drawn toward an economist line that centers their struggle around, and reduces it to, the fight to improve their relative position in this commodity exchange with the capitalists, and, more generally, they can be appealed to by reformist political pro-

---

70. Fine, *Democracy and Law*, p. 120; explanatory words in brackets added by Fine.

71. Fine, *Democracy and Law*, p. 119.

72. Fine, *Democracy and Law*, p. 120.

grams. In regard to working classes which include a fairly extensive section of more privileged, bourgeoisified workers, fattened from the spoils of imperialism (such as the U.S. or English working classes, to cite two outstanding, if not unique, examples), this economist, reformist tendency will also contain a powerful element of national chauvinism. It is all this that Fine is actually seeking to encourage and pander to when he writes that Marxists "should relate to this rather than simply denounce private property as something entirely oppressive and bad, from which workers are entirely expropriated and in which they have no interest."[73]

The original Marxist was, of course, not unaware of this contradiction: Marx recognized it as central to capitalist relations of wage-labor. Marx stressed that the worker was *deprived of ownership of any means to live except* the sale of his labor power. But he went further: the very exchange of labor power for wages and the utilization of that labor power in production by the capitalist *constitute the very essence of the capitalist relation of exploitation and the basis for the revolutionary interests of the proletariat, as a class, in overthrowing these capitalist relations — and with them all exploitative relations.* That is why Marx insisted that the workers

> ought to understand that, with all the miseries it imposes upon them, the present system simultaneously engenders the *material conditions* and the *social forms* necessary for an economical reconstruction of society. Instead of the *conservative* motto, *"A fair day's wage for a fair day's work!"* they ought to inscribe on their banner the *revolutionary* watchword, *"Abolition of the wages system!"*[74]

It is for the same reason that, with the development of imperialism and the split in the working class of the imperialist countries, Lenin insisted on building a revolutionary, internationalist movement based among the lower, proletarian sections of the working class, in opposition to a reformist and chauvinist bourgeois labor movement based among the upper, aristocratic sections of the working class.

But it is with the latter that Fine's inclinations lie.[75] Hence, he

73. Fine, *Democracy and Law*, p. 120.

74. Marx, *Wages, Price, and Profit* (Peking: Foreign Languages Press, 1975), p. 78.

75. Fine shares in the general characteristic of the social democrats that they

is concerned not only with stressing the commodity-owning aspect of the workers but with emphasizing the *identity* of different commodity owners in capitalist society rather than the fundamental *opposition* between the capitalists, as owners of the means of production and the class that dominates the entire process of capitalist commodity production and exchange, and the workers, whose dependence on their unique commodity, labor power, expresses their basic position as the exploited class within capitalist commodity relations. And this links up with Fine's treatment of the superstructure, the law, and the state especially. Fine writes that

> the state presupposes the divorce of labor from all rights except ownership of one's own labor-power. This exception is not insignificant: the juridic freedom and equality of labor distinguish capitalism from other forms of class society and serve as a necessary counterpoint to the power of capital and the state.[76]

Nor is that all. According to Fine, the state itself, while it "derives from private property," nevertheless "assumes unto itself the rights associated with private property" and comes into conflict with private property:

> Private property and the state are complementary poles: depen-

---

give scant (if any) attention to the basic division in the world between a handful of predatory imperialist states, on the one hand, and the vast numbers of countries subjugated to colonial (or neocolonial) domination by these imperialists, on the other, and that they put no emphasis on the problem of overcoming the lopsidedness attendant to this division – if indeed they recognize it at all. We shall see that such "neglect" is apparent in Heller's writings; we have already seen the peculiar form this chauvinism assumes with someone like E. P. Thompson, who even goes so far as to acknowledge that some of the liberties enjoyed in the imperialist countries rest on a foundation of colonial depredation, but then stops short of pointing to the need to overcome and uproot such an international imperialist "division of labor"; with Arendt the Eurocentric (or, more generally, imperio-centric) chauvinism characteristic of the social democrat sometimes assumes more grotesque expression, for example in her analysis that "the chances for totalitarian rule are frighteningly good in the lands of traditional Oriental despotism, in India and China, where there is almost inexhaustible material to feed the power-accumulating and man-destroying machinery of total domination, and where, moreover, the mass man's typical feeling of superfluousness – an entirely new phenomenon in Europe, the concomitant of mass unemployment and the population growth of the last 150 years – has been prevalent for centuries in the contempt for the value of human life"! (Arendt, *Totalitarianism*, p. 311.)

76. Fine, *Democracy and Law*, p. 153.

dent on each other for their mutual survival, but antithetical to each other not merely as competitors for the lion's share of surplus value but as embodiments of private right and socialized power respectively. The state represents the socialization of power in an alien, capitalist form.... [77]

Then comes the real kicker: the state's "relation both to capital and to labor is inherently contradictory."[78] Once again, but with its implications more fully developed, we are told that the state – the *bourgeois* state – is not an instrument of class rule but a force that is in contradiction to – and capable of being influenced and utilized by – both the capitalist class and the working class.

How does Fine's analysis of the place and function of law relate to all this? Fine argues that the "perspective from which Marx approached *Capital*" – that is, "starting with economic forms" – has given rise to the "impression that the economic expression of relations of production is their only expression, as if there is an exclusive association between economics and social relations of production which is not shared by other forms of social life." The result, Fine says, "is that law, politics and ideology are in one way or another dissociated from relations of production: 'determined' by them perhaps, or 'relatively autonomous' of them, or only 'determined in the last instance,' but not themselves a direct expression of relations of production in the same way as economics."[79] Actually, the correct answer to this is: "(d) all of the above." That is, law, politics, and ideology – the superstructure as a whole – are determined by the economic base; they are at the same time "relatively autonomous," or they have, relatively speaking, a "life of their own," yet they are "determined in the last analysis" by the economic base, but are not themselves part of this base. Fine is actually arguing that such things as politics, law, and ideology cannot be separated from and made dependent on the economic relations; as noted earlier, he specifically asserts that law is "an essential relation of production"[80] itself.

It might seem, superficially, as if Fine is polemicizing against a crude economic determinism, but at bottom he is taking issue with a fundamental principle of Marxism which flows from

77. Fine, *Democracy and Law*, p. 154.
78. Fine, *Democracy and Law*, p. 154.
79. Fine, *Democracy and Law*, p. 96.
80. Fine, *Democracy and Law*, p. 146.

Marx's whole method, not just in *Capital* but in all his analysis of society and the dynamics of its historical development overall. It is worth repeating here Marx's basic summary that

> in the social production of their existence, men enter into definite, necessary relations, which are independent of their will, namely, relations of production corresponding to a determinate stage of development of their material forces of production. The totality of these relations of production constitutes the *economic structure of society,* the real foundation *on which there arises* a *legal and political superstructure* and *to which there correspond definite forms of social consciousness.*[81]

Ordinarily, it would seem redundant to underline the words placed in italics in the above statement – specifically it would seem self-evident that production is an economic activity (and, vice versa, that economics refers to the sphere of production) – but it is perhaps necessary here to highlight the basic way in which Fine is trying to rewrite Marxism; similarly, in this context it is not being picayune to point out that in introducing the above statement Marx calls it "the guiding principle of my studies."[82] And, of course, this same analysis of the relationship between the economic base, on the one hand, and the politics, law, etc., that make up the superstructure that arises on and corresponds to this economic base, on the other hand, is what underlies (and is reflected in) Marx's comment (cited earlier) that "right can never be higher than the economic structure of society and its cultural development conditioned thereby." Right is precisely a part of law and politics – and in turn it is dependent on and ultimately determined by the economic structure (or base). Finally, Marx himself put this very point rather unambiguously: "human life has since time immemorial rested on production, and, in one way or another, on *social* production, whose relations we call, precisely, economic relations."[83]

Again, that this is the Marxist understanding of the relation between economics, on the one hand, and law (as well as the rest of the political and ideological superstructure), on the other, is so well established that the only really pertinent question can be:

81. Marx, *Preface to Critique*, p. 3, emphasis added.

82. Marx, *Preface to Critique*, p. 3.

83. Marx, *Grundrisse*, trans. Martin Nicolaus (London: Penguin Books, 1973), p. 489.

what is Fine up to with his attempt to make law part of the production relations – and to call this analysis "Marxism"?[84] The
answer is that, as suggested earlier, this is an important part of
Fine's attempt to negate, in the name of Marxism, the basic Marxist principle that the state is an organ of class suppression – a dictatorship of the economically dominant class. Fine's argumentation on the role of law and its relation to the state consists of a
complicated chain of reasoning, which is a distortion (and contor-
tion) in every one of its key links but which can be basically summarized as follows: if law is itself a production relation, and
therefore is on an equal footing, so to speak, with other aspects of
the production relations, then it can serve the development of a
state which is not merely the repressive instrument of the
economically dominant class but is an independent force itself
that is in conflict with the capitalist class as well as the working
class in capitalist society (and can be influenced by both classes).

Fine admits a coercive element in law, as an expression of
commodity relations, but the essential coercion he identifies is
that of the *state as such* over *individuals,* not the coercion of *one
class by another through its state;* and the essential contradiction he
identifies is this:

> The law presupposes that all, as individuals, possess a will, are
> free and equal human beings – and this is a great advance over the
> old order – but it recognizes only our will, freedom and equality as
> property owners. So it sees no contradiction in suppressing with
> the utmost vigor the real will of individuals in order that their ra-
> tional will may prevail, in treating people most unfreely so that
> they may be forced to be free.[85]

84. Ironically, the correct, actually Marxist, presentation of this relation is indicated in a passage from *Capital* that Fine cites in another context. As Fine quotes
it, this passage reads:

> [owners of private property] must place themselves in relation to one
> another as persons whose will resides in those objects and must behave in
> such a way that each does not appropriate the commodity of the other and
> alienate his own except through an act to which both parties
> consent.... This juridical relation, whose form is the contract, whether as
> part of a developed legal system or not, is a relation between two wills
> which *mirrors the economic relation.* (Cited in Fine, *Democracy and Law,*
> p. 109, emphasis added here)

85. Fine, *Democracy and Law,* p. 145. This is in many ways similar to Agnes
Heller's argument about the "paradox" of formal democracy, which will be
touched on shortly.

Then Fine says that the state is an extension of law, or that it "emerges out of law"; that "[t]he move from law to state should be regarded, like the move from money to capital, as a transition from a lower, simpler form of social life to one that is higher and more complex"; and that the state encompasses but is not limited to law, so that "law, which preexisted the state and makes up one of its presuppositions, now becomes only one of the forms assumed by state power."[86]

Fine thus insists that the state is a phenomenon associated with – is a function of – the bourgeois epoch and capitalist society. In the attempt to buttress this argument – and present it as a "Marxist" position – Fine quotes from Marx's *The Civil War in France,* as follows:

> Witness, for example, his comments in *The Civil War in France* that "centralized state power. . .*originating from the Middle Ages. . . developed in the nineteenth century* and with the development of class antagonism *between capital and labor. . .*assumed more and more the character of a machine of class rule."[87]

First off, a key word here that should be emphasized – but was not by Fine, for reasons that will become more apparent – is "centralized." Marx was here contrasting the capitalist state with the state as it existed in medieval society, which did not require, generally speaking, as powerful a *centralized state apparatus.* This becomes clearer by looking at Marx's observations more fully, including parts that are omitted by Fine:

> The centralized State power, *with its ubiquitous organs of standing army, police, bureaucracy, clergy, and judicature – organs wrought after the plan of a systematic and hierarchic division of labor –* originates from the days of absolute monarchy, serving nascent middle-class society as a mighty weapon in its struggles against feudalism. Still, its development remained clogged by all manner of medieval rubbish, seignorial rights, local privileges, municipal and guild monopolies and provincial constitutions. The gigantic broom of the French Revolution of the eighteenth century swept away all these relics of bygone times, thus clearing simultaneously the social soil of its last hindrances to the superstructure

86. Fine, *Democracy and Law,* pp. 146-47.

87. Fine, *Democracy and Law,* p. 151, emphasis in the quotation from Marx added by Fine.

of the *modern* State edifice raised under the First Empire, itself the offspring of the Coalition wars of old semi-feudal Europe against modern France....At the same pace at which the progress of modern industry developed, widened, intensified the class antagonism between capital and labor, the State power assumed more and more the character of the *national* power of capital over labor, of a public force organized for social enslavement, of an engine of class despotism. *After every revolution marking a progressive phase in the class struggle,* the purely repressive character of the State power *stands out in bolder and bolder relief.*[88]

Thus, what Marx was talking about when he referred to "centralized State power"—and what Fine treats as the *state in general*—is specifically the *modern* state corresponding to the emergence of the modern, bourgeois nation and the class rule of the bourgeoisie over the proletariat. There is no evidence to support—and there is overwhelming evidence to disprove—Fine's claim that "Engels's brief comments [sic] deriving the state from class antagonism in general and characterizing the state as the means of suppression owned by 'the most powerful, economically dominant class,' whichever that class may be...did not coincide with Marx's stated views."[89] While it turned out to be Engels, rather than Marx, who drew on the findings of American anthropologist Lewis Henry Morgan, as well as a wealth of other material, to systematize the Marxist view on the state, this was precisely a concentration of the basic position that had been contained in the works of Marx and Engels as a whole. Indeed Engels says in his "Preface to the First Edition, 1884," of *The Origin of the Family, Private Property, and the State:* "The following chapters constitute, in a sense, the fulfillment of a bequest. It was no less a person than Karl Marx who had planned to present the results of Morgan's researches in connection with the conclusions arrived at by his own—within certain limits I might say our own—materialist investigation of history and thus to make clear their whole significance."[90] But we don't have to take Engels's word for the fact that this work did "coincide" with Marx's views on the state; we can turn to another general survey of society's historical development, made by Marx himself:

check

—   88. Marx, *The Civil War in France* (Peking: Foreign Languages Press, 1966), pp. 64-65, emphasis added.

89. Fine, *Democracy and Law,* pp. 151-52.

90. Engels, "Origins," *MESW,* 3, p. 191.

What is society, whatever its form may be? The product of men's reciprocal action. Are men free to choose this or that form of society? By no means. Assume a particular level of development of men's productive forces and you will get a particular form of commerce and consumption. Assume particular stages of development in production, commerce and consumption and you will have a corresponding social system, a corresponding organization of the family, of social orders or of classes, in a word, a corresponding civil society. Assume such a civil society and you will get a political system appropriate to it, a system which is only the official expression of civil society. Mr. Proudhon will never understand this because he thinks he is doing something great by appealing from the state to civil society – that is to say, from the official epitome of society to official society.[91]

For all these reasons, while the modern bourgeois state is far more centralized and concentrates far more power in its hands than did previous forms of state in history, the state has existed since the split-up of society into antagonistic classes and it has always served as the instrument of the economically dominant class in suppressing the exploited classes: this is the Marxist – and the correct – understanding of the state. Fine has twice twisted reality – and the Marxist understanding of it – inside out: first, in asserting that "[i]t was only with the development of capital that class rule began to take the indirect form of state rule,"[92] and, more fundamentally, in his attempt to deny the Marxist analysis that the state is an instrument of class dictatorship, in bourgeois society certainly no less than in previous society. It is therefore hardly surprising that the lesson Marx and Engels singled out for emphasis in their 1872 "Preface to the German Edition" of the *Communist Manifesto* – that "the working class cannot simply lay hold of the ready-made State machinery, and wield it for its own purposes"[93] – is not a lesson to which Fine chooses to call attention. Nor is it surprising that Fine's "Marxism" does not include Marx's and Engels's repeated insistence not only on the need for a violent revolution to overthrow the bourgeoisie but also for the proletariat to exercise dictatorship over the bourgeoisie once having overthrown it, in order to advance to communism; or, as Marx

91. Marx, "Letter to Pavel Vasilyevich Annenkov" (28 December 1846), *MESL*, pp. 2-3.
92. Fine, *Democracy and Law*, p. 151.
93. Marx and Engels, *Communist Manifesto*, p. 2.

so succinctly put it:

> Between capitalist and communist society lies the period of the
> revolutionary transformation of the one into the other. There cor-
> responds to this also a political transition period in which the state
> can be nothing but *the revolutionary dictatorship of the proletariat.*[94]

Such a dictatorship will certainly not mean an extension of
democracy and individual liberty for the bourgeoisie.

When Marx pointed out that it is "vulgar democracy" which
"sees the millennium in the democratic republic and has no suspicion that it is precisely in this last form of state of bourgeois
society that the class struggle has to be fought out to a
conclusion,"[95] he was describing exactly the viewpoint of vulgar
democratic "Marxists" like Fine, who can go so far as to seriously
argue that, under the present system, workers have "the political
liberty to elect a government, protest against bad laws *and remove
from power those who oppress them,*"[96] and who goes on to insist:

> Thus it is no part of working class politics to reduce private prop-
> erty, law and the state to mere instruments of the ruling class or
> mere functions for the reproduction of class relations. A socialist
> politics which debases the coinage of individual liberty and
> political democracy – or which presents private property, law and
> the state as mere negations of these values – is unlikely to win
> favor among those it would champion: not because workers are
> bedeviled by false consciousness but because they understand
> what is important to them. The task of Marxism is not to negate
> this working class consciousness but to encourage its growth by
> giving it theoretical expression.[97]

At this point it would be beating a dead horse to explore and
expose further what Fine means by "Marxism" and "working class
consciousness." (Engels's remark seems appropriate here: if this is
Marxism, "just as Marx used to say, commenting on the French
'Marxists' of the late seventies: 'All I know is that I am not a Marxist.' "[98]) Instead, let's return to the assertion by Fine that "when

---

94. Marx, *Critique of the Gotha Programme,* pp. 27-28.
95. Marx, *Critique of the Gotha Programme,* p. 29.
96. Fine, *Democracy and Law,* p. 211, emphasis added.
97. Fine, *Democracy and Law,* p. 211.
98. Engels, "Letter to Conrad Schmidt" (5 August 1890), *MESL,* p. 72.

Marx referred to the withering away of private property, law and the state, he had in mind not merely their abolition but also their replacement by *more* democracy and *more* individual liberty than is possible within their confines." It is true that Marx made clear that individuals would have a far broader (and continually expanding) horizon of liberty under communism than they do in capitalist society (and all previous society). But "more individual liberty" was not at the heart of Marx's vision of communist society, nor, more fundamentally, was "more democracy" what Marx "had in mind" when he spoke of the withering away of private property, the state, law, and all the production relations and superstructure characteristic of capitalism. Marx had in mind first and foremost the abolition of all class distinctions. He had in mind not the linear extension of what exists under the present system—bourgeois democracy, which means bourgeois class dictatorship over the proletariat—but a revolution that would overthrow the existing state and replace it with the dictatorship of the proletariat, and would then continue forward to the complete overthrow of all hitherto existing social conditions and relations. He had in mind what he (along with Engels) said he had in mind: the most radical rupture with traditional property relations and traditional ideas. Finally, he had in mind the withering away, with the state, of democracy itself—and of personal liberty conceived of as liberty in opposition to a state or as the freedom of individuals in opposition to other, antagonistic forces in society—and their replacement by far more advanced forms of social organization and consciousness.

When Marx and Engels wrote in the *Communist Manifesto* that the proletariat must, as a first step, "win the battle of democracy," they meant, as they explained in the same sentence, that the proletariat must first raise itself "to the position of the ruling class."[99] And, as we have seen, they came to realize the profound importance of the fact that this could not mean taking over the existing state apparatus and utilizing it in the interests of the proletariat— this state apparatus must be smashed, broken up, and replaced by a new state, radically different from all previous states and serving as the transitional form to the abolition of classes and the state. Winning the battle of democracy, in the sense in which they came to understand the unprecedented tasks of the proletarian

---

99. Marx and Engels, *Communist Manifesto*, p. 59.

revolution, means winning the world-historic battle that will make possible the abolition of social conditions in which democracy exists and has meaning.

➤ Agnes Heller's efforts, like Bob Fine's, are aimed at reconciling Marxism with bourgeois democracy. But what makes Heller particularly interesting is that she is one of a small group of "dissident defectors" from the Soviet bloc who make their critique of Soviet society – and put forward their viewpoint generally – in the form not of outright repudiating but of seemingly upholding Marxism. As such, Heller has exerted significant influence on various people seeking what they regard as a democratic socialist alternative to what exists in the Soviet bloc (and also to what now exists in the West). *Marxism and Democracy: Beyond "Real Socialism,"* a collection of essays by Heller (and by Ferenc Feher, who, along with Heller, belonged to a group of followers of George Lukacs known as the "Budapest School"), is an attempt to posit such a democratic socialist alternative. On the one hand, this book makes clear that Heller et al. share not only the basic views on "totalitarianism" that were examined earlier in this chapter but also many of the basic articles of faith of classical bourgeois democracy, including the worship of the *Declaration of Independence*. On the other hand, however, people like Heller do attempt to combine this (at least up to a point) with what they consider Marxist principles. In opposition to a cold, grey, lifeless, mechanical, and economist "socialism" practiced (and preached) in the Soviet bloc, Heller stresses that humanity does not live by bread alone and that society and government must not be restricted to such concerns – and moreover that the state must not be allowed to determine what humanity's needs are. In these essays, a great deal of emphasis is placed on the importance of consciousness. But at bottom, Heller's viewpoint represents not a radical rupture with, but only the "logical opposite" of, the official Soviet ideology she criticizes: hers is an idealist emphasis on consciousness and not a dialectical materialist one that stresses the ultimate dependence of consciousness on material reality and the fact that it is precisely consciousness that corresponds to material reality in its motion and development that is capable of playing a tremendous role in transforming it.[100] As noted earlier, one of the things that

---

100. This is a point given particular emphasis by Mao Tsetung, for example in the formulation "matter can be transformed into consciousness and consciousness into matter" (see "Where Do Correct Ideas Come From?," Mao Tsetung, *Selected*

most characterizes Heller's views is the failure to correctly grasp the relationship between the economic base and the political and ideological superstructure of society, a failure which finds marked expression in her treatment of democracy as an ideal form that can be fitted onto either a capitalist or a socialist economic base. All this will become clearer by turning to *Marxism and Democracy*, especially the essay "The Past, Present and Future of Democracy" by Heller.

"Ho Chi Minh was right," Heller argues,

> to say that the whole of socialism is to be found within the Declaration of Independence, if one is referring to the ideal form of democratic socialism. But those who consider that capitalism is itself also embodied within the Declaration are also right, if what they are referring to is an "ideal" form of capitalism. For the same democratic principles, to the extent that they are formal principles, can serve as fundamental principles in the constitution of either a capitalist or a socialist society.[101]

And she adds the explanation that

> formal democracy, indeed, can be transformed into socialist democracy *without undergoing the slightest modification.* The principles of formal democracy prescribe how to proceed in dealing with the affairs of society, how to find solutions to problems, but in no way do they impose a limit on the content of various social aspirations.[102]

Leaving aside Ho Chi Minh's error in upholding the *Declaration of*

Readings [Peking: Foreign Languages Press, 1971], p. 503]. Heller is most emphatically not a Maoist, however. This can be seen in her comments on the "nouveaux philosophes" in France (people like Bernard Henri-Levy, et al.). While one can certainly agree with her dismissal of these people – "I don't think it is necessary to criticize the theory of the new philosophers because its level is so low that it doesn't warrant much attention" – Heller is fundamentally wrong in attempting to stress the identity, rather than the opposition, between the earlier (more or less) Maoist views of some of these people and their present bankruptcy – "From the beginning, then, social theory has taken for them the form of a myth" ("Introduction" to *Marxisme et Démocratie: Au-delà du "Socialisme Réel"* [Paris: Petite Collection Maspero, 1981], p. 14, my translation]. All passages cited from this book, hereafter referred to as *Marxism and Democracy*, are my translations from the French.

101. Heller, *Marxism and Democracy*, p. 223.

102. Heller, *Marxism and Democracy*, p. 224, emphasis added.

Independence,[103] what is striking here is how Heller completely fails to reckon with the historical context and class content of democracy. Without repeating everything that has been said so far (and without preempting the remaining discussion in the concluding chapters on socialist democracy as a system of class rule and the withering away of democracy with the abolition of classes), it should be clear that democracy, as a set of formal principles, cannot be made to serve socialism as well as capitalism "without undergoing the slightest modification." In fact, to repeat the most basic point, democracy under socialism must undergo a qualitative, radical transformation from what it was under capitalism – it must be inverted – so that democracy is practiced among the ranks of the new ruling class, the proletariat, while dictatorship is exercised by the proletariat over the former ruling class, the bourgeoisie.

Principles of formal democracy that, on the surface, grant equal rights to everyone without class distinction – while on a deeper level the very implementation of these formal principles works to enforce a fundamental relationship of exploitation and class oppression – can *not* serve socialism. There is absolutely no sense in Heller of the need for the two radical ruptures Marx and Engels spoke of as decisive, essential aspects of the communist revolution, no sense that in reality a bitter, in many ways uphill, battle must be waged *after* socialism is first established, not only to defend whatever socialist transformation has been achieved at any given point but to deepen and carry forward the socialist transformation of society toward the final goal of communism, worldwide. Without this, there is no socialism, let alone the ultimate achievement of communism. What are needed in the political realm are principles that reflect this and serve the struggle to overcome the resistance of the overthrown bourgeoisie (and newborn bourgeois class forces) and to enable the masses of people to become masters of society in every sphere. In other words, what is needed is the application of democracy (and dictatorship) with an *open, explicit, class content*, and *not* the principles of formal democracy "without the slightest modification."

103. As I wrote elsewhere, Ho Chi Minh's attempt to use the *Declaration of Independence* as an ideological and political weapon in the Vietnamese Revolution "is, unfortunately, an example of weaknesses and limitations in the Vietnamese Revolution and its leadership, *not* an indication of the value of the *Declaration of Independence* for revolutionary struggle in today's world" (*Horrible End, or End to Horror?*, p. 108).

As Mao Tsetung stressed:

> Those who demand freedom and democracy in the abstract regard democracy as an end and not as a means. Democracy as such sometimes seems to be an end, but it is in fact only a means. Marxism teaches us that democracy is part of the superstructure and belongs to the realm of politics. That is to say, in the last analysis, it serves the economic base. The same is true of freedom. Both democracy and freedom are relative, not absolute, and they come into being and develop in specific historical conditions.[104]

Heller is definitely one of those who regard democracy as an end in itself, and she actually believes that the consistent upholding of formal democracy, in practice as well as theory, is more radical than mere opposition to capitalism. Thus:

> One can describe as radical anyone who wishes to get beyond capitalism and all its nefarious implications; but only those who conceive of accomplishing this within the framework of formal democracy should be deemed left radicals. The left radical is not content to enlighten, although he also fulfills this role, but he also recognizes the reality of all human needs, except for those that imply the exploitation and oppression of other people, in accordance with the Kantian restriction prohibiting the using of others as merely a "simple means" [to an end]. The left radical must understand that intellectual knowledge is a specialized form of knowledge and that, when it comes to selecting values, all human beings are equally competent. He must recognize that, in deciding "what is to be done," no elite can play the decisive role. The left radical knows that the only valid social objective is that which is perceived as such by the majority of people, who would be ready to get involved to reach this goal in the same way as they are prepared to act to satisfy their own needs. All this is true for the simple reason that democracy is by definition the power of the people and the power of the people is by definition democracy.[105]

104. Mao, "On the Correct Handling of Contradictions Among the People," *Selected Works [SW]* (Peking: Foreign Languages Press, 1969 for volumes 1-4, 1977 for volume 5), Vol. 5, pp. 388-89.

105. Heller, *Marxism and Democracy*, p. 227. Note that here Heller takes the obligatory swipes at Lenin's line on the relation between the organized, politically conscious vanguard and the masses, and between consciousness and "spontaneity," especially as concentrated in his book *What Is To Be Done?* (it is not incidental that Heller is also an admirer of Rosa Luxemburg). It is also interesting to

The question of whether Heller really "wishes to get beyond capitalism and all its nefarious implications" will be returned to shortly, but it should be noted that the above is again a classical expression of bourgeois democracy, resting on several of its traditional pillars. In particular, the formulation that "when it comes to selecting values, all human beings are equally competent" is nothing if not Jeffersonian. And, of course, the principle that one must never treat people as merely a means to an end is pure Kant.[106] We shall see that in the final analysis it also turns out to be mere cant.

As I stated earlier, the Kantian maxim, "Act so that you treat humanity, whether in your own person or in that of another, always as an end and never as a means only," is not realizable — nor, for that matter, is it desirable.[107] First of all, this maxim presents things in terms of the relations between individuals; but in all human society individuals develop and assume their identity only in the context of social relations and not in isolation, "unto themselves." Further, in class society the most decisive relations — within which individual relations find their ultimate context — are the relations of classes, not individuals. And in a society divided into classes, it is impossible for any such maxim to be applied. Capitalist society is by definition a society based on exploitation and oppression. But socialist society, too, while its goal is the end of all exploitation, must depend on the oppression of one part of society — the bourgeoisie. As pointed out before, it is only in classless communist society that the exploitation and the oppression of one part of society by another will be finally eliminated, and moreover that the subordination of one individual *to another individual* will also be eliminated. But the subordination of individuals *to society as a whole* will *not* be

---

note that in the last line of the above-quoted passage, Heller uses exactly the same definition of democracy as the Soviet revisionist theoretician K. Zarodov in *The Political Economy of Revolution* (see p. 190) — which shows not that Heller has copied the Soviet authorities she detests (rightly, though not completely for the right reasons) but that they both adopt the classical bourgeois view of democracy and attempt (in different forms) to give this a "socialist" content.

106. An indication of how central this concept is to social-democratic — and generally to bourgeois-democratic — thought can also be seen in the statement by Michael Harrington invoking "Kant's magnificent dictum, that you cannot treat people as means to an end; or, as our own history puts it, that the individual has certain inalienable rights" (Harrington, *Decade of Decision*, p. 179).

107. See chapter 2, n. 99.

eliminated. Nor could it be, or else society could not function, and in actuality the freedom of all members of society would be severely restricted. Here we see once again the significance of Marx's statement: "Right can never be higher than the economic structure of society and its cultural development conditioned thereby." And this means that individuals will still be treated – by society – as a means to an end, though that end will then be nothing other than the continuing all-around advancement of society and of the people who make it up, and a continual broadening of the frontiers of their freedom.

As for Heller's insistence that "the only valid social objective is that which is perceived as such by the majority of people," having lived in one or another imperialist country for four decades (the overwhelming part of it in the USA), I am singularly unimpressed by such a concept. For much of the time that the U.S. was carrying out its criminal war in Vietnam (and "criminal" is really too weak a word for it), the majority of people in the U.S. did not consider it a "valid social objective" to oppose and defeat the U.S. in this war. But I do not think that, therefore, the Vietnamese people should not have tried to defeat the U.S., or that people in the U.S. – clearly constituting a minority for a considerable period – who opposed the war should have refrained from actively doing so until they had convinced the majority that this was a "valid social objective." Nor do I think that such opposition should have mainly taken the form of simply attempting, through discussion, to convince the majority in the U.S. of the validity of this objective. Or today, it is definitely the case that a majority of the people in the imperialist countries, while they may be opposed in a general, abstract sense to world war, nevertheless do not consider it a "valid social objective" to take a stand of particularly targeting their own ruling class (while opposing all imperialists) and moreover working toward proletarian revolution to overthrow that ruling class as their most important contribution toward preventing world war and eventually eliminating the system that gives rise to such monstrosity. But the majority's present opposition to such an objective does not make it any less valid – or urgent. Nor should those who do hold this objective wait for the majority to embrace it before undertaking active work toward realizing it – or concentrate their efforts mainly on persuading this majority through "reasoned dialogue."

Of course, if we were to put such questions to the people not merely in the imperialist countries but throughout the world – and if those who are the target of these objectives (the ruling classes) did not exist, or somehow did not exercise political power (class dictatorship) – then we might get quite a different answer from the "majority." And it is very relevant to raise such a perspective in responding to Heller's nostrums about the will of the majority, since (judging from these essays at least) she gives virtually no attention to the question of dealing with – to say nothing of overcoming – the lopsidedness in the world. But the reality is that we cannot put the question to the world's majority in this way now – and this is just the point; it will require a thoroughgoing world revolutionary struggle to create a situation where the exploited majority in the world can actually realize – in fact, fully recognize – its interests.

Even in socialist society, where for the first time it is actually true that the majority rules – since the class that represents the interests of the majority, the proletariat, will be in power – it is still not true that "the only valid social objective is that which is perceived as such by the majority of people." It may be true, to cite a dramatic example, that at the time of the revisionist coup in China right after Mao's death, a majority of the people either supported that coup or at least did not consider it a "valid social objective" to actively oppose it. But this was definitely a "valid social objective" all the same. It is true that the socialist revolution, and its ultimate objective of communism, must ultimately rely on the majority of the people and be realized through the conscious activism of the masses, but that does not in any way validate Heller's opposition to a vanguard leadership and her insistence on bowing to the spontaneous will of the majority. There is a dialectical relationship between the vanguard and the masses: the conscious activism of the masses is heightened by the leadership of the vanguard, and vice versa. And none of this can be considered outside the context of the continuing division of society into classes and the struggle between them. For all these reasons, it may be very democratic to preach about how social objectives can find their validity only in their acceptance by the majority – without class distinctions being drawn – but it is very bourgeois democratic, and it has nothing to do with achieving socialism and ultimately communism.

Here it might be objected that Heller's vision of socialism is after all quite different from the one I have been presenting. And that is most definitely true. In putting forward the principles she says should govern the society she envisions, Heller seeks to

resolve what she identifies as a "paradox" of formal democracy –
"that it reveals nothing concerning a society's economic structure,
social relations and corresponding power structure" – which explains why, according to Heller, "formal democracy can coexist
with capitalist society."[108] More specifically, "among the rights of
man there is one which has bearing on the economic structure [of
society]: the right of property."[109] In capitalist society, this means
the right to capitalist private property, but the problem is, as she
identifies it, that "exercising this right in effect deprives the
majority of people of ownership of property, except for ownership of their own labor power. This means that it prevents the
exercise of a right which is guaranteed as such."[110]

Thus, Heller says, it has understandably been tempting
historically to seek to resolve this contradiction by abolishing the
right to ownership of private property, concentrating all economic power in the hands of the state, and blurring over the distinctions between the state and civil society (here the image of
totalitarianism rears its monstrous head). This, according to
Heller, is what Marx termed the "negative abolition of private
property." But this is not a genuine socialist solution, she says,
because by concentrating such power in the hands of the state, including the right of the state to dictate the terms of all contractual
agreements, the people are deprived of liberty and equality, even
in the formal sense, whereas socialism should seek to maximize
these. The socialist solution is to work for the "positive abolition
of private property." This means that the *right* to private property
is not abolished (and the merging of the state and civil society, as
Heller sees it, is not effected). In elaborating on this, Heller
presents a portrait of a society where the right to property has
been generalized and guaranteed to every last individual, and
where everybody equally participates in all the key decisions in
all spheres of society and makes decisions regarding the distribution of the social product. Property is therefore "collective" and
the "contract" – defined as a "transaction between equals" –
becomes pivotal to the functioning of society. All this is to be
accompanied (gradually) by the decentralizing of economic
power and the breaking of the hold of privileged elements in such

108. Heller, *Marxism and Democracy*, p. 233.
109. Heller, *Marxism and Democracy*, p. 233.
110. Heller, *Marxism and Democracy*, p. 233.

key spheres as the media, education, and so forth, so that a system of pluralistic representation through elections can really work.[111]

It is little wonder that Heller finally feels compelled to comment in passing that she is not even so sure how much Marx can be used as a point of reference in working for such a goal, since, she says (indulging extravagantly in understatement), this is after all not exactly how Marx conceived of the abolition of private property.[112] It is not very difficult to see that, in opposition to Marx's view of the complete abolition of bourgeois property relations – and all relations in which human beings confront each other as owners (or non-owners) of property rather than through conscious and voluntary association – Heller's vision is that of a society of small property owners, equal in their contractual relations and cooperating in the ownership of what is still, at bottom, bourgeois property.

It is also not surprising that, in opposition to Marx's stirring call for the proletariat to arise and overthrow the bourgeois state (including in its ideal democratic form), to establish its own state and through it move forward to the abolition of the state itself with the abolition of classes; Heller insists that violence cannot be justified if the goal is to abolish altogether a system based on contractual relations – for this would sound the death knell of democracy; that the abolition of the state is an unrealizable utopian vision; and that in a truly democratic state, since "citizens have both the right and the obligation to institute and apply laws and to serve as judges," they therefore have the "right and obligation to obey the laws which they have formulated."[113] In opposition to the *Communist Manifesto*, Heller sees the realization of a democratic socialist society through "the putting into practice of the principles of the Declaration of Independence."[114]

For Marx,

socialism is the *declaration of the permanence of the revolution,* the *class dictatorship* of the proletariat as the necessary transit point to

111. See Heller, *Marxism and Democracy*, pp. 233-39, especially pp. 234-36.

112. See Heller, *Marxism and Democracy*, p. 237.

113. Heller, *Marxism and Democracy*, p. 221; see also pp. 236-38. The comment of a friend upon reading this particular passage in Heller's essay is very much to the point: "It's not too hard to see the iron hand underneath all the hippie-sounding gobbledy-gook about multiplicity of lifestyles, individual initiatives, etc."

114. Heller, *Marxism and Democracy*, p. 239.

the *abolition of class distinctions generally,* to the abolition of all the relations of production on which they rest, to the abolition of all the social relations that correspond to these relations of production, to the revolutionizing of all the ideas that result from these social relations.[115]

For Heller, one can only say – at the risk of being redundant – that socialism is the *Declaration of Independence,* bourgeois democracy, bourgeois ideals, and the permanence of all the production and social relations to which these correspond and upon which they rest.

* * * * *

In concluding this chapter, it is important to reemphasize that, despite their differences, there is a profound underlying unity between the social democrats and the revisionists focused on here. The social democrats of various kinds are more or less classical apologists for Western imperialism (whether openly such, as in the case of Arendt, or more indirectly so in the case of people like Heller, Thompson, or Fine – democratic forms and traditions *do* make a difference, they say, and these *do* exist in the West, as opposed to the Soviet bloc. . .so. . .). On the other hand, revisionists like Zarodov are obviously directly in the service of Soviet social-imperialism. But, even with opposite loyalties, and in some respects opposite forms of the same stupidity (to borrow from Engels), they all share the fundamental feature that their principles and ideals are grounded (ultimately but solidly) in relations of bourgeois domination, not only within particular countries but internationally. They all see democracy as inseparable from their vision of the most just and rational society; they all do not see beyond the bounds of bourgeois society and the bourgeois epoch.

115. Marx, "The Class Struggles in France," in *MESW*, 1, p. 282.

7

Democracy and the Communist Revolution

From all that has been said so far, should it be concluded that the communist approach to democracy is an entirely negative one? No, it is a dialectical materialist one. Concretely, this means that communists recognize that democracy is not an end in itself but a means to an end; that it is part of the superstructure and conforms to and serves a particular economic base; that it arises in certain historical conditions and is generally associated with the bourgeois epoch; that it never exists in abstract or "pure" form but always has a definite class character and is conditioned by the fundamental relation between classes; and that it has a distinctive character and role in the transition from capitalist society and the bourgeois epoch to the epoch of world communism, and will wither away with the achievement of communism.

Besides the discussion on these issues in the preceding chapters, I have written fairly extensively elsewhere on different aspects of these questions, in particular on two points: the role of democracy in colonial revolutions leading to socialism and the role of socialism itself as a transition to communism.[1] With this as background, this chapter will begin with a basic summary on these two points and then proceed to the questions of democracy and dictatorship under socialism and the withering away of dictatorship and democracy with the realization of communism.

New Democracy

It is true that in most of the world today – specifically in the Third World – the immediate transformations that must be carried out in social and international relations conform, as a general rule, to what can broadly be defined as democratic tasks: the winning of genuine national liberation and the elimination of various forms or vestiges of precapitalist economic relations and their reflection in the superstructure. In short, in these vast regions containing the great majority of the world's people and constituting the most volatile areas under imperialist rule, what is immediately on the agenda is what Mao Tsetung defined as the new-democratic revolution.

It was through the course of the several-decades-long revolution in China, led by the Communist Party, which eventually led in 1949 to the founding of the People's Republic of China and the emergence of China onto the socialist road, that Mao fully formulated the theory and political program of this new-democratic revolution. In one of the major works in which this is set forth, Mao makes this basic presentation of the question:

> What, indeed, is the character of the Chinese revolution at the present stage? Is it a bourgeois-democratic or a proletarian-socialist revolution? Obviously, it is not the latter but the former.
>
> Since Chinese society is colonial, semicolonial and semifeudal, since the principal enemies of the Chinese revolution are imperialism and feudalism, since the tasks of the revolution are to overthrow these two enemies by means of a national and democratic revolution in which the bourgeoisie sometimes takes part, and since the edge of the revolution is directed against imperialism and feudalism and not against capitalism and capitalist private property in general even if the big bourgeoisie betrays the

---

1. See, for example, *Mao Tsetung's Immortal Contributions* (Chicago: RCP Publications, 1979), especially chapters 1, 2, and 6; *For a Harvest of Dragons*, chapter 2; and *A Horrible End, or an End to the Horror?*, chapters 2 and 3.

revolution and becomes its enemy – since all this is true, the character of the Chinese revolution at the present stage is not proletarian-socialist but bourgeois-democratic.

However, in present-day China the bourgeois-democratic revolution is no longer of the old general type, which is now obsolete, but one of a new special type. We call this type the new-democratic revolution and it is developing in all other colonial and semicolonial countries as well as in China. The new-democratic revolution is part of the world proletarian-socialist revolution, for it resolutely opposes imperialism, *i.e.,* international capitalism....

The new-democratic revolution is vastly different from the democratic revolutions of Europe and America in that it results not in a dictatorship of the bourgeoisie but in a dictatorship of the united front of all the revolutionary classes under the leadership of the proletariat....

The new-democratic revolution also differs from a socialist revolution in that it overthrows the rule of the imperialists, traitors and reactionaries in China but does not destroy any section of capitalism which is capable of contributing to the anti-imperialist, anti-feudal struggle.[2]

Further, while in itself it is not yet the proletarian-socialist revolution – and while it may create more possibility for the development of national capitalism – this new-democratic revolution is not only part of the world proletarian-socialist revolution in a general sense; it is the prerequisite to and clears the way for the socialist revolution in the particular country itself, by overthrowing the domination of imperialism and making a qualitative break with the whole network of imperialist international relations, by uprooting precapitalist relations within the (formerly) colonized country, and by expropriating, as a first major step, the capital of the big bourgeoisie tied to and dependent on imperialism.[3]

Despite significant changes in the world and in various specific countries since the time Mao formulated the line of new-

2. Mao, "The Chinese Revolution and the Chinese Communist Party," *SW*, 2, pp. 326-27.

3. Mao estimated that in the Chinese new-democratic revolution this involved the expropriation of 80 percent of capital's industrial holdings – the amount controlled by big, bureaucrat capital. (See Mao, *A Critique of Soviet Economics* [New York: Monthly Review Press, 1977], p. 40.) Conversely, the political program of the socialist revolution comprehends what can be generally defined as democratic tasks; the point is that it is not limited to these but is distinguished by the objective of abolishing capitalist relations of exploitation and indeed all class divisions.

democratic revolution (the period before and during World War 2), and despite the fact that within the Third World today conditions may significantly differ from country to country (for example, some have undergone a fairly extensive industrial development while some others have experienced only an extremely limited one), it remains the case that imperialism dominates all these countries – and, in dominating, distorts and disarticulates their economies and social relations in various ways. Thus, as a general rule, the strategic orientation and program of new democracy, as the first stage of the revolutionary process – clearing the ground for and leading to socialism – illuminates the way forward throughout the Third World, and therein the way forward for the great majority of the people in the world who are exploited and oppressed under imperialist rule. As Mao emphasized, this revolution "is a stage of transition between the abolition of the colonial, semicolonial and semi-feudal society and the establishment of a socialist society, i.e., it is a process of *new*-democratic revolution."[4]

In sum, new democracy means not a bourgeois revolution, led by the bourgeoisie and leading to capitalist society – nor a revolution in the abstract, without class content and leading to a democratic state without a class character – it means a revolution against imperialism, precapitalist social relations, and the domestic class forces that represent and uphold all this, and it leads to the political rule of the classes that unite to carry out this revolution, under the leadership of the proletariat and its communist vanguard. It leads, in other words, to a particular form of the dictatorship of the proletariat – involving a broad class alliance but firmly led by the class-conscious proletariat – and thereby opens the way to socialism. In this way it forms a decisive component of the world-historic proletarian-socialist revolution and its ultimate goal of communism with the abolition of all class distinctions and all forms of the state.

Socialism as a Transition

In the previous chapter, attention was called to Marx's statement in his *Critique of the Gotha Programme* that the form of state dur-

---

4. Mao, "Chinese Revolution and Chinese Communist Party," *SW*, 2, p. 327, emphasis added.

ing the transition from capitalist to communist society can only be the revolutionary dictatorship of the proletariat. This was no facile formulation that Marx came up with on the spur of the moment. Already, some time before this, Marx had pointed out:

> As to myself, no credit is due to me for discovering the existence of classes in modern society, nor yet the struggle between them. Long before me bourgeois historians had described the historical development of this struggle of the classes, and bourgeois economists the economic anatomy of the classes. What I did that was new was to prove: 1) that the *existence of classes* is only bound up with *particular historical phases in the development of production*; 2) that the class struggle necessarily leads to the *dictatorship of the proletariat*; 3) that this dictatorship itself only constitutes the transition to the *abolition of all classes* and to a *classless society....*"[5]

As Chang Chun-chiao recounted:

> In this splendid observation, Lenin said, Marx succeeded in expressing with striking clarity the chief and radical difference between his theory on the state and that of the bourgeoisie, and the essence of his teaching on the state. Here it should be noted that Marx divided the sentence on the dictatorship of the proletariat into three points, which are interrelated and cannot be cut apart. It is impermissible to accept only one of the three points while rejecting the other two. For the sentence gives complete expression to the entire process of the inception, development and withering away of the dictatorship of the proletariat and covers the whole task of the dictatorship of the proletariat and its actual content.[6]

While Marx's sentence on the dictatorship of the proletariat does indeed give a succinct and at the same time sweeping summary along the lines Chang stresses, it is also true that since the

---

5. Marx, "Letter to Joseph Weydemeyer" (5 March 1852), *MESL*, p. 18.

6. Chang Chun-chiao, "On Exercising All-Round Dictatorship Over the Bourgeoisie," in *And Mao Makes 5*, ed. Raymond Lotta (Chicago: Banner Press, 1978), p. 216. Chang Chun-chiao, of course, was one of the "gang of four"—the leading core in the Communist Party that upheld Mao's line and was arrested and subsequently put on trial by the revisionists who seized power shortly after Mao's death. And he has remained one of the "gang of two"—the other being Chiang Ching—that has refused to capitulate to these revisionists, even in the face of a threatened death sentence. This article by Chang, in 1975, was a major theoretical salvo against the revisionists and a major exposition of Mao's basic line on continuing the revolution under the dictatorship of the proletariat.

time of Marx (and since the time of Lenin as well) a great deal of experience has been accumulated concerning the nature of the transition from capitalism to communism (Chang's article was, as noted, a major effort at summing up this experience in light of intense struggles within socialist China at that time). In particular, as I pointed out in a previous book:

> It would seem that when Marx referred to the transition to *communist* society he meant the lower phase of communist society and that he envisioned this as a society where there is no longer any private ownership of the means of production, and no longer either commodity production or wage-labor as such, although payment would be according to work and be received as certificates indicating the amount of labor performed, so that in this sense the principle governing commodity exchange would still be in effect. In *The State and Revolution,* written just before the October Revolution in Russia, Lenin argued that during the transition period there would still be the need to suppress the overthrown exploiters but that once the first stage of communist society had been reached (which is "usually called socialism," Lenin said) there will no longer be any class left which must be suppressed; "differences, and unjust differences, in wealth will still persist, but the *exploitation* of man by man will have become impossible because it will be impossible to seize the *means of production*—the factories, machines, land, etc.—and make them private property." The need for a state will nonetheless remain, he said, although its nature and function will be different than in the transition to this first, socialist stage of communism.[7]

♦ And further,

> As a matter of fact, in no socialist country that has existed, neither in the Soviet Union nor China nor elsewhere, has a society like that discussed in *The State and Revolution* (and described by Marx in the *Critique of the Gotha Programme*) actually existed. Under the leadership of Stalin, ownership in the Soviet Union was radically transformed in the late 1920s and early 1930s in industry and agriculture, but neither then nor later did this ever reach the point where all ownership of the means of production had become state ownership, as assumed by Marx and Lenin in discussing the lower stage of communism. Nor was commodity production and exchange or wage-labor ever eliminated. The same is true for all

---

7. Avakian, *Harvest of Dragons,* pp. 105-6; the quotations from Lenin are from "State and Revolution," chapter 5, *LCW,* 25, pp. 472, 471.

the countries which were at one time socialist. Stalin's approach to this question was to conclude that once small-scale production had been (overwhelmingly) eliminated and ownership almost entirely transformed into state *or collective* ownership (the latter by the peasants in agricultural production in particular) socialism had been achieved, antagonistic classes had been eliminated, the need to suppress internal class enemies no longer existed and the socialist state was still required only because of danger posed by international capital and the infiltration of its agents. This was, on the one hand, a muddled formulation. . . and on the other hand it was a departure from the analysis presented by Lenin who had said that even in socialist society as he defined it the state would still be necessary for the enforcement of "bourgeois law" in relation to distribution of consumer goods (and not merely because of imperialist encirclement and imperialist agents). Most seriously of all, Stalin was wrong in saying that antagonistic classes – and in particular the bourgeoisie – no longer existed in the Soviet Union. But it is important to grasp that Stalin's formulation was a response, however marred by error, to the fact that the transition from capitalist society to communist society, and in particular the phase of this transition after the basic elimination of private ownership has been carried out, has proved to be more protracted and complex than envisioned by Marx or Lenin.[8]

All in all, then, while in the few years between the initial victory of the proletarian revolution in Russia and his death in 1924 Lenin made some beginning analysis of the concrete problems that arise during the transition to communism, it remained for Mao Tsetung, several decades later, to achieve a new breakthrough on this question, on the basis of summing up a vast and rich store of experience, positive and negative, in the Soviet Union as well as in China itself. Mao summed up that, even after ownership of the decisive means of production had, in the main, been socialized (either in the form of state ownership or collective ownership by peasants in agriculture and some others in small factories, urban cooperatives, etc.), there still remained classes and class struggle. In particular, not only were many members of the old exploiting classes still around, but of greater significance – and increasingly posing the greatest internal danger to the socialist state – *new* bourgeois elements were constantly being engendered out of the very conditions – the basic contradictions – of

8. Avakian, *Harvest of Dragons*, pp. 107-8.

socialist society itself. Wage-labor and payment in relation to work performed, the production and exchange of goods in the form of commodities, the continued role of money, even aspects of commodity relations and money exchanges in the dealings between various discrete units of ownership (whether collectives, urban cooperatives, and so on, or even enterprises formally under state ownership) – all these things continue to exist and exert considerable influence in various ways. "Under the dictatorship of the proletariat," Mao summed up, "such things can only be restricted," and not yet eliminated, and therefore if people in authority who take the capitalist road usurp political power, "it will be quite easy for them to rig up the capitalist system."[9] Mao also linked this with the fact that, especially in the more economically backward countries where socialism has so far been established, the contradictions between town and country and between workers and peasants have continued to be very acute. At the same time, in all socialist societies, the division between mental and manual labor persists as does the division of labor along sexual lines, whose roots are intertwined with the very division of society into classes; and other important contradictions, such as that between the dominant nationality and minority nationalities, also continue in various forms.

Because of the long-term persistence of these basic contradictions and social inequalities inherited from the old society (Mao used the term "bourgeois right," in a broad sense, to refer to such social inequalities and their reflection in the superstructure, including the spheres of law and politics as well as ideology) – indeed out of these very contradictions and social inequalities – a new bourgeoisie will be constantly engendered under socialism, and socialism itself will constitute a long transition period between capitalism and communism – a transition marked by recurrent acute class struggles between the bourgeoisie, particularly the newly engendered bourgeoisie, and the proletariat. In these struggles, bourgeois right – and specifically whether to restrict or give full expression to it – will be a major focus, and the more privileged strata in socialist society (intellectuals, administrative personnel, professionals, and others) will tend spontaneously to support a program of not restricting but giving unrestricted scope to bourgeois right. For all these reasons, along

---

9. Cited in Chang Chun-chiao, "Exercising All-Round Dictatorship," in *Mao Makes 5,* p. 214.

with the encirclement and pressure – and, at times, direct military attack – by imperialism, as well as the connections between domestic counterrevolutionaries and various imperialist states, the danger of capitalist restoration remains very great throughout this socialist transition period. It is essential, Mao summed up, not only to uphold the dictatorship of the proletariat, but to continue the revolution under it. But that is not all. Mao

* made the unprecedented analysis that, in the conditions where ownership is (in the main) socialized and where the party is both the leading political center of the socialist state and the main directing force of the economy – in which the state is the decisive sector – the contradiction between the party as the leading force and the working class and the masses under its leadership is a concentrated expression of the contradictions characterizing socialist society as a transition from the old society to fully communist, classless society. Therefore, Mao concluded, while the party must on the one hand continue to play its vanguard role, on the other hand, the party itself, especially at its top levels, is also where the new bourgeoisie will assume its most concentrated expression, where its core and leading forces will be centered, among those who, as Mao described it, "take the capitalist road." To defeat the attempts of these forces, and the reactionary social base they mobilize, to seize power from the proletariat and restore capitalism, it is necessary, Mao summed up, to expose and wage struggle against the revisionist line and actions of these "capitalist roaders" and more than that to continually revolutionize the party itself as part of revolutionizing society as a whole by unleashing and developing the conscious activism of the masses and mobilizing them in ideological and political struggle in every sphere of society while directing the spearhead of that struggle against the revisionists in positions of authority.[10]

• "It was all this, and more, that burst forth in the Great Proletarian Cultural Revolution in China beginning in the mid-'60s," as I put it in *For a Harvest of Dragons.* And I cannot here better summarize the importance of this Cultural Revolution than by repeating the assessment of it in that work:

Adjectives such as "unprecedented," "historic," "earth-shaking" and so on have frequently been used to describe this mass revolutionary movement, and if anything they understate its impact and

10. *Basic Principles for Unity of Marxist-Leninists*, paragraph 126.

importance. With the reversal of the revolution in China in 1976 and the suppression of everything revolutionary there in the years since, and in the present world situation, there is a strong tendency to forget what it meant that there was a country, with one-quarter of the world's population, where there had not only been a successful revolution leading to socialism, overcoming tremendous obstacles and powerful reactionary forces in the process, but even after that there was again a mass revolutionary upheaval, initiated and inspired by the leading figure in the new socialist state, Mao Tsetung, against those in authority who sought to become the new party of order, restoring capitalism in the name of "socialism," using their revolutionary credentials as capital. The Cultural Revolution involved literally hundreds of millions of people in various forms and various levels of political struggle and ideological debate over the direction of society and affairs of state, the problems of the world revolutionary struggle and the international communist movement. Barriers were broken down to areas formerly forbidden to the masses of people—science, philosophy, education, literature and art. Putting self above the interests of the revolution, in China and the world, was an outlook under attack and on the defensive and few were those who would openly utter such phrases as "my *career*." Through all this, transformations were brought about in the major institutions in society and in the thinking of masses of people, further revolutionizing them. Through all this as well, new breakthroughs were made and new lessons gained in moving, through the exercise of the dictatorship of the proletariat itself, toward the eventual withering away of the state—striking at the soil engendering class distinctions and at the same time drawing the masses more broadly and more consciously into the running of society.[11]

What is noteworthy about this Cultural Revolution is not—as conventional wisdom insists today (including in a China now ruled by revisionists)—that mistakes were made by the revolutionaries; it is not that the new shoots of the communist future that sprung up through this Cultural Revolution were in many ways fragile or imperfect, nor that some of the innovations made were not viable; nor even that in the end this Cultural Revolution failed to prevent a revisionist takeover and capitalist restoration. What is noteworthy is that this was the first mass revolutionary struggle under socialism consciously aimed at bourgeois usurpers that had arisen within the structure of the new proletarian state itself; that it turned back and held off their attempts to seize

11. Avakian, *Harvest of Dragons*, pp. 110-11.

power and restore capitalism for a full decade; and, of more lasting significance, that it indicated a means and method (as Mao said) for waging this struggle and, before it was reversed, brought into being new, indeed unprecedented, transformations in the economic relations and the political and ideological superstructure of society, new breakthroughs on the path to communism.

At the same time, it is important to stress that the struggle for communism is, and must be, an international struggle, and that the class struggle within a particular country, even a socialist country, is, and must be, subordinate to the overall world revolutionary struggle to achieve the dictatorship of the proletariat and carry through the transition to communism. Here my purpose is not so much to repeat the criticism I have previously made that the Cultural Revolution, while it indeed represented the highest pinnacle yet reached by the international proletariat, was still treated, even by Mao, a bit too much as a thing unto itself and "too much apart from the whole, worldwide struggle against imperialism, reaction, and all exploiting classes," and "even though support was extended to revolutionary struggles elsewhere and it was stressed that the final victory of a socialist country requires the victory of the world proletarian revolution, it was not firmly enough grasped and popularized that the socialist transformation of any particular country can only be a *subordinate* part of the overall world proletarian revolution."[12] But what must be emphasized here is that the overcoming of the social inequalities characterizing the old order – the eventual elimination of bourgeois right in the broadest sense – must be approached, above all, on the world level in order to carry through the transition to communism. It is this which sets the most fundamental basis and most comprehensive context for the discussion of the content and tasks of the dictatorship of the proletariat.

Democracy and Dictatorship Under Socialism

Why is a dictatorship necessary in socialist society, if it is actually the case that socialism is a qualitative advance over capitalism

---

12. Avakian, *Horrible End, or End to Horror?*, p. 154; see also Avakian, "The Philosophical Basis of Proletarian Internationalism," *Revolutionary Worker*, No. 96 (13 March 1981).

and other forms of exploitative relations; if the proletariat represents the real interests of the majority of people, and stands for the elimination of all exploitation, then why does it need a dictatorship to enforce its rule over society? This is a question that is not infrequently asked, including by people who are not necessarily opposed to some kind of socialist transformation of society (as well as, of course, many who definitely are). And, in any case, it is a question that deserves discussion here.

The basis for answering this question is found in the nature of socialist society as a transition, as summarized in the last section. To put it in a nutshell, in many ways, in socialist society, even after the bourgeoisie has been overthrown and the old exploiters have been expropriated and the means of production formerly owned privately by them have been converted into public ownership (in one form or another), it is still an uphill battle to carry through the transition to classless, fully communist society. The struggle to achieve this goal is going up against those traditional property relations and traditional ideas with which there must be a radical rupture – thousands of years of the accumulation and deep implantation of these traditions have made them formidable obstructions that must be thoroughly uprooted. There are all the contradictions and inequalities inherited from the old society, which cannot be overcome all at once but in varying ways and varying degrees will persist for some time. And on top of all this, experience has shown that it is extremely unlikely that socialism will be established all at once in anything like all, or even a majority of, the countries in the world, but is likely to be established in only one or a few in any particular conjuncture of world contradictions, after which it is necessary to consolidate the breakthroughs achieved in these countries while supporting the revolutionary struggle in other countries and preparing for the next major conjuncture with its heightened possibilities for the advance of the world revolution.[13] So, especially viewed in light of all this, it becomes clear that not only does the bourgeoisie still retain the upper hand in the world as a whole – and is likely to for some time – but this interpenetrates with, and indeed sets the overall framework and foundation for, the struggle to carry

13. For a fuller exposition of this point, see *For a Harvest of Dragons*, chapter 3, part 2; *A Horrible End, or an End to the Horror?*, chapter 2, especially pp. 149-51 and chapter 4, especially pp. 195-99; see also *Conquer the World? The International Proletariat Must and Will*, especially section 2.

forward the revolutionization of society in any particular socialist country.

• Already, in the first years of the dictatorship of the proletariat in the infant Soviet Republic, Lenin made an extremely incisive and farsighted analysis of key aspects of this problem, and it is worth quoting at length from one of his major polemics on this point:

> The exploiters can be defeated at one stroke in the event of a successful uprising at the center, or of a revolt in the army. But except in very rare and special cases, the exploiters cannot be destroyed at one stroke. It is impossible to expropriate all the landowners and capitalists of any big country at one stroke. Furthermore, expropriation alone, as a legal or political act, does not settle the matter by a long chalk, because it is necessary to *depose* the landowners and capitalists in actual fact, to *replace* their management of the factories and estates by a different management, workers' management, in actual fact. There can be no equality between the exploiters—who for many generations have been better off because of their education, conditions of wealthy life, and habits—and the exploited, the majority of whom even in the most advanced and most democratic bourgeois republics are downtrodden, backward, ignorant, intimidated and disunited. For a long time after the revolution the exploiters inevitably continue to retain a number of great practical advantages: they still have money (since it is impossible to abolish money all at once); some movable property—often fairly considerable; they still have various connections, habits of organization and management; knowledge of all the "secrets" (customs, methods, means and possibilities) of management; superior education; close connections with the higher technical personnel (who live and think like the bourgeoisie); incomparably greater experience in the art of war (this is very important), and so on and so forth.
>
> If the exploiters are defeated in one country only—and this, of course, is typical, since a simultaneous revolution in a number of countries is a rare exception—they *still* remain *stronger* than the exploited, for the international connections of the exploiters are enormous. That a section of the exploited from the least advanced middle-peasant, artisan and similar groups of the population may, and indeed does, follow the exploiters has been proved by *all* revolutions, including the [Paris] Commune (for there were also proletarians among the Versailles troops, which the most learned Kautsky has "forgotten")....
>
> The transition from capitalism to communism takes an entire historical epoch. Until this epoch is over, the exploiters inevitably

cherish the hope of restoration, and this *hope* turns into *attempts* at restoration. After their first serious defeat, the overthrown exploiters – who had not expected their overthrow, never believed it possible, never conceded the thought of it – throw themselves with energy grown tenfold, with furious passion and hatred grown a hundredfold, into the battle for the recovery of the "paradise," of which they were deprived, on behalf of their families, who had been leading such a sweet and easy life and whom now the "common herd" is condemning to ruin and destitution (or to "common" labor...). In the train of the capitalist exploiters follow the wide sections of the petty bourgeoisie, with regard to whom decades of historical experience of all countries testify that they vacillate and hesitate, one day marching behind the proletariat and the next day taking fright at the difficulties of the revolution; that they become panic-stricken at the first defeat or semi-defeat of the workers, grow nervous, run about aimlessly, snivel, and rush from one camp into the other – just like our Mensheviks and Socialist-Revolutionaries.

In these circumstances, in an epoch of desperately acute war, when history presents the question of whether age-old and thousand-year-old privileges are to be or not to be – at such a time to talk about majority and minority, about pure democracy, about dictatorship being unnecessary and about equality between the exploiter and the exploited! What infinite stupidity and abysmal philistinism are needed for this![14]

When all this is taken into account – and when, moreover, what has been learned since Lenin's time is added to it – we can return, with a deepened understanding, to the fundamental conclusion Lenin drew: for all these reasons the dictatorship of the proletariat is essential.[15]

Here we must return also to the fundamental point that democracy is not and cannot be an abstract thing unto itself or an end in itself, it cannot exist in "pure" form: it always assumes form

---

14. Lenin, "Proletarian Revolution and Renegade Kautsky," *LCW*, 28, pp. 252-54. This, by the way, should help explode the much-propagated myth that the Marxist view of the future society is a utopian one – as Lenin stressed in this very polemic, and repeatedly elsewhere, it is necessary to build socialism and advance to communism by beginning with conditions, and with people, as they are "bequeathed" by the old society (however much they undergo some dramatic *initial* changes in the very process of seizing power through the mass armed struggle).

15. See also Lenin, "'Left-Wing' Communism, An Infantile Disorder," chapter 2, *LCW*, 31, pp. 23-26.

as part of the state – that is to say, the dictatorship – of one class or another, and specifically in this era, of the bourgeoisie or the proletariat. But there is a profound qualitative difference in the content of democracy under the rule of the one class and the other, that is, between democracy under socialism and democracy under capitalism. As Lenin also laid bare in his polemic against the "Renegade Kautsky,"

> Bourgeois democracy, although a great historical advance in comparison with medievalism, always remains, and under capitalism is bound to remain, restricted, truncated, false and hypocritical, a paradise for the rich and a snare and deception for the exploited, for the poor....
>
> The learned Mr. Kautsky has "forgotten" – accidentally forgotten, probably – a "trifle," namely, that the ruling party in a bourgeois democracy extends the protection of the minority only to another *bourgeois* party, while the proletariat, on all *serious, profound and fundamental* issues, gets martial law or pogroms, instead of the "protection of the minority." *The more highly developed a democracy is, the more imminent are pogroms or civil war in connection with any profound political divergence which is dangerous to the bourgeoisie.* [16]

In contrast, Lenin stressed, "Proletarian democracy is *a million times* more democratic than any bourgeois democracy."[17] In fact, it is not only a million times more democratic, it is democratic in a qualitatively new and profoundly different way: it represents and depends on the broadest, and ever-deepening, participation of the formerly oppressed and exploited masses in every sphere of society – and more than that requires their increasing mastery of affairs of state, of economic management, and other aspects of administration, and indeed of the superstructure as a whole, including culture as well as other spheres of ideology. All this goes far beyond – again, it is qualitatively different from – the mere question of formal democracy and formal rights. As Mao penetratingly pointed out in criticizing those modern-day renegades, the Soviet revisionists:

> we find a discussion of the rights labor enjoys [in socialist society] but no discussion of labor's right to run the state, the various

16. Lenin, "Proletarian Revolution and Renegade Kautsky," *LCW*, 28, pp. 243, 245.

17. Lenin, "Proletarian Revolution and Renegade Kautsky," *LCW*, 28, p. 248.

enterprises, education, and culture. Actually, this is labor's greatest right under socialism, the most fundamental right, without which there is no right to work, to an education, to vacation, etc.

The paramount issue for socialist democracy is: Does labor have the right to subdue the various antagonistic forces and their influences? For example, who controls things like the newspapers, journals, broadcast stations, the cinema? Who criticizes? These are a part of the question of rights. If these things are in the hands of right opportunists (who are a minority) then the vast nationwide majority that urgently needs a great leap forward will find itself deprived of these rights.... Who is in control of the organs and enterprises bears tremendously on the issue of guaranteeing the people's rights. If Marxist-Leninists are in control, the rights of the vast majority will be guaranteed. If rightists or right opportunists are in control, these organs and enterprises may change qualitatively, and the people's rights with respect to them cannot be guaranteed. In sum, the people must have the right to manage the superstructure. We must not take the rights of the people to mean that the state is to be managed by only a section of the people, that the people can enjoy labor rights, education rights, social insurance, etc., only under the management of certain people.[18]

Here Mao has expressed in striking and concentrated terms the fundamental difference between capitalist democracy and socialist democracy and between bourgeois dictatorship and proletarian dictatorship, as well as the relationship between proletarian dictatorship and socialist democracy, and between both of them on the one hand and the role of the proletariat's vanguard leadership on the other hand. Notice that Mao does not say that the rights of the vast majority – including their most fundamental right to control the economy and "manage the superstructure" – will be guaranteed if people who *call themselves* Marxist-Leninists are in control (for such is the situation in the Soviet Union, where bourgeois dictatorship and a peculiar form of capitalist democracy, revisionist democracy, are in force). Nor is it *automatically* the case that if people who genuinely are Marxist-Leninists are in leading positions the basic rights of the masses under socialism will be assured. When it is said that in socialist society the masses of people, led by a proletarian vanguard, are the masters of both the economic base and the superstructure (and when this is ac-

18. Mao, *Critique of Soviet Economics*, p. 61.

tually true – that is, when there is really a socialist and not a revisionist state), it is true in a dialectical, not a metaphysical, sense. In other words, this must be understood as something contradictory and in motion, not something absolute and static. The mastery by the masses of the economic base and the superstructure, of society as a whole, is a question, or a process, of their continually increasing that mastery – and more than that, it is a process through which the economic base and the superstructure are themselves transformed in the direction of communism, a process through which, ultimately, democracy and dictatorship, and vanguard leadership, are eliminated, surpassed, because the conditions making them necessary, in any form, have been eliminated and superseded. And, finally, as we have seen, this is a process that proceeds not smoothly and in a straight line but through intense, complex, tortuous class struggle, in which the contradictions and struggles within the particular socialist country intertwine with and are ultimately determined by the contradictions and struggles on a world scale.

'   Before entering further into discussion of the withering away of democracy and dictatorship, and other political phenomena attendant to them, it is necessary to more deeply explore the issue of democracy and dictatorship in socialist society, how this differs from capitalist society, and in particular how the general principle that democracy is not an end in itself but a means to an end applies to socialist democracy. In one sense, to give a basic answer to the latter question, it would be sufficient to recall what has just been stressed: democracy, along with dictatorship, is a means under socialism to achieve the end of communism and all the transformation of society that implies (and in this regard it would be highly relevant to invoke once again Marx's decisive analysis that "right can never be higher than the economic structure of society and its cultural development conditioned thereby"). What poses a more concrete problem, however, is how to understand – and beyond that, how to handle in practice – the actual relation between democracy among the masses and dictatorship over the exploiters that is at the heart of the proletarian state. It is fairly easy to say (at least for those not befogged by bourgeois-democratic miasma) that it is necessary to exercise dictatorship over the exploiters while applying the broadest and deepest democracy among the masses; but in reality it is far from easy to carry this out correctly. During the height of the Cultural Revolution in China, Mao remarked that one of the

most difficult things was to sort out the two different types of contradictions—on the one hand, those among the people, which
must be resolved by democratic means, and, on the other hand,
those between the people and the enemy, which require the exercise of dictatorship—because in the swirling turbulence of this
mass upheaval, these two types of contradictions became very
closely intertwined. While this problem was acutely posed in the
Cultural Revolution, it finds expression, in one form or another
and with one degree of intensity or another, throughout the
socialist transition period. One extreme, and crucial, expression
of this, to which Mao also drew pointed attention, is the
phenomenon of capitalist-roaders right within the Communist
Party itself, especially at its top levels. Mao described this with
dramatic irony:

> You are making the socialist revolution, and yet don't know where
> the bourgeoisie is. It is right in the Communist Party—those in
> power taking the capitalist road. The capitalist roaders are still on
> the capitalist road.[19]

It is because of this, and the other ways in which the two different types of contradictions intertwine and are likely to be con-
fused, that Mao focused attention on the question of ideological
and political line and the struggle over this—which assumes concentrated expression within the vanguard party in the form of the
struggle between the Marxist-Leninist line and opportunist lines
of one kind or another, but which must be taken up and battled
out by the masses of people broadly, both in terms of how this line
is expressed theoretically and in terms of its implications and application in practice. As a matter of basic policy—and basic principle—Mao insisted, dictatorship must be exercised over particular people and social groupings only on the basis that it has
been clearly established that their line, the program they adhere
to, and the activities they engage in represent a determined position antagonistically opposed to socialism, the world revolution,
and the advance to communism (of course, the overthrown exploiters, whose fundamental antagonism with the revolution has
long since been demonstrated, will have been stripped of all
power, and there will be no question of granting them the same
political rights exercised by the masses of people). And in

19. Quoted in "Reversing Correct Verdicts Goes Against the Will of the People"
(*People's Daily* editorial, 12 March 1976), in Lotta, ed., *Mao Makes 5*, p. 262.

suppressing counterrevolutionaries it is necessary to bring to light the line and outlook guiding them, to thrash out among the masses the key questions this raises and concentrates, and to fundamentally rely on the support – but more than that, the conscious activism – of the masses.

Here we see, once again, democracy among the masses in its most profound sense, and in its dialectical relationship with dictatorship over the exploiters. Clearly, in cases of actual criminal activity against the interests of the revolution which assumes acute form and poses an immediate problem demanding action – to be specific, such things as murders, robberies, rapes, theft of the property of others, or theft or destruction of public property, and so on, as well as such things as actual armed attacks on organs or representatives of the proletarian state – the repressive apparatus of this state must be brought to bear forcefully and decisively. But even here, the underlying political and ideological questions involved, and their implications in terms of what kind of society is being upheld, must be brought out to the masses and thrashed out among them – and in this way fundamental reliance must be placed on the support and ultimately the conscious activism of the masses.

• This raises the question of the relationship between the law and mass revolutionary struggle in the enforcement of proletarian dictatorship and the exercise of democracy among the masses in socialist society. "The rule of law" is another basic bourgeois ideal, another principle which is treated as an end in itself by bourgeois theorists of freedom and democracy.[20] In this conception, dictatorship is the antithesis of "the rule of law." But in fact, "the rule of law" can be part of a dictatorship, of one kind or another, and in the most general sense it always is – even where it may appear that power is exercised without or above the law, laws (in the sense of a systematized code that people in society are obliged to conform to, whether written or unwritten) will still ex-

20. Thus, in *The Social Contract*, for example, while insisting that "All legitimate government is 'republican'," Rousseau explains that "any state which is ruled by law I call a 'republic'," and he adds that by "republic" he means "not only an aristocracy or democracy, but generally any government directed by the general will, which is law" (Rousseau, *Social Contract*, p. 82). It may be helpful to recall here the distinction pointed to in chapter 2 between Rousseau's concept of *sovereignty*, which he insisted must be popular (democratic), and of *government*, which Rousseau thought should, preferably, not be democratic, while it must represent the popular will.

ist and play a part in enforcing the rule of the dominant class.[21] Conversely, all states, all dictatorships, include laws in one form or another. In socialist society, too, law has a definite class character: it must reflect and serve the exercise of dictatorship over the exploiters and the exercise of political power by, and democracy among, the broad masses of people. As Mao put it, applying this to social organization in particular, and socialist society more specifically, "An organization must have rules, and a state also must have rules. . . ."[22] In short, law is a part of the superstructure, it has a definite class character. Under socialism it serves the transformation of society toward the goal of communism, and with the achievement of communism, law too will wither away. But beyond this general principle, the fact that law is a subordinate part of the rule of a particular class must find expression in socialist society in the practice of combining the implementation of the laws with mobilization of the masses – and fundamental reliance on the conscious activism of the masses in the functioning of the socialist state and the correct handling of the two different types of contradictions and the two interrelated aspects of democracy among the masses and dictatorship over the exploiters.

It is in line with the same fundamental orientation that Mao also called attention to the fact that, as he put it, "Marxism is a wrangling *ism*, dealing as it does with contradictions and struggles,"[23] and that he emphasized the need for ideological struggle

21. In this regard it must be remarked that when Lenin said that "Kautsky accidentally stumbled upon *one* true idea (namely, that dictatorship is rule unrestricted by laws)" (Lenin, "Proletarian Revolution and Renegade Kautsky," *LCW*, 28, p. 235), he was mistaken in granting Kautsky even this much. For as Lenin makes clear in this very passage, all states, whatever their form and whatever the "rule of law" within them, are dictatorships. In one sense, then, all states, all dictatorships, are "unrestricted" by laws, in that laws conform to the relation of classes, and specifically to the rule of one class over others, and not vice versa (the laws do not fundamentally determine, but reflect and form part of, the state – the dictatorship – of whichever class). But in the sense in which Kautsky means this – and in which Lenin assents – this statement that dictatorship is unrestricted by laws is wrong, because laws do after all *form a part of* and *give some content to* the *specific character* of the dictatorship, even if only secondarily.

22. Quoted in "Report on the Revision of the Constitution" (delivered by Chang Chun-chiao [13 January 1975]), in *Documents of the First Session of the Fourth National People's Congress of the People's Republic of China* (Peking: Foreign Languages Press, 1975), p. 33; also in Lotta, ed., *Mao Makes 5*, p. 186.

23. Mao, "Talks at a Conference of Secretaries of Provincial, Municipal and Autonomous Region Party Committees," *SW*, 5, p. 364.

and debate over the major questions of politics and world affairs, but also science, philosophy, education and culture, and other spheres. Any particular truth, when it is first being grasped, is always recognized only by a minority and has to fight for general recognition, Mao repeatedly pointed out.[24] It is also in line with this same fundamental orientation, and drawing from the emphasis Mao gave to it, that in discussing this point in a previous book I stressed that truth should not "be directly equated (and sometimes it should not be equated at all) with the governing ideas and policies of any particular proletarian state at any given time (even a *genuine* socialist state) to say nothing of a nonproletarian, reactionary state, whether openly such or in 'Marxist' disguise."[25] At the same time, however, I also stressed that the wrangling over such major questions, the confrontation of opposing views, the thrashing out of diverse ideas, and indeed the role of dissent from the governing ideas and policies – all this too is not an end in itself but a means to an end: arriving at a more profound grasp of the truth and utilizing this to further transform society, and nature, in the interests of humanity. And I stressed the fundamental difference between this orientation and approach and the principle of "pluralism":

> Pluralism as such is an expression of agnosticism, which – wrongly – denies objective truth. That is, it denies such truth on one level while actually defining truth (openly or implicitly, consciously or "by default") as whatever is in accord with and serves the outlook and interests of the ruling class. (This is closely akin to the pragmatism that is upheld and promoted by the U.S. imperialists especially.) . . . The "pluralists" say (at best) that the conflict of opinions and ideas itself is more important, higher than objective truth – or even that there *is no* objective truth, only different points of view, with each as true (and untrue) as the other. But in the final analysis the "pluralists," by acting as if all ideas are equal and can compete equally – when in reality the bourgeois ruling class has a monopoly on the dissemination of ideas and exercises dictatorship in the realm of ideas, as it does in every other sphere – actually aid this ruling class in defining and enforcing as truth whatever suits its own class interests and outlook. . . .

---

24. See, for example, "Talks at the Chengtu Conference," in *Chairman Mao Talks to the People*, ed. Stuart Schram, trans. John Chinnery and Tieyun (New York: Pantheon Books, 1974).

25. Avakian, *Horrible End or End to Horror?*, p. 163.

. . . The reason and purpose of communists in encouraging and unleashing this wrangling over ideas, the critical spirit, the challenging of convention, the dissent from the established norms, is that this is in accordance with the basic laws of development of all life and society and with the interests of the proletariat, which must also *lead* all this to contribute in various ways to the advance to communism. This is possible only with the establishment of Marxism in the commanding position and the exercise of the all-around dictatorship of the proletariat – in the way summarized here, and in particular in dialectical unity with the long-term policy of "100 flowers" and "100 schools" [let a hundred flowers blossom and a hundred schools of thought contend in the arts and sciences, a policy put forward by Mao beginning in the mid-1950s].[26]

Here it might be instructive to make a detour and discuss, in relation to what is said above, the views of John Stuart Mill, a nineteenth-century English philosopher, political economist, and political theorist, about whom it can justly be said that "more than anyone else" (or at least as much as anyone else), he has "bequeathed to us" (that is, to the Western liberal-democratic tradition) "the idea of the free and sovereign individual."[27] More specifically, Mill was an ardent champion of the rights of the individual not only as against the state but against society in general and its "prevailing opinion and feeling." For, as Mill wrote in *On Liberty*, "when society is itself the tyrant – society collectively over the separate individuals who compose it – its means of tyrannizing are not restricted to the acts which it may do by the hands of its political functionaries."[28] The mere existence of a democratic form of government, then, is no guarantee of the rights of the individual: "The limitation, therefore, of the power of government over individuals loses none of its importance when the holders of power are regularly accountable to the community, that is, to the strongest party therein."[29] Indeed, Mill affirms, "as the tendency of all the changes taking place in the world is to strengthen society and diminish the power of the individual, this encroachment [of the power of society over the in-

---

26. Avakian, *Horrible End or End to Horror?*, pp. 188-89.

27. Gertrude Himmelfarb, "Editor's Introduction" to John Stuart Mill, *On Liberty* (Middlesex: Penguin Books, 1984), p. 8.

28. Mill, *On Liberty*, p. 63.

29. Mill, *On Liberty*, p. 62.

dividual] is not one of the evils which tend spontaneously to disappear, but, on the contrary, to grow more and more formidable."[30]

᠊ *On Liberty,* first published in 1859, was a major manifesto by Mill dedicated to the proposition of the sovereignty of the individual. As he himself expressed it:

> The object of this essay is to assert one very simple principle, as entitled to govern absolutely the dealings of society with the individual in the way of compulsion and control, whether the means used be physical force in the form of legal penalties or the moral coercion of public opinion. That principle is that the sole end for which mankind are warranted, individually or collectively, in interfering with the liberty of action of any of their number is self-protection. That the only purpose for which power can be rightfully exercised over any member of a civilized community, against his will, is to prevent harm to others. His own good, either physical or moral, is not a sufficient warrant. He cannot rightfully be compelled to do or forbear because it will be better for him to do so, because it will make him happier, because, in the opinions of others, to do so would be wise or even right. These are good reasons for remonstrating with him, or reasoning with him, or persuading him, or entreating him, but not for compelling him or visiting him with any evil in case he do otherwise. To justify that, the conduct from which it is desired to deter him must be calculated to produce evil to someone else. The only part of the conduct of anyone for which he is amenable to society is that which concerns others. In the part which merely concerns himself, his independence is, of right, absolute. Over himself, over his own body and mind, the individual is sovereign.[31]

In this general affirmation – and more specifically in his insistence that it is essential that the expression of all opinions, above all minority and unpopular opinions, be allowed without suppression or coercion to prevent or obstruct their expression – Mill's arguments raise significant points highly relevant to what has been stressed in this book, and in this chapter in particular, and Mill's arguments run directly counter to what has been presented here. Examining and dissecting Mill's central arguments in *On Liberty* should therefore help to further clarify, and sharpen up, these questions – and the profoundly different

30. Mill, *On Liberty,* p. 73.
31. Mill, *On Liberty,* pp. 68-69.

and opposed views on them, the bourgeois and the proletarian.

Mill makes his most powerful argument against the suppression of opinions (even through indirect means such as intimidation) as follows:

> the peculiar evil of silencing the expression of an opinion is that it is robbing the human race, posterity as well as the existing generation – those who dissent from the opinion, still more than those who hold it. If the opinion is right, they are deprived of the opportunity of exchanging error for truth; if wrong, they lose, what is almost as great a benefit, the clearer perception and livelier impression of truth produced by its collision with error.. . .
>
> . . . We can never be sure that the opinion we are endeavoring to stifle is a false opinion; and if we were sure, stifling it would be an evil still.
>
> He who knows only his own side of the case knows little of that. His reasons may be good, and no one may have been able to refute them. But if he is equally unable to refute the reasons on the opposite side, if he does not so much as know what they are, he has no ground for preferring either opinion. The rational position for him would be suspension of judgement, and unless he contents himself with that, he is either led by authority or adopts, like the generality of the world, the side to which he feels most inclination. Nor is it enough that he should hear the arguments of adversaries from his own teachers, presented as they state them, and accompanied by what they offer as refutations. That is not the way to do justice to the arguments or bring them into real contact with his own mind. He must be able to hear them from persons who actually believe them, who defend them in earnest and do their very utmost for them.. . . So essential is this discipline to a real understanding of moral and human subjects that, if opponents of all-important truths do not exist, it is indispensable to imagine them and supply them with the strongest arguments which the most skillful devil's advocate can conjure up.[32]

Consistent with this, Mill even poses and gives an answer to the argument that while it is wrong to lightly or arbitrarily suppress opinions, once it can be determined with great certainty that something is true and must be acted upon, it is not only not wrong, it is necessary to bar the dissemination of contrary ideas, since they run counter to established truth and obstruct action

32. Mill, *On Liberty*, pp. 76-77, 98-99.

that must flow from it. Acting as devil's advocate, Mill concludes the argument opposed to his own and then answers it:

There is no such thing as absolute certainty, but there is assurance sufficient for the purposes of human life. We may, and must, assume our opinion to be true for the guidance of our own conduct; and it is assuming no more when we forbid bad men to pervert society by the propagation of opinions which we regard as false and pernicious.

I answer that it is assuming very much more. There is the greatest difference between presuming an opinion to be true because, with every opportunity for contesting it, it has not been refuted, and assuming its truth for the purpose of not permitting its refutation. Complete liberty of contradicting and disproving our opinion is the very condition which justifies us in assuming its truth for purposes of action; and on no other terms can a being with human faculties have any rational assurance of being right. . . .

. . . To call any proposition certain, while there is anyone who would deny its certainty if permitted, but who is not permitted, is to assume that we ourselves, and those who agree with us, are the judges of certainty, and judges without hearing the other side.[33]

First, it should be said that in what Mill argues here there is much that is true and very important, and much that should be applied in socialist society. Mao, in explaining the philosophical basis for the "hundred flowers" and "hundred schools of thought" policy, emphasized:

Truth develops through debate between different views. The same method can be adopted in dealing with whatever is poisonous and anti-Marxist, because in the struggle against it Marxism will develop. This is development through the struggle of opposites, development conforming to dialectics.

. . . Only by comparing can one distinguish. Only by making distinctions and waging struggle can there be development. Truth develops through its struggle against falsehood. This is how Marxism develops. Marxism develops in the struggle against bourgeois and petty-bourgeois ideology, and it is only through struggle that it can develop.

We are for the policy of "opening wide"; so far there has been too little of it rather than too much. We must not be afraid of "opening wide," nor should we be afraid of criticism and

33. Mill, *On Liberty*, pp. 79, 81.

poisonous weeds. Marxism is scientific truth; it fears no criticism and cannot be overthrown by criticism. The same holds for the Communist Party and the People's Government; they fear no criticism and cannot be toppled by it. . . .

. . . All erroneous ideas, all poisonous weeds, all ghosts and monsters, must be subjected to criticism; in no circumstances should they be allowed to spread freely. However, the criticism should be fully reasoned, analytical and convincing, and neither rough and bureaucratic, nor metaphysical and dogmatic.[34]

And:

Ideological struggle differs from other forms of struggle, since the only method used is painstaking reasoning, and not crude coercion. . . .

Fighting against wrong ideas is like being vaccinated – a man develops greater immunity from disease as a result of vaccination. Plants raised in hothouses are unlikely to be hardy. Carrying out the policy of letting a hundred flowers blossom and a hundred schools of thought contend will not weaken, but strengthen, the leading position of Marxism in the ideological field.[35]

It is in coming to grasp this more deeply that I have also stressed:

Ideas need challenging. Even wrong ideas or incorrect criticism may raise important questions, besides the fact that criticism of prevailing ideas may be correct. The masses – as well as party members and especially the leaders of the party and the state under socialism – need to be exposed to controversy and the struggle over conflicting ideas and criticism of and challenges to accepted ideas and norms. This is certainly no less necessary under socialism than in capitalist society. And when we are in power we must struggle to maintain the same willingness – no, more, eagerness – we have now to take on and demolish through exposure and debate counterrevolutionary or just plain wrong ideas, theories, and so on. . . .

All this is related to the crucial question of overcoming the division of labor left over from capitalism and previous class-divided societies. The radical rupture with all that could hardly be accomplished without tradition-challenging, convention-breaking initiative and without ferment and upheaval in socialist society,

34. Mao, "Speech at the Chinese Communist Party's National Conference on Propaganda Work," *SW*, 5, pp. 433-34.

35. Mao, "Correct Handling of Contradictions," *SW*, 5, p. 410.

certainly involving the criticism of, shaking up, and in some cases the pulling down of leading people.[36]

This, however, brings us to the crucial point that, in seeking to make an absolute—an end in itself—out of the free expression and conflict of opinions, Mill has vitiated the truth, has actually turned it into a profound falsehood.[37] Just as in general the superstructure reflects and serves a certain economic base—and in class society the superstructure reflects the domination of a particular class—so the battle over ideas, the exchange of opinions, and so forth, which is part of the superstructure, also takes place within and is fundamentally conditioned by the basic class relations in society and the struggle between classes. And in class society—of necessity, and whether one likes it or not, or even understands it—one class or another (whichever is the ruling class) will in fact determine, on any really significant question, which ideas will be favored and which will be discredited or even suppressed. It can be no other way, so long as society is divided into classes, and so long therefore as there is a state and that state represents the dictatorship of one class over another. And in today's world this means:

> Either the Marxist method and proletarian forces—concentrated through the party but also involving the masses and mass initiative broadly—will be in command and leading in the arts and sciences (and the superstructure generally) or the opposite methodology and forces will: classes do and will sharply contend over this, so long as classes (and their social basis) exist. One class or another must win out. There is no "pure" knowledge or search for knowledge (and no "art for art's sake" standing outside or above class contradiction and struggle), just as there is no "pure" democracy (without class content). But fortunately, *one* of these methodologies does provide a comprehensive basis for arriving at, and making a powerful material force of, the truth: the outlook and interests of the proletariat do correspond to the further emancipation and enlightenment of humanity, in a qualitatively greater way than ever before.

---

36. Avakian, *Horrible End or End to Horror?*, pp. 185, 187.

37. Gertrude Himmelfarb has pointed out that with Mill, "If any distinction between means and ends can be made, one might say that he sometimes spoke as though liberty were the means and individuality—not happiness—the end" ("Introduction" to *On Liberty*, p. 30).

It is not that truth itself has a class character. . . .

But to fundamentally know and change the world (including society) in accordance with its basic laws, Marxism-Leninism-Mao Tsetung Thought must be in command as the guiding orientation and methodology, and politically the proletariat – in a concentrated way through its vanguard party but through its own mass initiatives and struggles as well – must lead in the struggle to grasp and apply the truth in the process of changing the world. Otherwise reactionary class forces and ideology will occupy the commanding posts, obscure the truth, keep knowledge – flawed, corrupted, and crippled knowledge (at best) – the province of an elite and impose reactionary economic and social relations throughout society.[38]

The impossibility of Mill's position and its ultimately reac-

---

38. Avakian, *Horrible End or End to Horror?*, pp. 184, 162-63.

As for why it is that "the outlook and interests of the proletariat do correspond to the further emancipation and enlightenment of humanity, in a qualitatively greater way than ever before," this is rooted in the proletariat's position and role in modern, capitalist society and in the fact that, as opposed to all other social classes in contemporary society – and throughout human history – the proletariat has nothing to gain by seeking to arrest social development, even after it has risen to the position of the ruling class – its interests lie not in perpetuating or solidifying its existence as a social class but in eliminating it along with the elimination of all class distinctions, and therefore its interests are not opposed to but in conformity with the most thoroughgoingly scientific, critical, revolutionary approach to investigating and changing society and reality generally. As I have previously summarized it:

> The outlook of the proletariat, the scientific worldview and methodology of Marxism, unlike all other class outlooks, is not only partisan, it is also true. It represents a class outlook but it is not blinded or prejudiced by class *bias*. This is because of the fact that the position and role of the proletariat in society and human history are radically different from those of any other class. The proletariat carries out socialized production in a society (and world) marked by large-scale industry, the widespread application of science, highly developed means of communication, etc.; it is the exploited class in capitalist society, a society split in the main into two directly antagonistic classes, the bourgeoisie and the proletariat; because of its propertyless condition it is subjected to domination and exploitation by capital and subordinated to the dynamics of capitalist accumulation, and its interests lie in the thorough revolutionization of society, in bringing about the most radical rupture with traditional property relations and traditional ideas, as it is put in the *Communist Manifesto* – the proletariat can emancipate itself only by abolishing not just capitalism but all exploitation, indeed all class distinctions and their material and ideological bases. It is for this reason that Marxism openly proclaims its class character and ruthlessly exposes the class character and interests in all relations, institutions and ways of thinking in present-day (and past) society. (Avakian, *Harvest of Dragons*, p. 44)

tionary implications in today's world begin to suggest themselves in examining a few key phrases in the passages cited from Mill earlier. There is a world of difference, he says, between presuming something true because "with every opportunity for contesting it, it has not been refuted, and assuming its truth for the purpose of not permitting its refutation." While, again, there is some truth to what Mill says, the key phrase here is *"every opportunity* for contesting it"—the meaning of which is repeated and reemphasized by Mill shortly after that, when he sharply criticizes the approach of setting ourselves up as judges to call something true (or "certain") "while there is *anyone* who would deny its certainty." If Mill means this literally, it is quite apparent how his position cannot be ultimately defended: discussion over something cannot go on *infinitely* before something can be declared true, and there is (or theoretically might be) always one more "anyone" who might deny its certainty. Philosophically, what Mill fails to understand is that:

> Knowledge is accumulated in spirals, involving the continuous interaction and interpenetration between practice and theory—in which the former is principal overall—but also involving leaps from one level to another. Knowledge is acquired, humanity does add to its store of knowledge, but not in a continuous, unbroken straight line.... [T]he state or store of acquired knowledge—what can be determined to be true—at any stage must be taken as the foundation from which to struggle to acquire further knowledge (even though that further knowledge involves discarding or correcting part of the previous "state or store of acquired knowledge"). Without this one plunges into relativism, a form of idealism (nothing is objectively true, it is all ideas... one opinion is as good as another... and so on), and the very process of acquiring knowledge, of knowing and changing the world, is fundamentally disrupted.[39]

In fact, the contradiction in Mill's position is suggested in Mill's own (conscious or unconscious) "qualifier" (my choice of word) that "if opponents of *all-important* truths do not exist" (emphasis added here) it is indispensable to invent them and make the best possible argument for them. Here (again, wittingly or unwittingly) Mill has let the cat out of the bag: someone, some group of people in society, has to decide what constitutes "all-important truths," even all-important questions for debate, and so on.

---

39. Avakian, *Horrible End or End to Horror?*, pp. 159-60.

Whether Mill meant to say so or not, the reality is that some kind of authority, in one form or another, has to provide guidance, direction, leadership—and in the final analysis, dictatorship, so long as we are talking about class-divided society—in determining what will and will not be discussed, and in what terms, in society at large. . .indeed what will be available for people to think about and discuss. What this reflects is that:

> It is also impossible to arrive at the truth without centralism— leadership (though this will take a qualitatively different form in communist society). All ideas should not get "equal time" nor *could* they, under any social system or set of circumstances. There has to be some means for determining what will be given priority, what will be posited as true, and what will be focused on as a target of criticism. What these means are and whether they correctly reflect material reality as fully as possible will depend on the social system. Further, it is impossible not only to arrive at an all-around understanding of the truth but to make it a material reality without social struggle—which means above all class struggle in class society.[40]

And, particularly in opposition to Mill's attempts at absolutizing individual sovereignty, it is worth repeating what I recently wrote on an often misunderstood aspect of all this:

> This touches on the question of "thinking for yourself." While it has some value to the degree that it implies critical rather than slavish thinking, this notion is ultimately a truism (everyone thinks and can only think with his/her own brain and not anyone else's) and/or it is a fundamental falsehood: everyone's thoughts are based largely on indirect knowledge, facts and concepts presented (in "distilled form") by *others*. This is especially obvious in a society where the media and means of communication generally play such an influential role. The essential question is not "thinking for yourself" but thinking according to *what method*—a correct or incorrect one—leading to what *basic result*— truth or falsehood.[41]

Here it might be objected that the essential argument Mill is making has to do not with the declaration that certain ideas are true so much as—and most centrally—the suppression of ideas, by one means or another, that conflict with these declared truths. But once we recognize that, in any society, at any given point

40. Avakian, *Horrible End or End to Horror?*, p. 161.
41. Avakian, *Horrible End or End to Horror?*, p. 184.

there are limited (and not infinite) productive forces, and therefore limited (and not infinite) means of communication (of printing books, making films, broadcasting over radio, television, etc.), then we must recognize that some decisions will have to be made by someone about all this. And once we acknowledge this, we must go on and acknowledge that *within this very process there is an aspect of suppression of ideas.* Even if, in communist society, this does not mean *political suppression,* representing and expressing the power of one part of society (one class) over another, it still means that society – "society collectively over the separate individuals who compose it" (to use Mill's formulation) – will have to make decisions that very directly affect what ideas people are exposed to, how discussion and struggle over ideas is taken up and resolved, and how this fits into social organization and the functioning of society overall. Again, this is inevitable and unavoidable – and if correctly handled, not a bad thing. But again, it is also inevitable and unavoidable that in class society all this will be conditioned by and take place within the overall framework of class relations, class contradictions and struggles – and the exercise of political power (dictatorship) by one class or another – and the decisive question will be which class rules, which methodology and approach is in command, and toward what end or result are things being led?

Mill argues that if the state – and society as a whole, as represented in the state (even a democratic state as he envisions it) as a force above the individuals making up society – is kept from suppressing ideas or intimidating people from expressing and debating them, then there will be the best possible situation: the freest exchange of ideas and the greatest good for humanity. This is Mill's fundamental philosophical idealism. But at the same time, it is also an expression of his bourgeois class outlook in other spheres, in particular political philosophy and political economy.

One of the central concepts that Mill is calling attention to – and pointing to the danger of – is "the tyranny of the majority," an idea that was contained in de Tocqueville's *Democracy in America,*[42] a work which exerted considerable influence on Mill,

---

42. See de Tocqueville, *Democracy in America,* especially Vol. 1, chapter 15: "Unlimited Power of the Majority in the United States, and its Consequences" and chapter 16: "Causes Which Mitigate the Tyranny of the Majority in the United States."

in this aspect particularly. This very concept ("the tyranny of the majority") is itself a bourgeois idealization – and fundamental distortion – of bourgeois society. In reality, this is a society in which not a majority (an idealized majority of modest property-owners) but a minority, the capitalist exploiters, rules – and exercises tyranny (that is, dictatorship) over the proletariat in particular. As Lenin made clear in his polemics with Kautsky (as well as more generally), under capitalism the protection of the minority – a basic notion of bourgeois democracy – is actually applied only to the minority within the bourgeoisie (that is, to parties, groups, or individuals that are in opposition to the prevailing views within the ruling class but constitute a *bourgeois* opposition). In short, capitalist society means exploitation and oppression for the majority – and the tyranny of the *minority.*

Underlying his political-philosophical views are Mill's political-economic conceptions. Gertrude Himmelfarb's phrase describing the fundamental tenets in *On Liberty* is very apt: "Mill's doctrine [is] a form of *moral laissez-fairism* in which each individual was encouraged to do as he liked so long as he did not injure another."[43] One of the more interesting observations in Bob Fine's *Democracy and the Rule of Law* is that "[Adam] Smith analyzed the mechanisms, which Rousseau was unable to discover, by which a person 'by pursuing his own interest' can promote the general development of civilization."[44] Leaving aside the question of to what degree Fine himself actually believes that these mechanisms really work as Smith said they do, we can focus on the all-important point here that John Stuart Mill's conception of liberty (his "moral laissez-fairism") is an idealized reflection of capitalist commodity relations: Ideas, like commodities literally exchanging through the mechanisms of the capitalist market, must be allowed free exchange and be allowed to find their fair price (or acceptance). We have seen that the reality and result of these relations is, however, that they contain, while also concealing, a fundamental relation of exploitation and oppression, and they lead, ever increasingly, to a situation where "accumulation of wealth at one pole is, therefore, at the same time accumulation of misery, agony of toil, slavery, ignorance, brutality, mental degradation, at the opposite pole."[45] And they have led to the imperialist stage of

43. Himmelfarb, "Introduction" to Mill, *On Liberty*, p. 39, emphasis added.
44. Fine, *Democracy and Law*, p. 38.
45. Marx, *Capital*, 1, p. 645.

capitalism, which has profoundly internationalized and intensified this great division. Further, capitalist commodity relations necessitate the capitalist state – the dictatorship of the bourgeoisie – precisely because Adam Smith's "invisible hand" does not work as he said it does – the dynamic of capitalist accumulation, the functioning of society through capitalist relations, does not lead to a situation where each pursues his personal interest and somehow through this different interests are harmonized to the general benefit of all – but instead the fundamental class antagonisms of the capitalist system are progressively accentuated.[46]

Mill, like other bourgeois ideologists, believes he is articulating universal, transcendental principles, not merely mirroring capitalist commodity relations. And that itself is revealing of Mill's bourgeois outlook. Marx cited Mill as an example of the bourgeois political economist who attempts to "represent production, as distinct from distribution, etc., as governed by eternal natural laws independent of history, and the opportunity is taken to smuggle in *bourgeois* relations surreptitiously as irrevocable natural laws of society *in abstracto*" – the problem then being to eliminate the arbitrariness that (according to people like Mill) has reigned in distribution and to make the latter conform to these eternal, natural bourgeois production relations.[47] Reflecting this,

---

46. The conflict between the bourgeois ideals of freedom, in particular the free exchange of commodities, on the one hand, and the reality of exploitation and oppression bound up with bourgeois relations, on the other, is reflected in many parts of *On Liberty* – for example, in Mill's statement that China's restrictions of the opium trade were "objectionable" – though "not as infringements on the liberty of the producer or seller, but on that of the buyer"(!) – in his argument (in the course of criticizing, not upholding, slavery) that the slave "by selling himself for a slave" in fact "abdicates his liberty," and in his insistence that, however repugnant might be a situation where a man has more than one wife, "this relation is as much voluntary on the part of the women concerned in it, and who may be deemed the sufferers by it, as is the case with any other form of the marriage institution" (Mill, *On Liberty*, pp. 165, 173, 160). While there may be an aspect of irony in the last comment cited here ("as is the case with any other form of the marriage institution"), Mill really does believe that such relations, or institutions, are entered into voluntarily (even if in some cases ill-advisedly) – unless there is actual coercion – he really does not see the coercion, the denial of liberty, that results not so much from political repression (or social pressure) as much as *economic compulsion*...that is, from the "normal functioning" of prevailing social relations. All these examples reflect that in one way or another.

47. Marx, *Preface to Critique*, p. 13; see also p. 14. For further criticism by Marx of Mill's political economy, see *Capital*, especially Vol. 1, pp. 516-17; Vol. 3, p. 878; and *Theories of Surplus Value* (Moscow: Progress Publishers, 1968), especially Part 2, p. 123; Part 3, pp. 191-92, 200-202, 506.

Mill makes essentially the same attempt in the realm of politics and ideology with his "moral laissez-fairism." And the result is just as much that Mill articulates not universal natural laws, or eternal principles, but ideas reflecting an historically contingent economic system—and reflecting them in such a way that the ideal must turn back on itself in obedience to the commands of the reality.

Hence, it only seems that Mill has made an absolute out of the sovereignty of the individual. In fact, in *On Liberty,* he himself says that his guiding principle is that "the sole end for which mankind are warranted, individually or collectively, in interfering with the liberty of action of any of their number is self-protection . . . to prevent harm to others."[48] But here again we come right up against reality: even if we were to accept this criterion, someone, or some group of people, must determine what constitutes harm to others and legitimate self-protection. Even in the case of dealings more or less restricted to two (or a small number of) individuals, their sense of what constitutes harm and what is necessarily part of self-protection will be *socially determined*—that is, it will be conditioned by the prevailing economic system and its corresponding laws, institutions, values, ideals, and so on, and by the forces in conflict with these and the struggle between them (above all, again, class struggle in class society). And where society as a whole is more directly involved (since it is *ultimately* involved in anything that takes place within it), it is all the more obvious that the governing institutions in society, corresponding to the dominant economic relations, will determine these questions (of harm, self-protection, etc.)—and when necessary will forcibly cause individuals' actions to conform to these determinations (so long, again, as society remains divided into classes and is therefore ruled by a class dictatorship of one kind or another).

It is therefore not surprising that Mill is obliged to allow for a number of situations where it is justified—indeed required—that society and government compel individuals to do (or not to do) certain things. Here, too, a number of the instances Mill cites are extremely revealing for what they say about the specific class outlook and interests Mill's ideas represent. First of all, Mill says that this guiding principle set forth in *On Liberty* is not applicable everywhere and to everyone; more specifically, it is not ap-

48. Mill, *On Liberty,* p. 68.

plicable to children or (note well) "young persons below the age *which the law may fix* as that of manhood or womanhood."[49] Nor, moreover, is it applicable to "those backward states of society in which the race itself may be considered as in its nonage," since "despotism is a legitimate mode of government in dealing with barbarians, provided the end be their improvement and the means justified by actually effecting that end."[50] (Here I will only note in passing the self-evident fact that "somebody" must determine who are "barbarians" and what constitutes their "improvement" and the means justified to achieve this; but it is hardly irrelevant that not only did Mill work for that infamous institution of British colonialism, the East India Company, but in *On Liberty* itself can be found numerous expressions of English and "white man's burden" chauvinism.) Finally, where Mill does say his basic doctrine is applicable, he makes such observations as the following:

> The laws which, in many countries on the Continent, forbid marriage unless the parties can show that they have the means of supporting a family do not exceed the legitimate powers of the State; and whether such laws be expedient or not (a question mainly dependent on local circumstances and feelings), they are not objectionable as violations of liberty.

> [If someone has] infringed the rules necessary for the protection of his fellow creatures, individually or collectively. . . [t]he evil consequences of his acts do not then fall on himself, but on others; and society, as the protector of all its members, must retaliate on him, must inflict pain on him for the express purpose of punishment, and must take care that it be sufficiently severe.

> An opinion that corn dealers are starvers of the poor, or that private property is robbery, ought to be unmolested when simply circulated through the press, but may justly incur punishment when delivered orally to an excited mob assembled before the house of a corn dealer, or when handed about among the same mob in the form of a placard.

> There are also many positive acts for the benefit of others which he [a person] may rightfully be compelled to perform, such as to

49. Mill, *On Liberty*, p. 69, emphasis added.

50. Mill, *On Liberty*, p. 69; see also pp. 18, 135-38, 184-85, for evidence of this chauvinism and of Mill's support for British colonialism in particular.

give evidence in a court of justice, to bear his fair share in the common defence or in any other joint work necessary to the interest of the society of which he enjoys the protection, and to perform certain acts of individual beneficence, such as saving a fellow creature's life or interposing to protect the defenceless against ill usage – things which whenever it is obviously a man's duty to do he may rightfully be made responsible to society for not doing.[51]

It should be abundantly clear that, in the final analysis, Mill is the champion not of absolute individual sovereignty but of the capitalist system – Mill is quite willing to see anticapitalist opinions suppressed so soon as they pose any danger to the system, and he is quite willing to allow for people to be deprived (and to deprive others) not merely of their right to speak but of their very lives in wars to defend that system ("the common defence" is clearly a euphemism for wars to defend the system and the national capitalist state against enemies and rivals, since "society," that is, government, does not wage wars other than for this purpose, although the *oppressed* within society do). In reality, then, Mill is an upholder not just of capitalist economic relations and their corresponding morals and ideals but also of the bourgeois political rule – the dictatorship of the bourgeoisie – that is necessary to enforce these. He cannot help himself, since his ideals are those of the bourgeoisie, and since – to repeat what cannot be repeated too many times (especially in the face of overwhelming efforts to distort and obscure this fundamental point) – so long as society is divided into classes, everyone will (wittingly or unwittingly) support one kind of dictatorship or another, representing one class interest or another.

Given this, Lenin's answer to the accusation that he was a dictator – an accusation hurled at him by upholders of the capitalist system (open and disguised) – can stand as an answer to Mill and all other apologists of this system: better me than you, better the dictatorship of the proletariat than the dictatorship of the bourgeoisie. When such apologists (and also many people who are not apologists of this system but are nonetheless under the sway of its ideology) insist on equality for all opinions and denounce attempts at dictatorship not only in the sphere of action but in the ideological sphere as well, they are actually (and, again, wittingly or unwittingly) insisting on the continued domination of the bourgeoisie in the domain of ideas – and in society as a

51. Mill, *On Liberty*, pp. 179, 146, 119, 70.

whole. An issue that has recently been the focus of sharp struggle in the U.S., at Brown University and some other places, exemplifies this point. In the face of attempts by the CIA to openly recruit on campus, students and others have openly disrupted these efforts and actually attempted to keep the CIA recruiters from carrying out their business. This has brought howls of hypocritical denunciation – as well as repressive measures – from the authorities and has created a great deal of controversy, with the question being raised: what about the CIA recruiters' "right to free speech" (and the right of students to be recruited by the CIA!)? Besides the fact, pointed out by the protesters, that it is not a matter of speech (or recruitment) in the abstract but efforts to recruit people for murderous actions that the CIA is carrying out all over the world, there is also the basic fact that the CIA, whose "right to free speech" is being raised here, is part of the bourgeois state; it is an important arm of the dictatorship of the bourgeoisie, which has complete domination in the dissemination of ideas and the molding of public opinion in the present society, along with thousands of years of tradition of class-divided, exploitative society going for it. Even if everyone in the CIA, and every last spokesman for the bourgeoisie, were not allowed to communicate a single word for a century, while proletarian revolutionaries had unlimited access to the media, etc., the revolutionaries still would not yet have achieved "equal time" with the reactionaries! This is an important aspect of why, with the overthrow of capitalism, the exercise of the dictatorship of the proletariat over the bourgeoisie and over counterrevolutionaries generally is essential and indispensable.

The exercise of this dictatorship does not mean that those who are the objects of it – the overthrown bourgeoisie and others who aim at the restoration of capitalism in one form or another – will literally and absolutely be deprived of the right to voice political opinions and so on. But it does mean that a clear-cut political identification will be publicly made of them as enemies of the revolution based on an analysis of the class interests they uphold, and that their political activity will be strictly supervised and controlled, restricted, and, as necessary, suppressed by the proletarian state. In some circumstances, it may be very desirable not only to allow but to require them to voice their opinions (their *real* opinions, not pretended acceptance of the new system) in order to use them as teaching material by negative example and to unfold mass debate and criticism around their ideas, further exposing the reactionary nature of their outlook and the class interests they uphold, and thereby deepening the understanding of the masses, and of leading people, of the correct versus the incorrect lines in all their various manifestations. It was on this basis and in this spirit that, projecting ahead to the situation in socialist society, I stressed:

> They want to whine about how they're going to be suppressed and not even allowed to speak up—well, let 'em speak up. But we're going to determine the context in which they speak up and in that context we're going to *make* them speak up, and let's have some fun while we thoroughly dissect and destroy their outmoded, rotten and vicious theories, credos, nostrums, and bromides.[52]

Speaking more generally to the basic principle that must guide all this, I also pointed out:

> How to handle the dialectical relationship between "100 flowers" and "100 schools" on the one hand and on the other hand the need for the proletariat to (in Mao's phrase) "exercise all-round dictatorship over the bourgeoisie in the realm of the superstructure, including the various spheres of culture"? This is similar to the phenomenon that while truth itself does not have a class character, the struggle to grasp and apply it is most definitely a class question—a question of class struggle—in class society. All-around dictatorship does not mean crude imposition of whatever the current policies of the government are. It does mean that the Marxist method must be in command and leadership must be in the hands of those who have demonstrated the ability to grasp and apply it—in a *critical* way, without turning it into a static, sterile state religion. This too will be a question of sharp struggle.[53]

It is a struggle that can and must be carried out and carried through as part of the overall struggle to exercise the dictatorship of the proletariat, to continue the revolution under it, and to carry forward the advance to communism. And in light of this, we can once again answer the accusation of the apologists of capitalism, who assail the communists for openly proclaiming the need for the dictatorship of the proletariat: better us than you—far better,

52. Avakian, *Horrible End or End to Horror?*, p. 187.

53. Avakian, *Horrible End or End to Horror?*, p. 183. The statement by Mao quoted here is from "Chairman Mao on Continuing the Revolution Under the Dictatorship of the Proletariat," *Peking Review*, 26 September 1969.

infinitely better the dictatorship of the proletariat than the dictatorship of the bourgeoisie. This answer given, let us turn to the question toward which all the preceding has been pointing.

The Withering Away of Democracy

This can only be understood as part of the withering away of the state. And the withering away of the state, in turn, must be seen not as the "evaporation" or "dissolving" of the state apparatus one fine day, suddenly or all at once out of nowhere, but as the result of a dialectical process – and a determined struggle – through which the relations and the people in society undergo revolutionary transformation. As Marx already emphasized, in summing up the historical experience of the first (and short-lived) proletarian state, the Paris Commune of 1871, the proletarians "in order to work out their own emancipation, and along with it that higher form to which present society is irresistibly tending by its own economical agencies, . . . will have to pass through long struggles, through a series of historic processes, transforming circumstances and men."[54] This process – this struggle – is dialectical in a twofold sense: it involves the dialectical relationship between dictatorship and democracy in socialist society, as discussed in the last section; and it involves the dialectical relation – the unity and opposition – between strengthening the dictatorship of the proletariat and, at the same time, by the same means, creating step by step, but also through a series of revolutionary leaps, the conditions whereby the dictatorship of the proletariat will no longer be necessary . . . or possible. The process – the struggle – involving the elimination of the inequalities and contradictions left over from and characteristic of capitalism and the bourgeois epoch is the path along which communism will finally be achieved worldwide, and the state – and along with it democracy – will finally wither away: the transformation of circumstances and people to achieve the elimination of "bourgeois right" and the division of labor attendant to class-divided society, in all their manifestations; the abolition of commodity production and exchange and the necessity of money as a medium of exchange, and their replacement by conscious plan-

54. Marx, *Civil War in France*, p. 73.

ning of production and exchange–involving both unity and diversity, both centralized guidelines and widespread initiative – all in accordance with the basic principle "from each according to his ability, to each according to his needs"; the overcoming of inequalities and antagonisms between women and men, and between different nationalities and regions. . . the transcending of national as well as class divisions and the creation of a true world community of humanity, consciously uniting – and wrangling – to achieve the continuous, all-around development of human society and of the human beings who comprise it.

Obviously, all this is not something that will be achieved overnight, or in a short time after the bourgeoisie and other exploiters have been overthrown and initially expropriated. As stressed earlier, even within particular countries, taken by themselves, the contradictions involved in carrying forward the socialist transition toward communism are extremely profound and complex and the struggles they give rise to extremely tortuous and, especially at key concentration points, extremely acute. But beyond that, a decisive point which the historical experience of the socialist transition so far has underscored is that this transition cannot be approached, fundamentally, within particular countries, taken by themselves, but must be approached, above all, as a worldwide process, involving the overcoming and elimination of the lopsidedness in the world and all the material and ideological conditions associated with it. But the basis does exist for carrying through this worldwide, and world-historic, struggle, exactly because of the previous development of human society, even with all its exploitative and oppressive divisions, and more particularly because the present society is "irresistibly tending by its own economical agencies" – by the very motion its underlying contradictions give rise to – toward that "higher form" of human society. Here again, it is the dialectical interplay between that irresistible tendency and the resistance the rulers of this society put up against that tendency – and between that irresistible tendency, on the one hand, and the need for the conscious, determined struggle of the proletariat to transform that tendency into its full realization, on the other hand – that constitutes the process through which that "higher form," communism, can be achieved.

This serves as the foundation and framework for the withering away of the state – and, with it, democracy. As the inequalities and contradictions "bequeathed" by the old world are attacked and overcome, through all the intense, complex, and world-embracing struggle spoken to here; as the distinctions between mental and manual labor, between intellectual and worker, between state functionary and "ordinary member of society" are uprooted, together with all the other social distinctions that make class, national, and male-female divisions and antagonisms possible, and indeed unavoidable; and as, in dialectical relation with all this, a whole new ideology and social consciousness defeat and supersede the narrow, obscured, inverted, and egoistic outlook generated by previous human history with its low level of productive forces and its thousands of years of class divisions, social antagonisms, and the battle for mere existence pitting people against each other – then the point will be reached where the state will wither away. The state arose with the split-up of society into antagonistic classes and it represents the irreconcilability of class contradictions; it became established as an institution standing above society while being controlled, shaped, and utilized by the economically dominant class as its instrument of class dictatorship; and as the material and ideological conditions for communism are attained, this state – a state of any kind – will no longer be necessary, it will no longer have a basis as such an institution and such an instrument, it will be superfluous, and more than that a hindrance to the functioning and further advancement of society. . .it will wither away. . .it will be replaced by the cooperative running of society by society's members generally. The Great Proletarian Cultural Revolution in China – the most advanced revolutionary experience in human history so far – despite the fact that it did not and could not solve all the problems associated with the historical leap to communism, and even despite the fact that it could not ultimately prevent the temporary triumph of capitalist restoration in China itself, has shown that the withering away of the state is not an airy, unrealizable fantasy but will be the outcome of world-stirring and truly world-historic struggle; and more, this great revolutionary movement, involving nearly one-quarter of humanity, has indicated, in basic terms, the means and methods for carrying forward that struggle and achieving that great historical leap, which will realize the withering away of the state with the abolition of class distinctions.

As stressed repeatedly throughout this book, democracy too will wither away with the state. The explanation of this was set forth in fundamental terms by Lenin in *The State and Revolution*, and, with what has been said so far as background, his analysis there still stands as a basic and crucial guidepost:

> In the usual arguments about the state, the mistake is constant-
> ly made against which Engels warned and which we have in pass-
> ing indicated above, namely, it is constantly forgotten that the
> abolition of the state means also the abolition of democracy: that
> the withering away of the state means the withering away of
> democracy.
>
> At first sight this assertion seems exceedingly strange and in-
> comprehensible; indeed, someone may even suspect us of expect-
> ing the advent of a system of society in which the principle of
> subordination of the minority to the majority will not be observed
> – for democracy means the recognition of this very principle.
>
> No, democracy is *not* identical with the subordination of the
> minority to the majority. Democracy is a *state* which recognizes
> the subordination of the minority to the majority, i.e., an organiza-
> tion for the systematic use of *force* by one class against another, by
> one section of the population against another.
>
> We set ourselves the ultimate aim of abolishing the state, i.e.,
> all organized and systematic violence, all use of violence against
> people in general. We do not expect the advent of a system of
> society in which the principle of subordination of the minority to
> the majority will not be observed. In striving for socialism,
> however, we are convinced that it will develop into communism
> and, therefore, that the need for violence against people in
> general, for the *subordination* of one man to another, and of one
> section of the population to another, will vanish altogether since
> people will *become accustomed* to observing the elementary condi-
> tions of social life *without violence* and *without subordination*.

> And the dictatorship of the proletariat, i.e., the organization of
> the vanguard of the oppressed as the ruling class for the purpose of
> suppressing the oppressors, cannot result merely in an expansion
> of democracy. *Simultaneously* with an immense expansion of
> democracy, which *for the first time* becomes democracy for the
> poor, democracy for the people, and not democracy for the
> money-bags, the dictatorship of the proletariat imposes a series of
> restrictions on the freedom of the oppressors, the exploiters, the
> capitalists. We must suppress them in order to free humanity from
> wage slavery, their resistance must be crushed by force; it is clear
> that there is no freedom and no democracy where there is sup-
> pression and where there is violence. . . .
>
> Democracy for the vast majority of the people, and suppres-
> sion by force, i.e., exclusion from democracy, of the exploiters and
> oppressors of the people – this is the change democracy undergoes
> during the *transition* from capitalism to communism. . . .

. . . Communism alone is capable of providing really complete democracy, and the more complete it is, the sooner it will become unnecessary and wither away of its own accord.

From the moment all members of society, or at least the vast majority, have learned to administer the state *themselves,* have taken this work into their own hands, have organized control over the insignificant capitalist minority, over the gentry who wish to preserve their capitalist habits and over the workers who have been thoroughly corrupted by capitalism – from this moment the need for government of any kind begins to disappear altogether. The more complete the democracy, the nearer the moment when it becomes unnecessary. The more democratic the "state" which consists of the armed workers, and which is "no longer a state in the proper sense of the word," the more rapidly *every form* of state begins to wither away.[55]

*   *   *   *   *

It is not only in a general sense, and not only in society as a whole, that a radical rupture with tradition is required, including specifically on the question of democracy. It is also the case that much of the tradition of the international communist movement, on this question in particular, must be ruptured with. Especially in the period after Lenin,[56] there has been a marked tendency, even on the part of genuine communists (leaving aside various kinds of revisionists and of course bourgeois socialists who are more or less open apologists of imperialism), to ignore, or actually distort, the communist position on this question. This assumed a very stark, and rather grotesque, expression during the period leading up to and during World War 2, and was given concen-

55. Lenin, "State and Revolution," *LCW,* 25, pp. 460-61, 466-68, 479.

56. Actually, as I pointed out in *For a Harvest of Dragons,* there was a tendency on Engels's part, in the last years of his life, to vitiate somewhat the Marxist position on the state and revolution, particularly in the form of exaggerating the possibilities of peaceful transition to socialism, in Germany specifically. However, as I also stressed there, Engels certainly never renounced the armed struggle, and he waged a fierce struggle against attempts to use some conjecturing on his part about the possibility of peaceful transition as justification for a whole strategy based on this, as people like Kautsky were already doing (see *Harvest of Dragons,* especially pp. 64-68). And to give further perspective to this, it is important to remember that it was during this same general period that Engels systematized the Marxist position on the state, as well as making other theoretical contributions, in his landmark work, *The Origin of the Family, Private Property, and the State.*

trated expression in the line of the Seventh Congress of the Communist International (Comintern) as represented in the speeches by Comintern leader Georgi Dimitrov setting forth the "United Front Against Fascism" line. Not only was the Leninist line on the nation in the imperialist era openly reversed – it was stated that the communists should be the best representatives of the nation, even of the imperialist nations, whereas Lenin had insisted that the statement in the *Communist Manifesto* that the workers have no fatherland applied precisely to the imperialist countries – but, despite talk about finding the ways to make the transition to the struggle for the dictatorship of the proletariat, it was actually argued, "Now the working masses in a number of capitalist countries are faced with the necessity of making a *definite* choice, and of making it today, not between proletarian dictatorship and bourgeois democracy, but between bourgeois democracy and fascism."[57] In other words, the program that was put forward for fighting fascism in the capitalist countries was explicitly not a program for proletarian revolution – that was to be put off into the future – but a program for defending bourgeois democracy. Along with this – and in defense of it – the Marxist-Leninist view of democracy was (to put it extremely charitably) distorted, even to the point where the imperialist states opposed to Germany (and its allies) were portrayed as progressive upholders of a sort of classless democracy. It was not emphasized that bourgeois-democratic rule means bourgeois *dictatorship*, and fascism was presented as a dictatorship only of the most reactionary sections of the bourgeoisie – rather than as the dictatorship of the bourgeois class *as such* – in open terroristic form.[58]

57. Georgi Dimitrov, "Unity of the Working Class Against Fascism" (concluding speech before the Seventh World Congress of the Comintern, 13 August 1935), in *For a United and Popular Front* (Sofia, Bulgaria: Sofia Press, n.d.), p. 209; see also, in the same volume, "The Fascist Offensive and the Tasks of the Communist International in the Struggle of the Working Class Against Fascism" (report before the Seventh World Congress of the Communist International, delivered 2 August 1935). For Lenin's position on the question of the fatherland in imperialist countries, see, for example, his statement that "whoever refers today to Marx's attitude towards the wars of the epoch of the *progressive* bourgeoisie and forgets Marx's statement that 'the workers have no fatherland,' a statement that applies *precisely* to the epoch of the reactionary, obsolete bourgeoisie, to the epoch of the socialist revolution, shamelessly distorts Marx and substitutes the bourgeois for the socialist point of view" ("Socialism and War," in *Lenin on War and Peace, Three Articles* [Peking: Foreign Languages Press, 1966], p. 17; see also *LCW*, 21, p. 309).

58. See, for example, J. V. Stalin, "Report to the Eighteenth Congress of the C.P.S.U. (B.) on the Work of the Central Committee" (10 March 1939), in *Problems*

After World War 2, similar deformations of the Marxist-Leninist line on democracy – involving democratic questions and tasks in the broadest sense, including the national question – have continued to be put forward in the name of Marxism-Leninism, including by leaders of the international communist movement. For example, Stalin, in a speech in 1952, called on the communists in the imperialist countries (at least those other than the USA) to take up the banner of democratic liberties and the banner of the nation, because, Stalin said, the bourgeoisie in these countries had thrown these banners overboard and was no longer willing or able to uphold them.[59] And even Mao – who opposed the notion that democracy is an end in itself and showed that instead it can only be a means to an end, and who stressed the struggle against bourgeois-democrats turned capitalist-roaders in socialist society – did not break with the erroneous view that communists should uphold the national banner not only in colonial countries (where such a stand is correct as a political program) but also in the imperialist countries (where it is most emphatically incorrect).[60] On the one hand, such errors were strongly influenced by the exigencies of the foreign policy of the socialist states (this is very obvious in the case of Stalin and the Soviet Union, but it is also true, to some extent at least, with Mao and China during the time Mao was leading it overall). But on the other hand, there is also a significant aspect in which these positions were upheld in their own right – and erroneously – as communist positions.[61]

The continuing influence of such errors – and the need for a

---

of Leninism (Peking: Foreign Languages Press, 1976), Stalin, *On the Great Patriotic War of the Soviet Union* (Moscow: Foreign Languages Publishing House, 1954), as well as the speeches by Dimitrov in *For a United and Popular Front*.

59. See J. V. Stalin, *Speech at the Nineteenth Party Congress* (Calcutta: Books & Periodicals, 1978), especially pp. 12-14; and also *Basic Principles for Unity of Marxist-Leninists*, paragraph 117.

60. See, for example, *A Proposal Concerning the General Line of the International Communist Movement* (Peking: Foreign Languages Press, 1963), especially pp. 18-20.

61. I have made a fairly extensive critical analysis of these positions, and of their connection to such foreign policy exigencies, in *Conquer the World? The International Proletariat Must and Will* and "Advancing the World Revolutionary Movement: Questions of Strategic Orientation," *Revolution*, No. 51 (Spring 1984). An important analysis of one very significant focus of all this, the Spanish Civil War of the late 1930s, is contained in "The Line of the Comintern on the Civil War in Spain," *Revolution*, No. 49 (June 1981).

rupture with them – has been furthered by the lopsidedness in the world and the deviations within the Marxist movement associated with it – toward social democracy in the imperialist countries and toward nationalism (as well as some other manifestations of bourgeois-democratic tendencies) in the oppressed nations (though, again, the latter does have the virtue of often assuming a revolutionary expression, even if not a fully Marxist-Leninist one). And the need for such a rupture is all the more urgently accentuated in the present situation, with the approaching world-historic conjuncture – holding the potential not only of danger and destruction but also of revolutionary advance, of truly unprecedented dimensions. The formation and the *Declaration* of the Revolutionary Internationalist Movement represent an extremely important, if still beginning, step, including in terms of making such a rupture. But much more indeed cries out to be done – and urgently.

8

The Future of Humanity and the Historical Place of Democracy

We have seen that from its earliest forms in antique society democracy has been an expression and an integral part of the division of society into classes and the exercise of dictatorship by one class or another and that in modern society democracy is a phenomenon associated with, an expression of, capitalist society and the bourgeois epoch – for even the existence of democracy under socialism, as radically different as it is from capitalist democracy, still reflects the fact that the divisions and contradictions characteristic of this epoch have not yet been completely transformed and overcome. Where it is possible to speak of democracy, of whatever kind, that is a sign that class distinctions and, in one form or another, social antagonisms – and with them dictatorship – are still to be found, indeed still characterize society. And when this is no longer the case, it will no longer be possible, or necessary, to speak of democracy. Then the determination of how society and the whole of humanity of which it is constituted should both meet their needs and expand their horizons, in an ever-widening spiral, will rest on a whole new foundation, materially and ideologically, and will be guided by whole new principles.

The economic basis of modern democracy – bourgeois democracy – is a generalized system of commodity production and exchange, but more specifically a system of production and exchange in which human labor power itself has become a commodity, labor has become wage-labor – and slavery has become wage-slavery. It is a system of production and exchange driven by a compelling force of anarchy, arising out of the very nature of commodity production, with its requirement that things produced command a value in exchange as a condition of the realization of their use value. It is at the same time a system where not merely value but surplus value, and the ever-greater accumulation of wealth as capital – as the command over the labor power of others – is the irresistible requirement and the only means through which social production can be carried out, regardless of the cost in human misery and the fettering of the productive forces themselves, above all the masses of people. It is a system which demands a strict hierarchy of social orders, in production and in social life generally, together with the subjugation of one half of humanity by the other half and the domination of a few nations over many – and all the force and violence that is required in the endeavor to insure this. In short, it is a system based on exploitation, an oppressive division of labor and antagonistic social inequalities; a society in which, for the majority, the means, the labor, whereby they earn their livelihood – if such they have – is reckoned not as part of their life but as a sacrifice of their life[1]; a society where the capitalists are "capital personified and endowed with consciousness and a will," where their bottom line and driving compulsion is "the restless never-ending process of profit-making."[2]

It is all this which sets the foundation and establishes the ultimate limits of the freedom, democracy, equality, and right that characterize bourgeois society – not merely in their practical application but even in their theoretical conception. That is why there is not a single theorist or ideologist – other than a communist one – who will not regard it as both impossible and horrifying to conceive not merely of abolishing private property in the means of production, commodity production and ex-

---

1. See Marx, *Wage Labor and Capital* (Moscow: Progress Publishers, 1976), p. 20.

2. Marx, *Capital*, 1, p. 152.

change, wage-labor, and all the other production and social relations marking the division of society into classes; not merely
uprooting all social inequality; not even just radically transforming the thinking of the people in society; but carrying through the
revolutionization of relations and people to the point where such
things as equality and democracy have lost their basis and meaning and have been superseded by far higher visions, and realiza-
tions, of human freedom.

Socialism, as we have seen, is a transition from capitalism to
communism, and retains many of the features of the former even
while advancing toward the latter. The economic base of
socialism is marked by the contradiction between incipient communist elements – such as public ownership of the means of production and the formal abolition of the right to exploit others –
and remaining capitalist elements (broadly defined as "bourgeois
right"). The superstructure of socialism reflects this profound
contradiction and struggle; in particular, it retains dictatorship
and democracy, but as compared with capitalism, these are
reversed and radically transformed, and they serve as the
political vehicle through which to carry forward the advance to
communism.

The economic base of communism will embody the reality
that not only private ownership of the means of production but
bourgeois right in its entirety and all the production and social
relations marking the division of society into classes have been
transformed and transcended. Engels, in the concluding pages of
Socialism: Utopian and Scientific, provided a sweeping vision of
this. If the division of society into classes has a certain historical
justification, he said,

> it has this only for a given period, only under given social condi-
> tions. It was based upon the insufficiency of production. It will be
> swept away by the complete development of modern productive
> forces. And, in fact, the abolition of classes in society presupposes
> a degree of historical evolution at which the existence, not simply
> of this or that particular ruling class, but of any ruling class at all,
> and, therefore, the existence of class distinction itself has become
> an obsolete anachronism. It presupposes, therefore, the develop-
> ment of production carried out to a degree at which appropriation
> of the means of production and of the products, and, with this, of
> political domination, of the monopoly of culture, and of intellec-
> tual leadership by a particular class of society, has become not
> only superfluous but economically, politically, intellectually, a

hindrance to development.

This point is now reached.... The possibility of securing for every member of society, by means of socialized production, an existence not only fully sufficient materially, and becoming day by day more full, but an existence guaranteeing to all the free development and exercise of their physical and mental faculties – this possibility is now for the first time here, but *it is here.*

With the seizing of the means of production by society, production of commodities is done away with, and, simultaneously, the mastery of the product over the producer. Anarchy in social production is replaced by systematic, definite organization. The struggle for individual existence disappears.... Only from that time will man himself, more and more consciously, make his own history – only from that time will the social causes set in movement by him have, in the main and in a constantly growing measure, the results intended by him.[3]

The epoch of world communism will be characterized, as Mao expressed it, by the fact that "all mankind voluntarily and consciously changes itself and the world."[4] These two words – "voluntarily" and "consciously" – express in a concentrated way the profound difference, in the realm of the superstructure, between communism and all previous human society, and reflect the profound difference in the economic base. But what do they mean? "Voluntarily" cannot mean that in some absolute sense there will be the absence of compulsion. Marxism recognizes that freedom does not lie in the absence of all compulsion – which is an impossibility – but in the recognition and transformation of necessity. Unless nothing new should ever appear again, unless the relation of human beings with the rest of nature, and with each other, were to remain frozen, unless all motion and change in the universe were to stop – all of which is, of course, an impossibility – then human beings and human society will constantly be confronted with necessity, which must be grasped in its essence and transformed. But the world, the universe, is not just necessity, it is also accident: necessity itself is in dialectical relation with accident – there is accident in necessity and necessity in accident – and if this too were not so, things would come to a standstill, indeed existence would be inconceivable. Thus communist society cannot help but be full of contradiction and strug-

---

3. Engels, "Socialism: Utopian and Scientific," *MESW*, 3, pp. 148-50.
4. Mao, "On Practice," *SW*, 1, p. 308.

gle – grappling with and solving new problems, with old ones reappearing, perhaps in somewhat different form, and in general constantly confronting and transforming necessity.

What will be radically new and different, however, is that this contradiction and struggle will not have to and will not go on in the form of social antagonism – there will still be contradictions among the people, and indeed the struggle to resolve these will be a driving force in society, but there will not be contradictions between the people and the enemy. . . there will not be people who are enemies. There will still be compulsion, in the sense of necessity, but there will *not be social compulsion in the sense of the political domination of one part of society over another or the domination of one individual over another.* In the absence of such antagonism and compulsion, people will voluntarily unite – and struggle, often sharply no doubt, but nonantagonistically – to continually confront and transform necessity.

It is similar with "consciously." This does not mean that people will have perfect knowledge. Just as motion and change in the material world are continual, so are motion and change in the realm of ideas. And just as there is the dialectical relation between necessity and freedom summarized here, so too there is a dialectical relation between ignorance and knowledge – which means ignorance can be and continually is transformed into knowledge (and the opposite transformation can also take place) – so that consciousness is not static and can never be absolute or "perfect," but is always undergoing development and change. But, again, the significance of the word "consciously" here is that, as opposed to previous society, social antagonisms will not exist and serve to obscure reality and vitiate knowledge and to obstruct the members of society as a whole from accumulating knowledge. There will still be – there will always be – ignorance, in dialectical relation with knowledge – *but there will not be suppression and distortion of knowledge and ideas, and there will not be the bias and limitation imposed by the domination of exploiting classes and the very division of society into classes.* A correct and comprehensive worldview and methodology, dialectical materialism, will be the common worldview and methodology of the members of society, although at the same time there will be continual struggle over how to apply this correctly to all the various spheres of knowledge and to all the new questions and problems continually posing themselves – and over how to continually develop this worldview and methodology itself through this ongoing process.

The abolition of social antagonism and political domination, and the unity of people around the basic principles of dialectical materialism – together with the struggle over how to apply and further develop them – will make possible, for the first time, the voluntary association of people in society on the basis of a fundamentally correct and ever-deepening understanding of the laws of motion of nature, of society, and of the relation between the two – it will make possible and involve the recognition and transformation of necessity on a whole new and far higher basis than humanity has previously been capable of.

One other phrase in this formulation by Mao must be briefly explored here: "all mankind." This, again, cannot be taken in an absolute sense. That is, it is possible, even probable, that particular individuals may not voluntarily (or consciously) carry out what society as a whole has decided upon in a particular situation – there may even be individual cases where someone uses violence in dealing with others. But the fundamental point is, once more, that there will not be the basis for this to become a *social antagonism,* or for the political domination of one part of society over another to be necessary, or realizable.

It is only possible today to conjecture, and to dream, about what expressions social contradictions will assume in the future communist society and how they will be resolved. How will the problem be approached of combining advanced productive forces, which require a significant degree of centralization, with decentralization and local initiative (whatever "local" means then)? How will the rearing of new generations of people – now carried out in atomized form, and through oppressive relations, in the family – be approached in communist society? How will attention be paid to developing specific areas of knowledge, or to concentrating on particular projects, without making these the "special preserve" of certain people? How will the contradiction be handled of enabling people to acquire all-around skills and knowledge and at the same time meeting the need for some specialization? What about the relation between people's individual initiatives and personal pursuits on the one hand, and their social responsibilities and contributions on the other? It seems that it will always be the case that, around any particular question, or controversy, there will be a group – and as a general rule a minority at first – that will have a more correct, advanced understanding, but how will this be utilized for the overall benefit while at the same time preventing groups from solidifying into "interest groups"? What will be the relations between different areas and regions – since there will no longer be different countries – and how will the contradictions between what might be called "local communities" and the higher associations, all the way up to the world level, be handled? What will it mean concretely that people are truly citizens of the world, particularly in terms of where they live, work, and so on – will they "rotate" from one area of the world to another? How will the question of linguistic and cultural diversity versus a world union of humanity be handled? And will people then, even with all their understanding of history, really be able to believe that a society such as we are imprisoned in now actually existed – let alone that it was declared to be eternal and the highest pinnacle humanity was capable of reaching? Again, these questions, and many, many more, can only be the object of speculation, and of dreaming, today; but even to pose such questions, and to attempt to visualize how they might be addressed – in a society where class divisions, social antagonism, and political domination no longer exist – is itself tremendously liberating for anyone without a vested interest in the present order.

At the same time, however, the future prospects of communism clash directly today with the future that imperialism holds out for humanity, with immediate menace. Humanity is today rapidly approaching a world-historic turning point without precedent. As I emphasized in *A Horrible End, or an End to the Horror?*, the danger of world war between the two imperialist blocs, with all its almost unimaginably destructive consequences, is very real and very immediate, but at the same time:

> the possibilities for revolutionary breakthroughs, for the overthrow of reactionary social systems and for profound revolutionary changes in the entire structure of world relations, are greatly heightened.

> The relation (or dialectic) between war and revolution is at the center of this historic drama being enacted in the world arena: a deadly serious struggle is going on between these two trends which will have everything to do with determining the direction of human society, and indeed the destiny of humanity itself. The question of revolution is very much alive – and more, it represents the only possible way forward. This, again, is all the more so because the whole world and its future are this time, quite literally, at stake. Any other attempted solution to this, which will leave the foundations of imperialism untouched and bring no

fundamental changes in world relations and social systems, is utterly incapable of providing a way forward out of this howling madness; *only* proletarian revolution holds the possibility for doing so. . . .

. . . A horrible end – at least to human civilization as it has developed to this point – that is a very real possibility posed in the period ahead; it is to this threshold that the development of civilization under the domination of exploiting classes and their oppressive states has brought us. And such a horrible end is something to be actively, urgently fought against. But at the same time, it must never be forgotten that the daily workings of this system are a continual horror for the great majority of the world's people – this is no exaggeration but a profound, searing truth commonly overlooked in the preserves of privilege and comfort that exist for broad strata much of the time in the imperialist citadels. Nor must it be forgotten that, as stressed earlier, the only possible means of preventing such a horrible end, or in any case the only way forward in the face of it, is the advance of the world proletarian revolution.[5]

In concluding that book I argued that it cannot be said that the achievement of communism is inevitable – including for the reason that it is not theoretically inconceivable that humanity could be wiped out in such a world war – but that "there is plenty of basis at this stage of history and in today's world to achieve communism *and* to see the urgent necessity of fighting to achieve it – though that fight will be long, arduous, and tortuous – by straining to make the key breakthroughs and leaps toward that communist future that are demanded now."[6]

There is not a progressive tendency in history, understood in the sense of a conscious design or a predetermined, pre-programmed development. But there is, as Marx put it, a "coherence" in human history:

Because of the simple fact that every succeeding generation finds itself in possession of the productive forces acquired by the previous generation, and that they serve it as the raw material for new production, a coherence arises in human history, a history of humanity takes shape which becomes all the more a history of

5. Avakian, *Horrible End or End to Horror?*, pp. 9-10, 12-13.
6. Avakian, *Horrible End or End to Horror?*, p. 216.

humanity the more the productive forces of men and therefore their social relations develop.[7]

It is not the case that all of history has been preparing the ground for the communist future, in some metaphysical sense, but it is definitely the case that it has laid the basis for communism. Things do not proceed in an unbroken straight line forward, but through spirals; they do not have a preordained course, but they do have identifiable fundamental contradictions and a motion that can be grasped, in all its complexity. Great leaps backward are possible – and this possibility poses itself as an urgent danger today – but great leaps forward are also possible. . .and this possibility too is magnified with the unprecedented world-historic conjuncture shaping up. While imperialism is driven toward world war in this period, it is also true that this same system, even more than in Marx's time, is "irresistibly tending by its own economical agencies" toward "that higher form" of society – toward communism. Thus, there are two possibilities, two futures that are posing themselves very directly and urgently before us and that are locked in acute conflict. To seize the opportunities to leap forward, even if that means having to do so from a position of first being hurled back by war and devastation of a horrendous magnitude, it is necessary to grasp the enormity of the situation and of the leaps and ruptures that are demanded.

This brings me back to the main theme and to the conclusion of this book. Democracy: can't we do better than that? In the light of all that has been said here – we can and must. With the abolition of classes and the state, Engels wrote, communist society "will put the whole machinery of state where it will then belong: into the museum of antiquities, by the side of the spinning-wheel and the bronze axe."[8] And with them, in its rightful place, will be democracy.

7. Marx, "Letter to Pavel Vasilyevich Annenkov" (28 December 1846), *MESL*, p. 3.

8. Engels, "Origins," *MESW*, 3, p. 330.

Index

About Bob Avakian

Bob Avakian is Chairman of the Revolutionary Communist
Party, USA. A major voice on the revolutionary left since the
1960s, he was active in the Free Speech and antiwar
movements in Berkeley, worked closely with the Black Panther
Party, figured prominently in debates within the Students for a
Democratic Society, and founded the Revolutionary Union in
1968. Avakian quickly emerged as the leading Maoist thinker
in the United States, and has over the last seventeen years
written numerous analyses of the world situation and problems
of revolutionary strategy. In 1980, under threat of more than a
lifetime in jail—as a result of trumped-up charges stemming
from a demonstration against Deng Xiaoping in 1979—Bob
Avakian was forced into exile in France.

ROUSSEAUS

ROBESPIERRE

DETOCQUEVILLE

DEMOCRACY IN
AMERICA